Fixing the Musical

Fixing the Musical

*How Technologies Shaped the
Broadway Repertory*

DOUGLAS L. RESIDE

OXFORD
UNIVERSITY PRESS

OXFORD
UNIVERSITY PRESS

Oxford University Press is a department of the University of Oxford. It furthers
the University's objective of excellence in research, scholarship, and education
by publishing worldwide. Oxford is a registered trade mark of Oxford University
Press in the UK and certain other countries.

Published in the United States of America by Oxford University Press
198 Madison Avenue, New York, NY 10016, United States of America.

Library of Congress Cataloging-in-Publication Data
Names: Reside, Doug (Douglas Larue), 1978– author.
Title: Fixing the musical : how technologies shaped the
Broadway repertory / Douglas L. Reside.
Description: [1.] | New York : Oxford University Press, 2023. |
Includes bibliographical references and index.
Identifiers: LCCN 2023013839 (print) | LCCN 2023013840 (ebook) |
ISBN 9780190073725 (paperback) | ISBN 9780190073718 (hardback) |
ISBN 9780190073749 (epub)
Subjects: LCSH: Musicals—History and criticism. | Music publishing—
History—20th century. | Music publishing—Technological innovations. |
Music—Electronic publishing. | Music and the Internet.
Classification: LCC ML2054.R47 2023 (print) | LCC ML2054 (ebook) |
DDC 782.1/4—dc23/eng/20230512
LC record available at https://lccn.loc.gov/2023013839
LC ebook record available at https://lccn.loc.gov/2023013840

DOI: 10.1093/oso/9780190073718.001.0001

Paperback printed by Marquis Book Printing, Canada
Hardback printed by Bridgeport National Bindery, Inc., United States of America

For Marilyn

Contents

Acknowledgments

This book is, like every work of any significance, the result of many collaborations. An author's name on the cover of any book is, at best, an "above the title" credit for just one of the many roles that lead to its production. There are many to whom I am deeply indebted and sincerely grateful whose contributions have led to the book you are now reading. And I understand that the living referent of that second-person pronoun ("you," dear reader of these "Acknowledgments") is almost certainly someone named in the next few paragraphs (or, more sadly, one who expects to be named but, through my sin of omission, is not). Still, thanks is owed, and so I hope I can entreat the reader, even those who were previously strangers to me and my collaborators, to pause and at least cast their eye over these honored names.

Early versions of portions of the material in this book were read by Joanna Dee Das, Liza Gennaro, Raymond Knapp, Jeffrey Magee, Carol Oja, David Savran, Jessica Sternfeld, Dominic Symonds, Stacy Wolf, Tamsen Wolff, and Elizabeth Wollman, all of whom encouraged me to pursue this as a book project and continued to provide insightful help on drafts throughout the process. As I could mention them in almost every section of these acknowledgments, the reader should assume they are present at every stage.

I finally decided to turn these ideas into a book after presenting a paper at Dominic McHugh's conference "Reading Musicals: Sources, Editions, Performance—A Conference in Honor of Geoffrey Block" in Carmel, IN, in 2018. At that conference I reconnected with Norm Hirschy, who encouraged me to submit a proposal to him for Oxford University Press. Norm's guidance throughout this process has been invaluable as I stumbled through the process of writing my first book.

Conversations with Derek Miller in airport taxi cabs, conference coffee shops, and digital-humanities hackathons inspired me to think through some of the ideas that had long been percolating in my brain and develop these inchoate thoughts into chapters. Nic Leonhardt provided several opportunities to present early versions of the first fragments book in progress to an international audience, and offered advice and encouragement throughout the process. Laura MacDonald generously read many of the chapters in this book, a few in multiple versions, and deeply engaged with the text with in-sightful comments and roadblock-breaking suggestions. I am also grateful to MacDonald, Trevor Boffone, Jordan Ealey, and Bryan Vandevender for establishing the "Telephone Hour" Zoom colloquium during the height of the COVID-19 pandemic in 2020. These opportunities to present work-in-process were invaluable motivators to continue working toward deadlines when everything felt so uncertain.

Laura MacDonald, Arianne Johnson Quinn, and Sarah Whitfield were constant remote companions on various messaging platforms and were ever ready to provide encouragement and support when I was frozen in a writer's block. Quinn additionally shared some of her own work in progress and reviewed a draft of Chapter 6. In addition to agreeing to an interview for Chapter 6, Ted Chapin provided insightful feedback on the chapter as a whole. Laurence Maslon's detailed and insightful comments on Chapters 1 and 3 have made this a much better book. Brent Salter also generously shared some of his own research materials for the Samuel French section of Chapter 6. John Esche reviewed Chapter 5 and FedExed his annotated copy of the chapter to ensure I would have it before my deadline. Teresa Kilzi's insights and excitement about this book provided much-needed motivation when my own enthusiasm lagged.

Mana Allen, Larry Blank, Ken Bloom, Jaqueline Z. Davis, Fred Gershon, Abbie Van Nostrand, and Kevin Winkler all provided access to research materials and introductions to individuals whose memories were invaluable in the writing of this book. Ken Bloom additionally generously read a com-plete draft and provided invaluable feedback and copyediting. The always-generous members of the listserv CASTREC-L also helped point me in the right direction several times in response to my digital cries for help. The late David Hummel also provided me with a wealth of resources, and I am disap-pointed that I was not able to finish this book while he was still able to read it.

I am grateful to all those who took the time to speak with me on the record including Brad Bennett, Ted Chapin, Kathryn Doby, Karl Gallmeyer, Terry Hughes, Robert Schear, David Sheehan, Robert Sher, Grey Shepard, Joseph Sicari, and Bruce Yekko. I will not name, but cannot fully express my grati-tude to, those who spoke to me anonymously for the section on bootlegs in Chapter 5.

I am ever grateful to my local colleagues at New York Public Library, espe-cially the staff of the Billy Rose Theatre division (listed alphabetically): John Calhoun, Zachary Cohn, Pat Darby, Patrick Hoffman, Brendan Leonard,

Suzanne Lipkin, Kaia Lyons, Brendan Leonard, Louise Martzinek, Steve Massa, Jeremy Megraw, Wendy Norris, Annemarie Van Roessel, Sharon Rork, Misy Singson, Gabriella Steinberg, and Melisa Tien. I am also grateful to the constant support of the New York Public Library Theatre Committee: Emily Altman, Margot Astrachan, Ken Billington, Julie Boardman, Ted Chapin, Drew Cohen, Bonnie Comley, Trip Cullman, Van Dean, Kurt Deutsch, Scott Farthing, Linda Feinstone, Lori Fineman, Barbara Fleischman, Louise Hirschfeld, Joan Marcus, Elliott Masie, Arthur Pober, Jennifer Schantz, Edwin Schloss, Morwin Schmookler, Jenna Segal, Ted Shen, Henry Tisch, Kara Unterberg, Abbie Van Nostrand, and Kumiko Yoshii. My colleagues in other Library divisions, especially Stephen Bowie, Greg Cram, Jonathan Hiam, Bob Kosovsky, Rebecca Littman, Linda Murray, Jennifer Schantz, and Jessica Wood, all provided advice and support throughout the process. Every conversation with library volunteer and theatre historian Mana Allen inspired me to think of new avenues for research. She has provided inspiration for more books than I will likely ever be able to complete. I am especially grateful to the constant support of Library for the Performing Arts Associate Director Carolyn Broomhead, with whom I regularly discussed the process of the book and who was regularly able to help me break through a roadblock with a single sentence of advice or feedback.

I refer several times in the following pages to my early experiences with the materials that documented musical theatre in the 1980s and 1990s. These experiences were made possible by my parents, Dennis and Kathie Reside, who always supported and encouraged my interests as a child and continue to celebrate and support my work today.

Finally, I am regularly grateful and amazed at the blessing of partnering in life with my wife, Marilyn Reside. Nothing in my life would be possible without her constant support.

Introduction

As a child in the suburbs of St. Louis, MO, in the 1980s, I spent many Saturdays browsing through the LP and cassette collections of cast recordings (cataloged, I am afraid, as "Soundtracks") at the county library. Often the plot was all but incomprehensible from the album alone, so, if I enjoyed the music, I might seek out the libretto from the "non-fiction" shelves. Later, when my parents bought their first VHS player, I regularly checked out video recordings of live productions and movie adaptations to get a sense of what these musicals looked like on stage. This is not, I have discovered, an un-common experience among those American musical theatre fans who grew up in the late twentieth century. Browsing cast recordings in the public li-brary (a venue likely to have a larger selection than the usual middle-America record store) seems to have been something of a rite of passage for this tribe before streaming services threw open the doors to virtually the entire catalog.

St. Louis, I should note, was and still is a remarkably theatre-rich town. The Muny, a century-old municipal opera company, performs a slate of around half-a-dozen musicals each summer in an outdoor amphitheatre that can seat close to 11,000 and offers over 1,000 seats for free on a first-come, first-served basis at each performance. Equity tours of current Broadway shows regularly stop at the Fox Theatre. Scott Miller's New Line Theatre, still emerging in my own adolescence, offers regional premieres of smaller musicals. Although productions at these venues certainly informed my understanding of the repertory, the ability to replay, reread, and rewatch the records, books, and videos from the library did more to establish for me an understanding of the important works of American and British musical theatre.

It also seemed to me, in my youth, that the texts preserved on paper, tape, and disc in the library were more authentic than those I might have heard on stage. Mistakes are made in live performance, particularly in ama-teur productions, but the recordings, I thought, represented the texts as the creators intended them to be heard. While this was not, it turns out, an accu-rate understanding of authorial intention, the legal importance of recordings

Fixing the Musical. Douglas L. Reside, Oxford University Press. © Oxford University Press 2023.
DOI: 10.1093/oso/9780190073718.003.0001

over and above live performance is recognized and protected by the United States copyright law which applies to:

> original works of authorship fixed in any tangible medium of expression, now known or later developed, from which they can be perceived, reproduced, or otherwise communicated, either directly or with the aid of a machine or device.[1]

Under this code, performance becomes legally protected intellectual property only when it can be captured ("fixed") and sold as a commodity ("in any tangible medium of expression"). The rise of the American musical coincided with the proliferation of new tangible media of expression capable of fixing this very multimodal art form. In this book I will explore the impact that the technologies used to "fix" musical theatre works had on the art form from 1866 to 2022. Each new technology, from cheaper and faster printing to photography, audio recording, video recording, and virtual and augmented reality, has highlighted different elements of the work and made possible new kinds of musicals.

As the form changes, so too does the repertory—the set of titles that are best known by audiences and most frequently discussed and produced. I use the word "repertory" rather than "canon," because while the latter word suggests that the included titles were selected based on aesthetic values that may not be shared across all communities, the word "repertory" describes those musicals that are most frequently performed. A canon may be one community's idea of "the best that has been thought and said" or at least an estimate of "importance" or "influence." The repertory is largely a matter of historical record. The technologies used to fix musicals in tangible media certainly had an influence on both, but my argument here is largely focused on which titles were *best known* rather than which titles were, by anyone's judgment, considered the "best."

The repertory, of course, changes over time as new shows are introduced and old ones fade from memory. Different regions and different communities may have different local repertories; a Gilbert and Sullivan company will perform different titles than a Shakespeare festival. In this book, I am primarily focused on the repertory performed by major resident companies around the country that have existed for at least twenty-five years and that regularly produce at least two musicals each season. For this book, I have surveyed the seasons of the theatres in Table I.1 from their

Table I.1 Resident Theatres Surveyed

Goodspeed Opera House (East Haddam, CT, 1963–2019)
Zach Theatre (Austin, TX, 1990–2019)
Walnut Street Theatre (Philadelphia PA, 1983–2019)
Los Angeles Civic Light Opera (Los Angeles, CA, 1938–1987)
Lyric Theatre OK (Oklahoma City, OK, 1964–2019)
Ogunquit Playhouse (Ogunquit, ME, 1933–2019)
Utah Festival (Logan, UT, 1993–2017)
North Shore Music Theatre (Beverly, MA, 1954–2019)
St. Louis Muny (St. Louis, MO, 1919–2019)
Pittsburgh Civic Light Opera (Pittsburgh, PA, 1946–2019)
Papermill Playhouse (Millburn, NJ, 1992–2019)
Village Theatre (Issaquah, WA, 1979–2019)
Music Theatre of Wichita (Wichita, KS, 1974–2019)
Signature Theatre (Arlington, VA, 1990–2019)
Barn Theatre (Kalamazoo, MI, 1940–2019)

earliest published records to 2019. I end in 2019 because many theatres canceled or truncated their seasons between 2020 and 2022 due to the COVID-19 pandemic.

At these theatres, the musicals in Table I.2 were, in the aggregate, produced five or more times.

More recent musicals have obviously had less opportunity to be produced, so this list is perhaps a bit biased toward musicals written in the latter half of the twentieth century. Still, very early musicals like *The Desert Song* and *The Merry Widow* are included alongside titles from the 1990s (*Aida, Miss Saigon, Jekyll and Hyde*) and even the early 2000s (*Xanadu, The Drowsy Chaperone, Young Frankenstein*). Any such list will have omissions that grate against the expertise of a particular historian, but these 186 titles are a reasonable inventory of those the average American theatre goer would have had a chance to see in a professional production. These musicals entered the repertory, I propose, because the media technologies in use when they premiered captured enough of the work that it could be known and loved by audiences, most of whom did not see the first production.

In addition to the formation of the repertory, this book will also explore the multimodal texts behind the titles, and how audience expectations for the text the title represents are defined by technology. There is, of course, a

Table I.2 Most Frequently Produced Musicals at Theatres Surveyed in Table I.1.

Musical		Musical		Musical		Musical	
Fiddler on the Roof	51	A Chorus Line	29	George M!	16	Shenandoah	12
The Sound of Music	51	The Desert Song	29	La Cage aux Folles	16	Sweeney Todd	12
South Pacific	48	Evita	27	Sweet Charity	16	The Mikado	12
Show Boat	47	The Merry Widow	26	Les Misérables	15	The Rocky Horror Show	12
My Fair Lady	44	Funny Girl	24	Song of Norway	15	A Little Night Music	11
Oklahoma!	44	Jesus Christ Superstar	24	The Chocolate Soldier	15	Call Me Madam	11
The Music Man	43	Mame	24	Where's Charley?	15	Into the Woods	11
West Side Story	43	Singin' in the Rain	24	Bells Are Ringing	14	Li'l Abner	11
Guys and Dolls	42	Anything Goes	23	Can-Can	14	Me and My Girl	11
The King and I	41	Grease	22	Chicago	14	Pippin	11
Camelot	38	The Pajama Game	22	Godspell	14	Rose-Marie	11
Carousel	38	1776	21	Hairspray	14	The Will Rogers Follies	11
Man of La Mancha	37	Kismet	21	I Do! I Do!	14	Aida	11
Brigadoon	36	The Most Happy Fella	21	Roberta	14	Forever Plaid	10
Kiss Me, Kate	36	The Unsinkable Molly Brown	21	Beauty and the Beast	13	Mary Poppins	10
Annie	35	Cabaret	20	Big River	13	On the Town	10
Annie Get Your Gun	33	Joseph and The Amazing Technicolor Dreamcoat	20	Cats	13	Rio Rita	10
Hello, Dolly!	33	7 Brides for 7 Brothers	20	Finian's Rainbow	13	The Boy Friend	10
Peter Pan	32	Naughty Marietta	19	Little Shop of Horrors	13	The Fantasticks	10
Oliver!	31	A Funny Thing . . . Forum	17	The Pirates of Penzance	13	The Vagabond King	10
The Student Prince	31	Bye Bye Birdie	17	The Red Mill	12	Ain't Misbehavin'	9
Damn Yankees	30	Cinderella	17	Babes in Toyland	12	Bitter Sweet	9
Gypsy	30	How to Succeed in Business . . .	17	Crazy For You	12	Bloomer Girl	9

legal fiction that a standard, authorized text exists for each title. The second page of scripts licensed by Music Theatre International includes a stern warning to directors: "You are not permitted to make any changes to the music, lyrics, or dialogue of the Play including the interpolation of new material and/or the exclusion of existing material."[2] However, there is an implicit acknowledgment on the first page (and, on some editions, the cover) that this rule is most honored in its breach, for there is another warning that one should "not deface!" the rented copy, but "mark cues or cuts" with "a soft black lead pencil only" (a directive present, amusingly, even on digital editions). The exigencies of production regularly lead to small changes in the text as licensed.

In a more scholarly context, the editors of the Kurt Weill Editions, a series of critical editions of scores of the eponymous composer, make explicit their decision to present a text other than the one that might have been performed on any particular evening in the theatre.[3] In the introduction to each volume of the series, the editors write:

> The KWE employs a distinction between Script and Text (note capitalization), less as a firm rule than as a heuristic device to aid editorial decision making. In the case of a Script, performance materials (music, dialogue, stage directions, etc.) served to guide specific realizations of a given work. A Text, on the other hand, transmits a representation of the work transcending any specific realization in performance. The work is not synonymous with the event.[4]

The Weill editors posit that an "ideal" text exists that is modified by—one almost gets the sense that they would argue "corrupted by"—performance, and that their pages represent an attempt to fix this ideal text so that readers can know the "true work." Bruce Kirle in his much-lauded monograph, *Unfinished Show Business*, is much more critical of the notion of an ideal text and argues that musicals are more akin to organisms that live through change and growth.[5]

While regional and amateur productions may be legally bound by the licensed script and score, even these elements quickly come unfixed when a show is produced in a new First Class production (often on Broadway or in London's West End). Changes are sometimes made either because of authorial attempts to "improve" the show[6] or because changing sensibilities lead more of the theatre community (both creators and audiences) to realize the problematic nature of certain moments or songs (e.g., the 2022 revival of *The Music Man* featured revised lyrics for the song "Shipoopi").

Some musicals are more variable than others. Historian Miles Kreuger went so far as to say that the 1927 musical *Show Boat* "never had an official script or score,"[7] though a production missing "Old Man River," "Only Make Believe," or "Can't Help Lovin' That Man" would likely disappoint and confuse audiences. Director/producer Harold Prince affirms this in an interview conducted for the 2004 documentary, *Broadway: The American Musical*:

> When you rethink [*Show Boat*] 60 years later, suddenly the old fashioned stuff gives you a lot of trouble, but you can't get rid of all of it because the show depends on some of it. Because some of the songs—"Life upon the wicked stage"—are perennials. You cut it out [and] people will immediately say "Where is it?"[8]

The text of *Show Boat* changes from production to production, but the song "Old Man River" keeps on rolling along.

Likewise, the book of *Anything Goes* is rewritten for nearly every new production. Geoffrey Block, writing about the 1987 Lincoln Center revival, observes:

> At the conclusion of this critically well-received and popularly successful show a large silkscreen photograph of Porter (1891–1964) appeared behind a scrim to cast a literal as well as metaphorical shadow over the cast. More than fifty years after its premiere the message was clear: the real star of *Anything Goes* was its composer-lyricist, the creator of such classics as "I Get a Kick out of You," "You're the Top," "Blow, Gabriel, Blow," "All Through the Night," "Easy to Love," "Friendship," "It's De-lovely," and the title song. Readers familiar with *Anything Goes* from various amateur and semiprofessional productions over the past thirty years may scarcely notice that the last three songs named were taken from other Porter shows.[9]

The exact language of the libretto has arguably never been part of the essential text of *Anything Goes*, but the title accreted essential songs over the past nine decades, and a production that leaves them out, regardless of their original provenance, may disappoint.

Kirle argues, "Musicals are read by their audiences in theatres, not through scripts in a library."[10] He immediately follows this statement with a caution,

"I do not wish to overstate my case [. . .] but the text by itself is incomplete."[11] Kirle, citing Roland Barthes' 1977 work *Image, Music, and Text*, compares musicals to opera seria in which the "interpreter no longer tries to follow any authentic text but [. . .] becomes a co-author of the score." Following this theory, original authorial intention, to the extent it can be determined at all, does not particularly matter. The fixed text of the musical is left intentionally incomplete to allow for interpretation in performance.

Fixed texts leave gaps in which new interpretations may be introduced. If the most widely available fixed text of the musical is limited to the notes and words of the score and libretto, then the gaps are especially wide. However, most musicals are "read" on stage or the page less frequently than they are "read" on cast recordings or video, and via a multiplicity of other media in which their texts are fixed, if incompletely. When a song is not included on a cast recording (the prologue from *Godspell* for instance), amateur productions sometimes see the song as optional (even if the terms of the license explicitly state otherwise). The essential text of the musical in the twentieth century, the text the audience expects, is often composed of the songs recorded on the album (or, for later titles, the text used in a movie adaptation or video recording of the stage production).

These more fully fixed texts potentially limit the range of interpretative possibilities. Barthes values a text that requires the reader to "produce the text, open it out, set it going"—a text that cannot be simply consumed but requires of the reader imaginative and creative work.[12] Readers of a libretto may experience such an open, incomplete text fixed in the tangible medium of the codex. A cast recording is less open as some interpretations have already been made by the singers and musicians recorded. A video recording is, perhaps, the most closed of all. It is a transcription of an interpretation rather than a Barthesian Text. As technologies make it possible to "fix" more of the work, there is less room for new productions to make interpretations that do not subvert what the audience expects from a title.

Sometimes such subversion of audience expectation is intended. Ivo van Hove's 2020 production of *West Side Story* intentionally avoided much of the Robbins choreography that audiences had come to associate with the title and cut the song "I Feel Pretty" altogether. This kind of surprise is sometimes expected in revivals, but there is a sense that the text presented has been altered, rather than simply reinterpreted. When Lincoln Center Theater revived *My Fair Lady* in 2018, the design, choreography, and line readings were very different from those used in the original 1956 production, but only the final moment, when Eliza was shown to leave Higgins, attracted much controversy. The final staging choice had been fixed by the movie version and by other productions, while the rest were left open to interpretation. The 1961 movie version of *West Side Story* had, however, fixed Robbins' original staging such that its absence was missed even by those who had not seen earlier revivals on stage.

Each chapter of this book will examine a different medium into which the musical has been fixed. I will explore how these media shaped the art form, defined which titles were part of the repertory, and established the texts that audiences expected were represented by these titles. In the first chapter, I will discuss the printing of musical libretti and scores from the late nineteenth century through the dawn of the internet age. Although printing in the West developed in the fifteenth century, new printing technologies perfected in the nineteenth and twentieth centuries meant that texts and music could be printed more rapidly and cheaply. This led to an increased willingness of publishers to experiment with printing for niche markets (such as readers of musical theatre libretti). As the printing of libretti became more common in the early twentieth century, the musical theatre libretto, often little more than a functional and disposable scaffolding in the nineteenth century, became respected enough to be considered "drama" and win Pulitzer Prizes in the twentieth. As a result, the libretto became part of what was signified by the title of a musical and could not be dramatically changed without subverting audience expectation.

Chapter 2 examines how the technologies used to promote and create a visual identity for musicals as part of promotional materials began to establish certain staging and costume elements as essential. Posters and sheet music covers for late nineteenth-century musicals often included color lithographs that defined the visual identity for a musical. Later, the photographs used on album covers, in souvenir playbills, and in companion books helped to "fix" certain visual choices and also provided a way for audiences far from theatrical centers to appreciate musicals not adequately represented in other media. In later years, websites, both official and fan-made, provided a way for productions to create brand awareness through the distribution of both images and audio-visual material.

Chapter 3 explores how audio recording, reproduction, and distribution technologies developed in the nineteenth and twentieth centuries worked to "fix" the program of a musical from a relatively fluid set of interchangeable songs into an increasingly stable score. As new audio technologies emerged, the market for re-releases of content available on earlier formats helped to establish a musical theatre repertory as the titles that were considered most "important" were converted to the new formats most quickly. As the commercial market for recorded music grew, musicals that could be easily appreciated on the basis of the recording alone entered the repertory more quickly than those that depended on the unrecorded or visual elements of a production.

The fourth chapter explores the emergence of commercially released video recordings of musical theatre both as film adaptations and as video documentation of live stage performance. I argue that, as with audio recordings, musicals that could be appreciated on film quickly entered the repertory. Further, changes made for filmed versions became part of audience expectations even when these changes were not incorporated into the texts licensed for stage performance. Though the influence of non-commercial or bootleg recordings is discussed throughout the book, I dedicate Chapter 5 to a history of the technologies used to create these recordings and the impact they have had on the canon and reception of musical theatre over the past hundred years.

In Chapter 6 I review the technologies used to create production resources for companies that license production rights and how these technologies have managed to fix ever more of the performance text. Finally, the last chapter provides an initial analysis of the effects that technologies used for theatre production during the COVID-19 pandemic have had on live musical theatre.

Recommended Reading and Earlier Work

This book is in some ways a follow-up to the aforementioned Bruce Kirle's *Unfinished Show Business*.[13] Kirle identified the phenomenon of variable and ever-growing texts; I propose that as more elements of the musical can be reproduced and commercially distributed, it is increasingly possible to "fix" the variable text in a stable form, although it is not yet clear whether these technologies will be used to so fix elements that have been traditionally considered variable.

The technological focus of this work is similar to Jessica Hillman-McCord's volume of collected essays *iBroadway: Musical Theatre in the Digital Age* (Palgrave-MacMillan, 2017) to which I contributed a chapter—however, this book is concerned with many technologies that long predate the digital computer.

In my discussion of the history of the cast recording in Chapter 3, I build on the work of Laurence Maslon's *Broadway to Main Street: How Show Tunes Enchanted America*.[14] Readers interested in a dedicated history of musical theatre on television (as discussed briefly in Chapter 4) are advised to look to Kelly Kessler's *Broadway in the Box: Television's Lasting Affair with the Musical* (Oxford, 2020).[15] The discussion of bootlegs and the influence of copyright law on the epistemology of musical theatre texts found most specifically in Chapter 5 but present throughout this book continues the work begun by Derek Miller in his *Copyright and the Value of Performance 1770–1911*[16] and Brent S. Salter's *Negotiating Copyright in the American Theatre: 1856–1951*.[17] The latter also offers a more detailed history of the company Samuel French than I include in Chapter 6.

This book, it should be noted, is fixed in the medium of one of the oldest technologies here discussed. There are some modes of communication for which the word, whether printed on paper, formed from e-ink, glowing in pixels, or read by a voice (whether human or automatically generated) remains the best available mode. The long-form argument, I believe, is one of these. I do not come to bury the printed word, nor to praise it, but simply to name it as one of the ways in which ideas might be fixed, and I have chosen this method for these ideas. I have not included links to audio recordings or video clips assuming the interested reader is likely to find them online more easily and in better versions than those for which I am able to clear the rights to use. Further, although copyright law has determined that the hard drives that serve content to the web represent a fixed medium of expression, their stability is closer to a sand mandala than a cave painting, and so the functionality of such links would be unlikely to outlast the format in which you are reading these words. The text that you are reading on whatever medium you have chosen for its encoding is designed as a book. The reader, I hope, will find this form a convenient one for the discussion of musicals designed for the still mostly unfixed experience of live theatre.

1

Printing the Musical

In May of 1932, *Of Thee I Sing*, a satirical musical by George S. Kaufman, Morrie Ryskind, and George and Ira Gershwin, became the first musical to win the Pulitzer Prize for Drama. The award specifically recognized the text rather than the music or other production elements of the show. In the announcement of the award, the committee acknowledged, "This award may seem unusual, but the play is unusual. Not only is it coherent and well-knit enough to class a play, aside from the music, but it is a biting and true satire on American politics and the public attitude toward them."[1]

A month prior, Alfred K. Knopf published the libretto as part of their Theatre of Today series. The series, advertised as "A Library of Plays Significant in the Development of Modern Drama," had previously included Maurine Watkins' 1926 play *Chicago* (on which the Kander and Ebb musical was based) and Maurice Donnay's 1892 adaptation of Aristophanes' *Lysistrata*. The first printing quickly sold out, and a second run, offered the same month, did so as well. The following month a third and fourth print run were issued, and there were at least four additional runs in the following year.

The printing of a musical theatre libretto was so unusual that the editor of the series, critic George Jean Nathan, contributed an introduction in which he instructs readers in the art of reading such a text:

> The reading of a music-show script imposes upon the library armchair a somewhat different attitude from the reading of a dramatic play. [. . .] I accordingly invite the more sober species of reader to engage this script with his top hat cocked saucily over his mind, with his ear filled with the hint of gay tunes and with his eye made merry by the imagined picture of all the relevant and appropriate clowns in the persons of actors, of madly painted canvas, and of appetizing femininity.[2]

Whatever "importance" Nathan might have felt the text had, he still felt the need to alert his readers that the aesthetics of musical theatre were somewhat different from those of the other plays published in the series, and that part

Fixing the Musical. Douglas L. Reside, Oxford University Press. © Oxford University Press 2023.
DOI: 10.1093/oso/9780190073718.003.0002

of the work of the reader of musical theatre texts is to imagine the elements of spectacle that are an essential part of the work on the stage.

If Nathan was a bit defensive of his choice to publish the work in 1932, he is much more self-congratulatory two decades later in his 1953 book, *Theatre in the Fifties:*

> Though the [Theatre of Today] series was supposedly confined to drama, when I came across *Of Thee I Sing* it made such an impression on me as a landmark in American satirical musical comedy that I dismissed the rule and included it, marking, I believe, the first time any such native script had been published in this country. And it came as a doubled gratification that not only, as everyone knows, was the show a great success on stage but a surprising success in book form, the biggest seller in point of fact of any of the volumes that previously had figured in the project.[3]

Nathan's confidence in the text may have increased the confidence of the Pulitzer board in making the award, leading to a greater respect for the American musical as literature.

The choice to publish the musical so close to the announcement of the Pulitzer Prize was fortuitous for Knopf. The play had opened only four months prior to the publication, so Nathan had worked quickly. The rapid turnaround was made possible by the new technologies used to print the book. This chapter will explore how these and later technological advances in duplicating and distributing words led to greater access to the book and lyrics of musical theatre, and how the texts that were shared in this way established the titles included in the musical theatre repertory. Further, I will examine how more recent editors have started to establish best practices and an editorial theory for publishing musical theatre texts.

Although Nathan was likely the first editor of a major press to print the libretto of an *American* musical, plays and music had been printed almost since the invention of the printing press. Mary Kay Duggan describes the early printing of liturgical choir music in Europe in the 1480s.[4] Similarly, Julie Stone Peters notes that plays were being printed and sold in Europe as early as the late 1400s.[5] Still, Peters cautions, "even in the late sixteenth and early seventeenth centuries [. . .] many plays that had found performance venues still remained unprinted."[6] She argues this was due to the "absence of sufficient readership" and "authorial reticence or indifference" caused by "aristocratic disdain for the press; anxieties about 'self-publication,' the desire to preserve the perceived exclusivity of manuscript circulation; [and] the commercial stigma of print."[7] This distrust of a new communication technology's power to weaken authorial control over intellectual property and the uncertain effect of the technology on the reputation of work created with it is familiar even today, as some artists resist, for various reasons, technologies like live video streaming and virtual reality. Perhaps for this reason, it is often those artists whose work is not yet widely acclaimed who are the fastest to adopt, or even create, new technologies.

In 1791, Alois Senefelder, a young German law student with a love of the stage, decided to give up his studies and seek a career in the theatre. He had written a set of plays that had, in small productions, "won sufficient applause,"[8] and he decided to have them printed and sell them at the Leipsic Easter Fair. Unfortunately, the printer he had engaged was unable to complete the work in time. Senefelder tried to find another printer, but without success. He writes, "My hope of profit was lost. I had, however, seen the entire procedure of printing, because I had spent many a day in the establishments."[9] He decided to become a printer himself, but lacked the capital to build a press. After a series of experiments, he invented a process whereby a particular kind of ink inscribed on slabs of cheap limestone and then washed with acid could be used to rapidly and cheaply produce printing plates. He collaborated with a musical composer named Franz Gleißner and, after many experiments and soul-crushing setbacks, developed a method that allowed for relatively quick and inexpensive high-quality printing, not just of text, but also of music and images.

For those familiar with the printing of playtexts, it perhaps comes as no surprise that lithography was invented by a playwright and a musician. Every writer would, of course, prefer printing to be as fast and inexpensive as possible, but cheap and fast printing is especially important for performance texts like plays and musical scores. Interest in these texts is often greatest for a short window of time around a recent performance. A short article in the April 1902 edition of *Printer's Ink*,[10] a New York journal for print advertisers, described a mail-order company that had experimented with advertising discount editions of selections of sheet music from *Florodora* on the elevated railway cars. Sales, it seems, were disappointing, but since *Florodora* had recently closed, they were seeking to try again with another product. The advertisers understood that the market for musical theatre scores would be greatest among audiences who had recently heard the music performed live.

By the late nineteenth century it was common for very cheap editions of libretti of operas and operettas to be sold in theatres. The texts of Gilbert and Sullivan's comic operas were often printed in this way in England and sold for as little as six pence (or roughly a dollar in 2021 values).[11] In an interview with *Dracula* author Bram Stoker in the January 2, 1908, edition of London's *Daily Chronicle*, William S. Gilbert described the financial success he had enjoyed as the result of the sales of printed libretti of his comic operas: "During the years we were running new operas at the Savoy I generally had royalties on my librettos to an average of about £3,000 a year. In all, I have had somewhere about £25,000 or £30,000 on this account."[12] Even at modest prices, print sales of popular libretti proved profitable.

Customers' expectations as to the quality of the printing and binding of these libretti would have been low. These were essentially souvenir programs. An early such edition of Gilbert and Sullivan's 1871 libretto for *Thespis* includes advertisements for sewing machines and cocoa.[13] A libretto for *H.M.S. Pinafore*,[14] distributed for free to audiences at the then-newly constructed San Francisco Tivoli for what seems to have been a pirated production of the show, was printed by "Bacon & Company, Book and Job Printers." The term "job printing" suggests short-run, cheap, quickly printed pieces rather than permanent, elegant, hard-bound volumes. At the turn of the century, the publication of musical theatre libretti seems to have been largely the provenance of "job printing."

Gilbert and Sullivan editions still enjoyed greater circulation than American musical theatre libretti, which remained largely unprinted, even in cheap editions, until the 1930s. In part this was because the libretti of most American musicals were generally considered little more than an excuse for the performance of the songs and dances. American librettists generally lacked the critical recognition to merit the permanence of print afforded to writers like Gilbert and Sullivan. As many historians have noted, it was not until the second decade of the twentieth century, when smaller-scale musicals like the Princess Theatre shows of Guy Bolton, P. G. Wodehouse, and Jerome Kern appealed to audiences through the wit of the book and lyrics, that the American musical theatre libretto started to earn critical notice, but these productions were intentionally designed for a very small theatre, and so the demand for the libretti was limited.[15, 16, and 17] None of the Princess Shows were published until many years later.

When George Jean Nathan selected *Of Thee I Sing* for Knopf's Theatre of Today series, the hardback volume needed to look and feel worthy of the imprint. The rapid pamphlet-printing technologies used for the souvenir Gilbert and Sullivan libretti would not suffice. Fortunately, Nathan's series had been built on the use of new printing technologies capable of creating a high-quality product more quickly and less expensively than had previously been possible. The final page of the libretto includes a note that the book was "composed, printed, and bound by Vail-Ballou Press, Inc., Birmingham, N.Y." and that the type was set "on the Linotype." This note, likely ignored by most readers, reveals the technological secret that made the risk of printing the libretto financially acceptable.

Vail-Ballou was a printing house founded in Ohio in 1900 using the technology of "Linotyping," a process wherein text is imprinted on strips of molten metal by means of something like a typewriter. A short history of the company, compiled by staff members Herbert and Everett Woodward, explains that in the first decade of the twentieth century:

> many publishers, particularly some of the older, more substantial concerns, were still prejudiced against linotype work. They didn't believe it good enough for their books, most of which were still set by monotype or hand. Linotypes were originally designed for use by newspapers. Types [fonts] available were largely newspaper faces and sizes and there was a lack of variety. There was occasional trouble, too, with broken letters. Many publishers wanted 12-point type while the early linotypes handled nothing larger than 11-point.[18]

The authors claim "By 1908 most of the early objections to linotype composition for books had been overcome, and the quality of work provided by Vail-Ballou was found equal to almost every demand."[19] The technology had made possible high-quality, cheap editions for short print runs like the volumes in the Theatre of Today series.

Of Thee I Sing seems to have benefited from an even newer and more efficient printing technology developed by the Vail-Ballou Press. In the Woodward history, the authors discuss Vail-Ballou staff Jim McGarrity and his invention of a new kind of "stereotype printing."[20] The invention addressed an inefficiency created by the fragility of the metal lines generated by the linotype, which made them unusable for printing in large volumes. Until the 1930s the lines were transferred to sturdier copper plates by an electrochemical process called "electrotyping." This could be expensive. Another method, "stereotyping," created plates using papier-mâché molds to cast the metal. This resulted, according to the authors, in "a substantial reduction in plate costs." The process had been used by newspapers, but McGarrity perfected it for book printing. All of the editions of the Theatre of Today prior to *Of Thee I Sing* included a note that they had been "set up, electrotyped, printed, and bound by Vail-Ballou press." *Of Thee I Sing*, and Vail-Ballou editions that followed, genericized "electrotyped" to "composed" in this description. It is likely, then, that *Of Thee I Sing* was printed with the cheaper "stereotype" method that became the Vail-Ballou standard for books that needed to be printed quickly and cheaply.

The technologies that led to the groundbreaking printing of *Of Thee I Sing*'s libretto did not, after all, earn the title a particularly prominent place in the musical theatre repertory. As time went on, the contemporaneous satire of political figures of the 1920s was lost on audiences, and the Gershwins' next work, *Porgy and Bess*, quickly eclipsed the score. However, the Pulitzer Prize and the commercial success of the printed libretto have nonetheless ensured it is remembered (it has been anthologized at least twice) and opened the door for musicals to be considered dramatic literature and distributed as such. Knopf, again using Vail-Ballou, printed the sequel to *Of Thee I Sing*, (*Let 'Em Eat Cake*) in 1933 with an introduction by Nathan wherein he reprised his instruction to the reader to saucily cock the mental top hat. In 1934, London Production Service and T. B. Harms printed an edition of Oscar Hammerstein's libretto for *Show Boat* (originally staged in 1927). Knopf printed the 1937 edition of the libretto of the Paul Green and Kurt Weill musical, *Johnny Johnson* (again using Vail-Ballou Press). By the end of the 1930s, the libretto of the American musical was regularly printed by commercial presses.

In 1938, Random House printed the libretto for Marc Blitzstein's musical *The Cradle Will Rock* with an introduction by playwright Archibald MacLeish. MacLeish puts forward a Brechtian argument for the printed libretto as an instrument for the destruction of theatricality. He begins with a call for the destruction of the passive Broadway audience (a "monster [. . .] that must be killed"[21]) and ends with the hope that the "faked realism of the modern stage [. . .] be replaced by the honest realism of a poetic theatre."[22] The printed libretto, stripped of every accoutrement of theatricality, must therefore be the pinnacle of this "honest realism" for the readers must by the participation of their imagination create everything except the text itself, all the while hyper-aware of the artificiality of the experience. The technology of print had created for MacLeish the perfect Brechtian medium for this very

Brechtian musical and left to the reader the Barthesian work of "making the text go."

In the 1940s musical theatre libretti continued to be published with regularity. It was not an enormously profitable enterprise for publishers. Bennett Cerf, an editor at Random House, was cited in Publisher's Weekly in 1953 saying his company "publishes plays [. . .] for the fun of it," although he notes that at a break-even point of only 2,000–3,500 sales, the company very rarely loses money on a title.[23] In the same article, Cerf acknowledged that the speed of publication was important because "in the six weeks it takes to produce the book, the original excitement over the play's opening had largely died out, especially in the New York area."[24] Publishers largely relied, therefore, on the regional market for plays. The anonymous Publishers Weekly journalist notes, "Many out-of-town New York book reviewers and drama critics give the Random House plays considerable review space. [. . .] When a Broadway show goes on a road tour, Random House provides the show's advance agent with books and jackets for display in bookstores and libraries in connection with the road company's posters."[25] The availability of the libretto, then, came to be a marker of the importance of a musical to audiences outside of New York.

Book Clubs

The production and sales of these libretti increased when a couple from Indianapolis, Nancy and Paul Briney, founded the Fireside Theatre Club. The couple loved theatre but, living inconveniently far from New York, relied on published scripts to track the art form. Although both were employed in full-time jobs, Nancy as a journalist and employee of the Army Map Service and Paul in public relations, the two decided to start a small, mail-order company to sell libretti to like-minded theatre fans far from New York. They used their personal savings to purchase a mailing list of those who had demonstrated a comfort with "buying by direct mail."[26] Nancy Briney recalls, "We made up a letter and sent it out. We sent it mainly to people in far places, such as Texas and California, because we thought the people in these parts might be more likely to think that Indianapolis was nearer to New York than easterners would."[27]

From the list of 10,000 names they found 106 subscribers who would select (at a cost of $1.89 each) four plays a year each from a list of twelve.[28]

They sold all genres of scripts including musicals. In 1949, when the couple moved to New York, Nancy approached the president of the Literary Guild, A. Milton Runyon, and asked him if the guild would be interested in taking over the club. Runyon agreed and appointed Nancy the editor (her husband, Briney said at the time, was "entirely out of it, now, except that he goes with me to see all the shows").[29] On January 27, 1950, *The New York Times* ran a short article announcing the club and its first offering under the new organization—the libretto of Rodgers and Hammerstein's *South Pacific*. Within four years, the number of subscribers had grown to around 15,000.[30]

An article in the 1954 volume of *Current Biography* summarizes the reception of the series among those in the theatrical community:

> Playwrights like "the immortality of covers" and most producers of plays which are still running on Broadway regard a published script as prestige. Only occasionally does a producer hesitate. Mrs. Briney recalls that she met with resistance from the producers of *Bell, Book and Candle*, since two road companies were going on tour [. . .] However they finally agreed to allow a Fireside Theatre version. It is believed that the published play created additional interest and increased audiences.[31]

The club continued to grow over the next two decades and at its peak in the 1970s had "close to 40,000 members on its mailing list."[32] The technology of the direct-mail list expanded a market for printed libretti, and the list of titles offered to these readers started to form an American repertory of musical theatre texts.

Theatre Arts Magazine

At around the same time as the emergence of the Fireside Theatre Club, libretti started to be included in theatre magazines. In spring of 1948, *Theatre Arts Magazine* combined with *Stage* magazine and promised to offer, as part of their new format, "a complete, unabridged publication of some recently produced stage success."[33] Although the majority of the works published were straight plays, the magazine did regularly publish both musical and opera libretti including the following sixteen titles:

Finian's Rainbow (January 1949)
Lost in the Stars (December 1950)
Brigadoon (August 1952)
Paint Your Wagon (December 1952)
Kiss Me, Kate (January 1955)
The Pajama Game (September 1955)
Plain and Fancy (July 1956)
Damn Yankees (November 1956)
Double Entry (July 1957)
The Most Happy Fella (October 1958)
Bells Are Ringing (April 1959)
West Side Story (October 1959)
Once Upon A Mattress (July 1960)
Fiorello! (November 1961)
Gypsy (June 1962)
The Unsinkable Molly Brown (February 1963)

Most of these opened in New York less than three years before their inclusion in the magazine, so the selections represent an attempt to provide a contemporaneous representation of the form rather than to publish earlier classics (like *Oklahoma!* or *Show Boat*). Rights may have been difficult to obtain from certain writers or for certain shows (the magazine never published a libretto of a Rodgers and Hammerstein musical or the enormously successful *My Fair Lady*). Still, the editors show remarkably prescient judgment in the titles they selected. All except *Lost in the Stars*, *Once Upon a Mattress*, and *Double Entry* (a double bill of two short musicals by Jay Thompson) have been performed frequently enough to be included in the regional theatre repertory listed in this book's introduction. With a peak distribution of 77,000 copies in 1957,[34] the magazine would have, unsurprisingly, been a niche publication (*The New Yorker* was circulating around 430,000 copies in the same period[35]). Still, many of those subscribers were likely theatre managers and artistic directors and so the editor's choices likely influenced the emerging American musical theatre repertory.

The relatively inexpensive cost of printing a magazine rather than a hardcover book, the built-in subscriber base, and the additional articles that might sell a magazine even if the script did not appeal to buyers also allowed the editors some freedom to experiment with both the selection and the presentation of the texts. The magazine printed, for instance, a heavily revised version of *Paint Your Wagon* in 1952 just months after the Broadway version had been published in hardcover by Coward-McCann. The introduction in the magazine version (titled "A Musical that Kept On Growing") includes a short production history of the show and introduces readers to the way in which musical theatre texts develop even after the Broadway run. The authors preferred the new version, but it would have been difficult for them to convince the publisher of the hardcover book to print it when the first edition had so recently been released. However, a new version of text appealed to the magazine's editors, as they could advertise the unique nature of their product.

Although most of the musicals selected for *Theatre Arts Magazine* had been relatively successful by the time they were printed, *Double Entry* had opened to mixed reviews and had only recently closed off-Broadway when it was printed in 1961. Thompson concludes his introduction for his pair of libretti in *Double Entry* by acknowledging the incomplete nature of the text as printed in the magazine:

> So, here is the blueprint for *Double Entry*. It is not the finished structure, which can only be erected by a director like Bill Penn using the extraordinary talents of a Rosetta LeNoire or a Jane Connell; or using the taste and ability of Brooks Morton and Rita Segree, who took my two-piano score and made honest-to-God music of it. What follows is a blueprint, but in reading it I hope you can visualize some of the fun that the above-mentioned people brought to it.[36]

Like Nathan before him, Thompson is asking the reader to approach the libretto as what Barthes would later describe as an "open text" and collaborate with the creators by providing enough imagination to fill in the gaps and "set it going."

Thompson's readers, though, needed to do less work than readers of the Random House editions of musicals. The libretti in *Double Entry*, like most in the series, included photographs of the production laid out in blocks along with the text of the scenes they depicted. This composition of text and photography was common in magazines, but less common in books that tended to isolate images to pages of photographic paper (often blank on the opposite side). In 1952, the magazine's edition of the libretto for *Brigadoon* included a single page of sheet music for four of the songs in the show along with the text. This kind of multimodal presentation became common in souvenir books in the 1970s (as will be discussed in the next chapter), but in the 1950s and early 1960s it would have been an innovative way to present the libretto.

Along with establishing a repertory, the magazine also worked to establish the musical as an important category of American drama. Articles by critics and artists alike discussed the form and history of musical theatre as a serious genre worthy of thoughtful consideration. There is some attempt to distance the musicals lauded by the magazine from less serious examples—the term "lyric theatre" is often used rather than "musical" or "musical comedy" to describe "important" titles. Historian Cecil Smith attempted to define the genre in a January 1947 article for the magazine titled, simply, "Lyric Theatre."[37] In the introduction to his libretto for "The Bible Salesman" (one of the two pieces in *Double Entry*) Jay Thompson struggles to find a definition for his work:

> "*Salesman* is not an opera or a musical comedy […]" he writes, "it is not a musical setting of the short story or of a one-act play based on the story; and it is certainly not a play with music. If you want to call the form 'washtub' or 'Tuesday afternoon,' those terms make about as much sense as any."[38]

In those days before internet forums or widespread scholarly acceptance of the genre, *Theatre Arts Magazine* was a place for those who wrote about the musical as a legitimate art form to publish their thoughts.

The decision of the editors of *Theatre Arts Magazine* to include musical theatre libretti without apology as part of their monthly publication of a script made it clear that musical theatre was an essential part of dramatic literature in America. While opera libretti, and in a few cases scripts written for television or film, were identified as part of a special issue focused on these related art forms, musical libretti were assumed to be as reasonable a selection for the play of the month as texts by Tennessee Williams, Mary Chase, Thornton Wilder, and Arthur Miller that were printed in the same venue. *Theatre Arts Magazine* ceased publication in 1963, and while later magazines like *Show Music* occasionally published libretti, and *American Theatre* regularly published scripts, no publication entirely filled the niche it vacated.

Anthologies

The reputation of musical theatre as a literary genre was further enhanced by respected publishers who started to print anthologies of libretti in the mid-twentieth century. The first such anthology was a single authored collection, *Six Plays By Rodgers and Hammerstein* published by Random House in 1955 and then given a second run under their Modern Library imprint in 1959. The Modern Library, in the words of the promotional text on their dust jackets, published "outstanding contributions to literature of the past and present, in authoritative editions, at a price within everyone's reach."[39] The 1955 Rodgers and Hammerstein anthology included all of the musicals the team had written to that point: *Oklahoma!, Carousel, Allegro, South Pacific, The King and I,* and *Me and Juliet* (each previously published as individual volumes by Random House).

Lise M. Jalliant has written about the effect of the Modern Library on the canonization of many modernist authors including Willa Cather.[40] Perhaps because of Bennett Cerf's own interest in theatre, the series was also rich in scripts, and so arguably had the same valorizing effect (at least in the popular accounting) on such playwrights as Tennessee Williams and Eugene O'Neill in addition to Rodgers and Hammerstein. Printing the libretti to American musicals alongside playwrights already considered "important" helped to establish the texts of musicals as legitimate works of dramatic literature (even if in the "light" category of Gilbert and Sullivan).

In the 1970s, the Chilton Book Company published three of the first multi-author anthologies of musical theatre texts: Stanley Richard's *Ten Great Musicals of the American Theatre,*[41] *Great Musicals of the American Theatre,* Volume 2,[42] and *Great Rock Musicals.*[43] These volumes, published in 1973, 1976, and 1979, respectively, represent an early first attempt to gather the most important texts of twentieth-century musical theatre into a kind of canonical collection. The contents of the first volume are somewhat idiosyncratic: *Of Thee I Sing, Porgy and Bess, Once Touch of Venus, Brigadoon, Kiss Me, Kate, West Side Story, Fiddler on the Roof, Gypsy, 1776,* and *Company.* The second volume is perhaps even more so: *A Little Night Music, Applause, Cabaret, Camelot, Fiorello!, Lady in the Dark, Leave It to Me, Lost in the Stars, Man of La Mancha,* and *Wonderful Town.* The absence of any of Rodgers and Hammerstein's musicals and the inclusion of *Brigadoon* and *Camelot* to represent Lerner and Loewe rather than *My Fair Lady* suggest that the choices were shaped by external forces. Richards himself obliquely apologizes for this in his introduction, writing, "Now for the omissions. It must be explained that publication rights for certain properties were unavailable at the time of compiling this volume."[44] He notes, though, that the anthology represents the first publication of the libretto of *Porgy and Bess* (though this is somewhat misleading as the piano/vocal score published in 1935 preserved the full text alongside the music[45]). Each volume was offered to members of the Fireside Book Club.

There were new attempts at anthologies at the turn of the twenty-first century. In 1997, a year before a Broadway revival of *On the Town*, Applause released a large-format three-title anthology of *The New York Musicals of Comden and Green: On the Town, Wonderful Town, and Bells are Ringing* featuring the full libretti and production photographs of the three shows in the title.[46] Applause followed this with *Four By Sondheim*,[47] which collected *A Little Night Music, Sweeney Todd, Sunday in the Park with George*, and *A Funny Thing Happened on the Way to the Forum* in a volume that was very similar in format and size to Stanley Richard's *Great Musicals* anthologies from the 1970s. Wiley Hausam's 2003 four-title anthology of *The New American Musical* (featuring *Floyd Collins, RENT, Parade*, and Michael John LaChiusa's *Wild Party*) attempted to make available and canonize new writers from, as the subtitle put it, "the end of the century."[48]

The market for these anthologies was limited, though, and only the TCG *New Musicals* volume remains in print as of this writing. In 2014, in an attempt to give some permanence to the printed texts of twentieth-century American musical theatre, historian Laurence Maslon edited a two-volume anthology of libretti for the Library of America. The Library of America was founded, in the words of their own website, when literary critic Edmund Wilson grew "concerned that many works by America's best writers were either out of print or nearly impossible to find."[49] Through endowments for each title, the company seeks to ensure that the works they publish stay perpetually in print, and that the volumes they produce are as durable as possible. The dust-jacket text introducing the Library of America makes special mention of the construction of the book:

> Library of America editions will last for generations and withstand the wear of frequent use. They are printed on lightweight, acid-free paper that will not turn yellow or brittle with age. Sewn bindings allow the books to open easily and lie flat. Flexible yet strong binding boards are covered with a closely woven rayon cloth.[50]

Indeed, by comparison with the glued bindings and soft paper covers of most of the TCG and Applause editions, the Library of America anthology does feel particularly sturdy.

The Library of America also has an explicit curatorial mission. On the "Why Library of America" section of the organization's website, the editors write:

> While millions of titles are now available in libraries and through on-line retailers, there are few places to turn for guidance in finding and appreciating the exceptional writing that best reflects this country's history and culture. To address this need, Library of America publishes carefully curated editions of works by the greatest and most significant American writers and develops nationwide and international initiatives to help readers discover these timeless works.[51]

Maslon's project, then, was a canon-forming one. He faced the self-limitation of avoiding works that depended too heavily on the music. "Of primary importance, beyond any other consideration," he writes in his introduction, "was that any musical selected should be enjoyable on its own merits in print form."[52] Perhaps it is for this reason that *Porgy and Bess*, which arguably depends so heavily on the score, was left out. It is notable, though, that despite Maslon's attempt to include "representation of the major contributors to the musical theatre form during this period,"[53] there is not a single Gershwin musical in the anthology. Maslon notes *Of Thee I Sing* had already been printed in "The Library of America volume *Kaufman & Co*," and so the brothers were felt to be already sufficiently represented by the Library of America.[54] *Annie Get Your Gun* would have represented Dorothy and Herbert Fields as well as Irving Berlin in a musical much better known than Maslon's Berlin selection, *As Thousands Cheer*, but Maslon explains in an article for *Slate* that he felt the musical seems "a little dimmer without the incandescent [performance] of Ethel Merman."[55] He defends his choice of *As Thousands Cheer* (one he admits is in large part a product of his "perverse opinion") as "the best, and one of the last, examples of the revue form."[56] Unlike Stanley Richards, who admitted his choices were in part shaped by the impossibility of acquiring printing rights in the 1970s, Maslon wrote to me in a personal email that "no estate ever said 'no' to any inclusion in the [*American Musicals*] anthology."[57] The contents represent the titles he wanted, and they were not significantly shaped by practical or legal limitations.

The Library of America anthology fixed a list of titles that most in 2014 would have acknowledged as "canonical" even if experts may have quibbled about whether they were the best representations of the musical theatre canon. The selection also represents a fair subset of the repertory compiled in this book's introduction. Only *As Thousands Cheer* is not included in that list, and of the sixteen titles Maslon selected, all but five have been performed at least twenty times by the regional theatres surveyed (placing them in the top 23 percent of the most performed works). Maslon's canon overlaps, perhaps unsurprisingly, with the established repertory and has the potential to further establish it.

More controversial than Maslon's selections, though, is his editorial approach. In his "Note on the Texts" at the end of the first volume, Maslon states his editorial goal is to "represent each musical, to the greatest extent possible, as it originally opened on Broadway."[58] That is, Maslon's textual ideal seems to be the "frozen" text as the creators intended it to be performed on opening night. Maslon reproduces the original published editions of *Oklahoma!*, *Finian's Rainbow*, and *South Pacific*, because they were "published within a year of opening night" and "reflect what is known about each musical's opening night state from the evidence of playbills, reviews, and subsequent scholarship." Maslon also considers the Knopf edition of *Kiss Me, Kate*, published five years after its opening, an accurate witness. The previously published editions of *On the Town*, *Pal Joey*, and *Show Boat*, however, have been, Maslon argues, modified based on later productions of the shows. *As Thousands Cheer* had never been published, and so he turned to unpublished archival sources for that text.

Maslon's choice to attempt to reproduce the text performed on opening night avoids the controversial and ultimately impossible project of discerning authorial intent and weighing *which* author's intention should matter most. Maslon also need not make aesthetic or editorial judgements about common variants. For example, in the original production of *Cabaret*, the song "If you could see her [through my eyes]" features the Emcee dancing with a gorilla. At the end of the song as written, the Emcee sings, "If you could see her through my eyes / she wouldn't look Jewish at all!" Fearing audiences would miss the point of the song, the line was changed to "She isn't a meeksite at all!" for most performances. In his textual notes for *Cabaret*, Maslon writes:

> In the Random House edition [which serves as his base text], both versions of the line were included:

> She isn't a meeskite at all!
>
> *Alternate*: She wouldn't look Jewish at all!

The present volume omits the "alternate" line just as it was omitted on opening night.[59]

Maslon seeks to present a single, historical performance of the text as accurately as possible (though he does record some alternative versions in endnotes as with the *Cabaret* example above).

Theoretically, the opening-night text was the version that would have been reviewed by critics and would have shaped the initial reception of the musical, so Maslon's editorial preference for this text makes a certain amount of sense. It is also the approach, Maslon explains, demanded by the Library of America. According to the editorial policy of the series, editors are expected to prefer "the first accepted, published text."[60] The first "published" and the first "accepted" are not, of course, the same in the theatre, if one assumes publication means commercial distribution of printed words. Maslon argues that the "opening night" text is the first "accepted," however, he often defaults to the first *published* text.

A live recording of opening night would, of course, transcribe the actual words spoken and sung that evening. Maslon's anthology, though, ends in 1969 and features only three musicals that opened after 1964 when the compact cassette tape was introduced in the United States, making surreptitious recordings much easier (as will be discussed later in this book). Non-commercial audio recordings of the original productions of *My Fair Lady*, *Gypsy*, *Fiddler on the Roof*, *Cabaret*, and *1776* all exist (if not necessarily of opening night),[61] though Maslon does not acknowledge, and does not seem to have used, these witnesses.

One might argue that if the goal is to document an important, single version of the text of a musical, a later version that is already safely fixed in a tangible medium would be a more realistic choice. We cannot recover what the original audience heard sitting in the seats of the St. James Theater on the opening night of *Oklahoma!* There is hard material evidence, however, documenting what the readers of the first edition of the published script read. Indeed, Maslon's use of a published libretto as a base text (instead of, say, the stage-manager bibles preserved in archives) suggests that he, or perhaps the Library of America series editors, also preferred a version of the text designed for commercial release rather than the text used in performance.

Digital Texts of Musicals

Regardless of what editorial theory is used, though, printed editions of musical theatre, at best, capture one version of a fragment of the full text of the musical. Any single edition offers not an "authentic" text, but a dim and partial reflection of one moment in the life of the work. Each performance of a musical represents a new version of the show created through the collaboration of many creative minds, all of whom share authorship in that particular edition. Editors of variorum editions have attempted to make the variability of texts legible to the reader, but the printed page demands finality while trying to represent a form that is, as Bruce Kirle noted, ever "unfinished."[62]

Further, musical theatre texts are not only variable, but also multimodal. They are meant to be sung as well as spoken, and much of the meaning of the lyrics depends on the music on which they are set. I have argued[63] that digital editions may be the best way to provide access to these texts, but, thus far, few have emerged, and the rapid development of technology has meant that even fewer last for many years after their initial publication. Nonetheless, like the advances in printing technologies in the 1930s, the advent of the commercial internet in the 1990s helped to both shape the musical theatre repertory and suggest new ways of reading these texts.

The earliest digital texts of musicals are as old as the commercial internet itself. Before the Hypertext Transfer Protocol (HTTP) became the most common way of accessing content on the internet, texts of all kinds were deposited in online directories accessed through the File Transfer Protocol (FTP). These could be found through early search tools such as GOPHER, or from links published on the online discussion forums called USENET. Musical theatre libretti were among the texts that could be found on these servers. The sources of the transcripts were rarely identified, though it seems likely most were based either on the commercially released cast recordings or published books, or from texts licensed for production.

Users of one of the most active musical theatre discussion forums on USENET, rec.arts.theatre.musicals, maintained a Frequently Asked Questions document, which included the question, "Where Can I Find the Lyrics/Scripts to xxxxxxx?" In 1997, the answer pointed readers to an FTP site for the group where one could find: "ROCKY HORROR, GREASE (the movie), LES MISERABLES, CHESS (Bway and London), HAIR, JESUS CHRIST SUPERSTAR, LITTLE SHOP, GODSPELL, and PHANTOM."[64] The FAQ also linked to a "Libretto of the Month Club" which published mostly transcribed lyrics from cast recordings. The libretti were usually presented as plain text (with no special formatting like italics or bold face) and intended to be downloaded rather than viewed while connected to the internet.

The authors of this FAQ also listed "Composers and frequently discussed musicals." Unsurprisingly given the mid-1990s vintage of the FAQ, the musicals listed are largely sung-through pop operas (e.g., *Les Miserables*, *Phantom of the Opera*, *RENT*, and *Jekyll and Hyde*), though lesser-known works such as *Carrie*, *Chess*, and, in later versions of the document, *You're A Good Man, Charlie Brown*, and *Snoopy!* received sections in the FAQ. The composers listed are Claude Michel Schönberg, Andrew Lloyd Webber, and Stephen Sondheim. These sections are meant to give new users to the group some background on the discussions they might encounter. (Simple, oft-asked questions from neophytes were often met with the curt instruction to "Read the FAQ!") Still, the shows that interested these newsgroup users (many of whom were also in the industry) formed a kind of canon both on and off the list, which in turn helped to shape the repertory at the turn of the millennium.

After the invention of the web browser (a technology specifically designed for multimodal texts), libretti moved from FTP repositories to web sites. Some of the earliest digital multimodal editions of musical theatre were the "Web Operas" of the Gilbert and Sullivan Archive, one of the first websites of any kind on the internet. Launched in 1993 on the servers of the Math Department of Boise State University (where the archive's webmaster, Alex Feldman, was a professor), the site first offered plain-text editions of the fourteen operettas by Gilbert and Sullivan and then, in the late 1990s, published what the site's editors dubbed "Web Operas."

Before internet speeds, disk space, and processing power made it possible to easily share recorded music, MIDI files (digital instructions for music synthesizers) were widely collected and shared on the early internet. Often compared to a player-piano roll, these files straddle the line between a musical recording and a score. They consist of instructions for playing a song, rather than a recording of the song itself, and the performance of the instructions varies greatly depending on the instrument (or computer) used to perform it. The Gilbert and Sullivan Web Operas were texts formatted in HTML with production photographs and downloadable MIDI files of the score (see Figure 1.1 for a screenshot of the Web Opera edition of *The Pirates of Penzance*).[65] These MIDI files sometimes included lyrics so those with a compatible MIDI player could sing along with them as a kind of karaoke track.

Gilbert and Sullivan were out of copyright by the 1990s, and so digital versions of their music could be legally produced and freely shared. Intellectual property was not, however, widely respected on the internet in the 1990s, and soon repositories of MIDI files of songs from more recent musicals sprung up around the web. One of the largest, Laura's Musical Haven, hosted tens of thousands of MIDIs from all genres until in January of 1999 the site owner removed the collection when, according to a note published on the site, the Harry Fox Agency (which enforces the mechanical rights for many music publishers) contacted the site manager with a takedown notice for "nine Rodgers and Hammerstein shows."[66]

It is noteworthy that it was mid-century musical theatre, rather than the top-forty pop songs of the 1990s, that led to the closure of the repository. The computer-generated melodies of MIDI files likely posed little market competition for commercial recordings of the Spice Girls, Madonna, or Nirvana. Indeed, it is unlikely that free access to a MIDI file of "My Favorite Things" from *The Sound of Music* would have prevented anyone from purchasing a cast recording (or film soundtrack). However, as will be discussed in a later chapter, in the 1990s licensing agencies for amateur productions had started offering packages of MIDI files as a kind of digital rehearsal pianist available for an additional fee with a performance license for one of their shows.

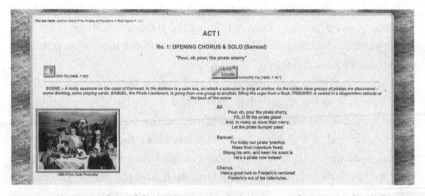

Figure 1.1 Screenshot of the Web Opera of *The Pirates of Penzance* from the Gilbert and Sullivan Archive (taken July 17, 2022).

Seeing a potential market, the Rodgers and Hammerstein Organization may have felt these free MIDI files posed a threat.

A similar story played out with libretti in the first years of the twenty-first century. Beginning around 2001 a Russian site, libretto.musicals.ru maintained a well-organized collection of both transcribed lyrics and full libretti (including some translated from languages other than English). Early titles transcribed for the archive included the shows that had entered the "internet canon" (*Carrie, You're A Good Man, Charlie Brown*, and *Snoopy!*). New titles were added regularly, including formatted HTML versions of yet unpublished musicals such as *Wicked* and *The Boy From Oz*, until the site was "temporarily closed" and then disappeared altogether in 2008 (a partial copy can still be viewed on the Internet Archive as shown in the screenshot in Figure 1.2). Although the reason for the shut-down was never publicly announced, Russia, in a bid to join the World Trade Organization, had passed a massive revision to their intellectual property laws in 2006, which went into effect at the beginning of 2008.[67]

Even digital editions created with the permission of the rights holders rarely last for very long online due to the rapid development of technology. In 2006 I completed my dissertation, which presented a prototype of an electronic edition of the musical *Parade* on a CD-ROM. The text was presented in a specially built HTML and JavaScript interface, which made it possible for the user to click a lyric and hear the related music if the cast recording was available on the user's computer. Over the years, QuickTime and JavaScript have both changed significantly, and so, as of this writing, the edition is no longer usable on modern web browsers.

Figure 1.2 Screenshot of Internet Archive capture of libretto.musicals.ru (screenshot taken July 10, 2022).

Over the next ten years I experimented with other methods of creating multimodal digital editions of musicals. In 2009, with support from a Digital Humanities Startup grant from the National Endowment for the Humanities, I led a team at the University of Maryland's Maryland Institute for Technology in the Humanities (MITH) to build a web application called Music Theatre Online.[68] The site published about fourteen variants of the Broadway musical *Glory Days*, letting users compare them, listen to different versions, examine photographs and Word files, and even watch videos of early productions. The site depended on Adobe Flash to play the media elements, however, and when Flash went out of fashion the site no longer functioned. By that time, I had accepted a new job at New York Public Library and was no longer able to maintain or update the site.

At the New York Public Library, I have published a semi-regular blog series called Musical of the Month, which makes available, in various electronic forms, libretti of musical theatre history from the library's archives.[69] Most of these texts are still available on the NYPL blogs, but my few attempts to connect the texts to music using online streaming services have broken, as these sites either ceased to operate or changed the way in which they allow third parties to access their content.

In 2014, again with support from a National Endowment for the Humanities Digital Humanities Startup grant, I published an Android app called Libretto that allowed users to read the text and click a lyric to hear a recording. Changes in Android over time have also meant this app has ceased to function. Digital innovations often have short shelf lives (at least in this still-early period of digital editions).

On the other hand, the simpler technologies of plain text and images have remained remarkably stable. The Gilbert and Sullivan Archive has survived a move from the University of Idaho servers at Boise to a private server, and the web operas continue to function (although they now must solicit donations from users for server fees). Amazon's Kindle eBook reader seems to have successfully created a sustainable market for commercially published electronic texts, and musical theatre libretti published by Applause or TDF are among the titles that can be purchased. These scripts are formatted to resemble their printed counterparts and do not tend to make use of the Kindle format's limited ability to include audio or video elements. The effect of the digital edition on the musical theatre repertory seems, thus far, to be about providing broader, if not always legal, access to digital surrogates of the paper documents. The technology's ability to offer functionalities beyond the affordances of the printed page has yet to be successfully used to create a stable, widely read, multimodal digital edition.

There may come a time, as digital publishing technologies continue to develop, when a multimodal digital edition of a musical can be published legally and in a form that will outlast the printed book. For now, however, the simple, commercially printed paper libretto has the power to bestow a certain legitimacy to both the title and the text itself. As musical texts were published by literary presses, anthologized, and discussed with seriousness by critics and practitioners in important magazines and journals, the potential for the form was better understood by artists and audiences. *Of Thee I Sing* and *The Cradle Will Rock* may not have entered the repertory despite their early publication, but those Knopf and Random House editions (with the accompanying critical acclaim) made possible new, serious works of musical theatre including those by Rodgers and Hammerstein and Stephen Sondheim. The Library of America printing of Maslon's anthology may not directly affect the repertory, but it is part of a corpus of work that recognizes the musical as a form that has classic texts on which new voices may build or else react against. "The immortality of covers" desired by the playwrights whose work the Fireside Theatre Club distributed bestowed on musical theatre the beginnings of the artistic respect that the form is, even now, still accreting.

2

Picturing the Musical

In today's era of music streaming, the time between the moment at which the thumbnail image of an album's cover art catches one's eye and one's first experience of the music from said album is roughly the time it takes to click a link. Browsing is now both a visual and aural experience. However, for most of the twentieth century, cover art might capture the imagination hours or even weeks before the music was ever heard. As I describe in the introduction to this book, I fed my early interest in musical theatre with the record collections of the St. Louis County Public Library. There was, as I remember, a limit of four records that a library patron could check out at any one time, and without a driver's license, I could generally only get to the library about once a week. So, even though borrowing was free, careful deliberation over which records to take out was required. I knew almost nothing of the history of musical theatre and so, for the most part, had to judge the album by its cover. Although many of the cast albums I remember had scores I grew to love, I recall certain titles for their cover art alone. I cannot recall ever listening to *Walking Happy*, for instance, but I do remember the boot on the yellow background.

The album cover was sometimes, though not always, the same artwork used on the *Playbill* cover, on the official poster, and in newspaper and magazine ads. For most outside of New York City, though, it was the most accessible visual representation of the musical. The promotional imagery associated with a production can fix the visual identity of the work so that later productions must either provocatively abandon that which came before or else pay homage to it in their own designs. The physicality of Tevye in *Fiddler on the Roof* as a stout man with dark hair and a relatively short beard has been fixed not only by the film adaptation but also by the poster illustrations and the many stage photographs reproduced in advertisements and in newspaper articles about the piece. Likewise, moments of staging are made iconic by the frequent reproduction of selected production photographs such as Dolly descending the staircase, Evita raising her arms on the balcony of the Casa Rosada, and Elphaba rising to defy gravity while the citizens of the Emerald

Fixing the Musical. Douglas L. Reside, Oxford University Press. © Oxford University Press 2023.
DOI: 10.1093/oso/9780190073718.003.0003

City fall back in amazement. This chapter will explore how the technologies used to create promotional imagery for musicals fixed audience expectations of the visual elements of titles in the musical repertory.

As with the other forms of documentation discussed in this book, promotional imagery depends on two technologies: that used to create or capture the image and the technology used to distribute it in mass quantities. One of the earliest and simplest forms of creating and printing images was block printing, a technology in which the subject is engraved on a piece of wood or metal and then painted before being pressed onto multiple sheets of paper. The practice was especially popular in Japan as a means of creating posters to promote Kabuki performances. In the West, engravings on metal were used to depict scenes from plays on posters and sometimes on the front pages of scripts. The title page of the 1615 quarto edition of *The Spanish Tragedy: Or Hieronimo Is Mad Again* featured an engraving depicting four characters each with a speech balloon in which are transcribed, in a meandering and somewhat squished typeface, lines from the play.[1] The somewhat absurd nature of the engraving has closely associated the image with the play, and it appears in most modern printings and in many histories that cite the work.

In the nineteenth century, lithography, a technology described in the first chapter, was used to print sumptuous full-color depictions of scenes from musicals on the covers of published sheet music. Within a year of the original production of *The Black Crook* in 1866, the sheet music for the songs "The March of the Amazons," "The Transformation Polka," and "The Fairy Queen March" had been printed with full color covers that announced their association with the title. These covers often depicted the supernatural female characters, often with legs bared (or in flesh colored tights) in a battle with fantastic monsters. The graphic covers of the sheet music were necessarily created by expert lithographers with a specialty in such work. The music portion of Dodsworth's publication of "March of the Amazons," for instance, was printed by "Russell," but the color cover was printed by Bufford Bros. (a well-respected lithography company at 735 Broadway, just across the street from the Astor Place location of Dodsworth's publishing offices). Music with these covers sold for around 6 cents rather than the 3.5 cent price for sheet music (like "You Naughty, Naughty Men") without a color cover.[2] The images on these covers helped to further cement the dubious reputation of *The Black Crook* as an erotic spectacle, one provocative enough to warrant the censure of the city's more conservative clergy, but innocent enough to fill the house with "respectable" audiences.[3]

Soon after the Civil War, photography had begun to replace sketches in theatrical advertising. Theatre and film scholar David Shields offers a detailed history of early theatre photographers on his website, "Photography and the American Stage," and those interested in a more complete history of the early days of the technology than can be covered in this chapter are referred there.[4] Both there, and in his printed book, *Still*, Shields writes about photographers like Charles Deforest Fredrick[5] and Napoleon Sarony,[6] who established themselves as portrait artists documenting the celebrities of the late nineteenth century and distributing the photographs both to the media and as souvenirs mounted on cardboard to create *cartes de visite* and slightly larger cabinet cards.[7] These artifacts, collected and displayed in fashionable society in the 1860s and 1870s, were some of the first to fix theatrical images in popular memory. Famously, in 1882, Napoleon Sarony photographed Oscar Wilde while the playwright was on a visit to America. The image was reproduced without permission by the Burrow-Giles Lithographic Company for a souvenir card provided with the "compliments of" the "trimmed hat department" of the New York store Ehrich Bros.[8] The lithographers argued that a photograph of a person could not be considered an invention and so could not be copyrighted.[9] The case went to the Supreme Court, which ultimately decided that the photograph represented enough artistic and intellectual creative work on the part of Sarony to merit copyright protection. This work included:

> posing the said Oscar Wilde in front of the camera, selecting and arranging the costume, draperies, and other various accessories in said photograph, arranging the subject so as to present graceful outlines, arranging and disposing the light and shade, [and] suggesting and evoking the desired expressions.[10]

The judgment left open the question of whether photographs of stage pictures created by others (say, for instance, the stage director) were also protected, and so there was perhaps less incentive for photographers to push the boundaries of the technology to attempt to capture scenes from a production itself.

According to Shields, although others had photographed tableaus of theatrical scenes in their studios, "Benjamin J. Falk received recognition as the first to take a production still of a commercial stage play [in the theatre] (Act II of 'Russian Honeymoon' in 1883, shown in Figure 2.1)."[11] A. I. Bowersox, in a piece printed in the 1894 edition of the *American Journal of Photography*,

Figure 2.1 Joseph Byron's 1883 photograph of *Russian Honeymoon* (courtesy New York Public Library for the Performing Arts, Billy Rose Theatre Division, MWEZ n.c.+ 19,348).

described the event as the first "electric light stage photograph."[12] An article in the 1883 volume of *The British Journal of Photography* describes the photograph as depicting the scene "exactly as presented to the audience."[13] *The New York Times* further describes the event as a post-curtain shoot, occurring at midnight and lit by "30 Brush arc lights" (i.e., Falk's own electric lights rather than stage lights).[14] According to the *Times,* the cast was "artistically grouped about the stage" and photographed for "about a dozen plates . . . obtained from the four 'sittings,' if they may be so called."[15] The language in the *Times* article, referring, even if with some reservation, to the shoot as a "sitting" and noting "the artistic arrangement" of the subjects and the photographer's careful choice of when to drop the shutter seems designed to emphasize Falk's creative work. The Sarony case was still working its way through the courts in 1883, but the article positions Falk's work in a way that would be most likely to earn protection under copyright law. One wonders if the report of this midnight photo shoot was supplied by Falk himself to the *Times* journalist in an effort to ensure his photographs would remain his own intellectual property. At the very least, Falk considered stage photography worthy of further experiments, and he later documented Charles Hoyt and Percy Gaunt's 1892 musical *A Trip To Chinatown.*

There soon emerged a market for creating and reproducing theatrical photographs, not just for sale as souvenirs or art, but as promotional material for producers. In a 1907 article for *Wilson's Photographic Magazine*, Sidney Allan, writing about early theatre photographer Joseph Byron, reported that early in his career "Byron went from one office to the other explaining the advantage of flashlight pictures, its merits as an advertising medium, as actual pictorial reports and records showing at a glance the character of a production, its scenery, costumes, and placing of accessories, but they would have none of it."[16] Allan notes, however, that Byron was eventually successful in his arguments and "No manager [in 1907] would think of sending out a production on the road without having secured a full set of all the principal scenes in the place. It has really become his helpmate in booking engagements and advertising plays, and seems to do its work more effectively than press clippings or any other method of recommendation."[17]

Despite the innovations of Byron and Falk during this period, though, most stage photographs from this period were portraits taken in a photographer's studio. Celebrities and young women were the most popular subjects. Magazines and newspapers regularly featured prints of chorus women or famous comics and tragedians, confirming that the heart of the musical stage was either female beauty or a well-known star. However, the printing of even these photographs was largely limited to specialty magazines (such as *Theatre*) or special photograph sections in the weekend papers. Printing technologies lagged beyond the ability of cameras to capture images and the distribution of photographs remained limited throughout the first half of the twentieth century.

By the late 1920s, though, photographs regularly accompanied news stories and were sometimes used in film and theatre advertisements. It could be expensive to do so, however. On the day of *Oklahoma!*'s opening in March of 1943, *Oklahoma!* published only a textual notice in the theatre listings. On the Sunday before, an advertisement in *The New York Times* featured a sketch of a cowgirl with a lasso, rather than any of the imagery used on the cast recording, the *Playbill* cover, or the poster.[18] The production did the same the following Sunday, but a feature story with photographs from the show ran at the top of the section, and so a photographic ad was likely considered unnecessary. The following Sunday, April 11, 1943, the production teamed up with Lux laundry soap to run a joint ad that included production photographs. The Theatre Guild found ways of introducing the public to the imagery of *Oklahoma!* without paying for expensive photographic advertisements.

The original Witold Gordon Theatre Guild poster for *Oklahoma!* features illustrations of characters from the show represented abstractly and colored with orange, green, brown, and red ink (or else left uncolored and white). The figures appear against a yellow background, but the colors are solid. Michael Patrick Hearn notes that this was the style of many of the Theatre Guild posters,[19] but it was especially well suited for *Oklahoma!*, which did not feature any well-known stars that might help sell tickets.[20]

The original *Playbill* cover for *Oklahoma!* included a photograph printed via rotogravure, a technique in which an image is imprinted on a cylinder. The image makes deeper impressions on the cylinder where it is darker, and shallower where it is lighter (so as to control the amount of ink that fills the impressions and is transferred to the page). As a new cylinder must be engraved for each page, it is a relatively expensive process. However, a single cylinder could be reused to print the program cover from night to night during the length of the run with the same picture—at least until the cast changed. A 1937 article in *The New York Times* reports that at that time *Playbill* dedicated two "flatbed cylinder presses" used "exclusively for printing the sepia covers that enclose the programs for legitimate playhouses" (three others were uses for color covers for the Metropolitan Opera and the Center Theatre).[21]

In her unpublished dissertation, Vicki Hoskins chronicles the history of *Playbill* and offers a short history of the covers noting that color sketches had often been used until the 1930s when the Great Depression made this an impossible extravagance.[22] She further notes that playbills during this period did not use photographs on its covers until competitors, like Radio City's program publisher *Showplace*, began to take clients who demanded photography.[23] Still, the company continued to resist cover photography for several decades. In September of 1957, Hoskins reports, producer Roger L. Stevens attempted to eliminate it altogether and introduced a standardized sketch that would be used on the cover of *every Playbill*. Audiences objected that this decision made the individual program less interesting to collect, and, notes Hoskins, "Producers criticized this change because they had promised their stars that their photographs would grace the covers."[24] Stevens relented and was forced to make a compromise with the League of New York Theatres (now the Broadway League) in an agreement that mandated cover photography but gave *Playbill* editorial control over the choice of photograph.[25]

Even in the 1940s, though, when *Playbill* often included photographs on the cover, the Theatre Guild and Rodgers and Hammerstein began to avoid using them for their own musicals. In 1943, it was extremely rare for a musical to run longer than a year. When *Oklahoma!* opened, the musical with the record for the longest run was the 1939 revue *Hellzapoppin*. The original program cover for that show, though, featured a photo of Harold "Chic" Johnson and John "Ole" Olsen, the book writers and lead performers. The show was so identified with the comedy pair that their faces would always fit the production even if the cast changed.

The Theatre Guild and Rodgers and Hammerstein seem to have learned over the course of the five-year run of *Oklahoma!* that the primary visual identity of a show that may run with several different casts should not feature images of individual cast members. By 1945, *Oklahoma!* had switched the cover of the *Playbill* to a black-and-white reproduction of Witold Gordon's poster art. Similarly, the original program of *Carousel* featured a single color reproduction of the poster art, which depicted abstract, solid color figures riding a carousel. *Allegro*'s program cover featured only the title on musical notes, and the poster used simple illustrations very similar to those of *Oklahoma!*.

The *Oklahoma!* cast album, on the other hand, featured a halftone photograph (a technology that used a series of pixel-like dots of a single color to create areas of heavier and lighter shading) depicting the cast in front of the original backdrop. It is crudely colored with blocks of red ink printed on top of a few of the costumes of the characters. The red is also used to shade the sky in a gradient and in the letters of the title. The cover of the *Carousel* cast album likewise featured a production photograph of the opening scene with the titular carousel. These recordings fixed particular performances by the original cast, and so a production photo allowed listeners to see the faces behind the voices on the discs and suggested the visual world of the musical in which these voices performed.

By the 1960s, scenic and lighting design had also become an increasingly essential part of the storytelling. From 1943 until about 1965, the scenic design of even spectacular musicals like *Hello, Dolly!* or *Camelot* were mostly functional and in service of the libretto. If the script called for a castle, a castle would be built (as impressively as the investors' money could afford). In the mid-1960s, though, designers and directors (especially Boris Aronson, Jerome Robbins, and Harold Prince) began to borrow the abstract theatricality of Russian theatre for the American musical. More than merely set dressing, the scenic design of, for example, *Cabaret* was an essential part of the dramatic text. The final moment in which the stage mirror was lowered to reflect the audience was not part of the libretto, but was an essential part of what Prince wished to convey with the piece. Prince continued this approach in his work with Stephen Sondheim in the 1970s. Scenic designer Boris Aronson had created designs for the sets of *Company* and *Follies* before the score or libretto were complete, and these designs helped to shape the text and music. By the 1980s, the visual elements of the British mega-musicals were at least as important to the enjoyment of the show as the score or lyrics.

Capturing the visual elements of these musicals in book form was complicated, but new technologies for cheaply printing pictures and text together led publishers to adapt an earlier document, the souvenir program, into the so-called coffee-table book. In 1973, Holt, Rinehart, and Wilson published *Two Gentlemen of Verona*, a large-format volume that included the libretto for the Public Theater's musical adaptation of Shakespeare's play. The cover describes the book as "A recreation, complete with pictures and sheet music."[26] Indeed, the volume includes not just the text but also reproductions of Theoni V. Aldredge's costume designs, photographs by Friedman-Abeles, and sheet music selections from the piano/vocal score. The text of the libretto appears in different sizes and different "weights" or thicknesses of bold typeface. The text wraps around the costume designs and photographs. In some cases the photographs are cropped to show only human figures without any background. Creating the plates for this kind of page-by-page collage of typefaces and photographs would have been challenging. Indeed, the editor dedicates a final page to credit the art director and production manager responsible for the book. This page also identifies the typeface ("Avant Garde Gothic"), the printer ("Halliday Lithographers Corp"), and the paper manufacturer ("Alling and Cory") and includes a small black-and-white photograph of two people, balanced on a suspended platform in front of the roof of the St. James Theatre, who seem to be finishing the placement of the show's billboard. The message seems to be that constructing this book was as risky a physical endeavor as hanging a billboard in Times Square.

This kind of companion book did not replace the souvenir program, but many productions began to produce them as another souvenir that could also be sold at venues (such as bookstores) unassociated with the production. In 1977, lyricist and director Martin Charnin published in hardcover *Annie: A Theatre Memoir*, a kind of "making-of" book about the musical without the libretto but filled with production photographs.[27] The final page of the book does not identify the manufacturing process, but does include photographs and biographies of the author, the photographers, and the book designer, Nancy Etheredge.

In 1978, the United Kingdom's Elm Tree Books, Ltd., published the libretto of *Evita* just before the opening of the show in London (an author's note dated March 1978 mentions that the text in the book includes changes made since the release of the original concept album).[28] Like the original concept album, the book features black-and-white photographs of the actual Eva Peron and her associates rather than production photos (perhaps because none were yet available when the book was edited). There is some creative arrangement of text and image, but for the most part the typeface is consistent throughout and the photos and text stick to fairly rectangular columns.

The souvenir companion book and libretto continued to flourish in the era of British mega-musicals of the 1980s and 1990s. In 1981, Faber & Faber published *Cats: The Book of the Musical* with the majority of the libretto (*sans* some repeating choruses) accompanied by full-color photos of the London production and John Napier's costume designs.[29] In 1983 Harcourt Brace Jovanovich released an American edition with most of the same content, but with photographs of Napier's American set model.[30] In 1987, London's Pavilion Books published *The Complete Phantom of The Opera*, the first of a genre of companion books that ambitiously described themselves as "The Complete" representation of the musical they documented.[31] In 1989 the London publisher Jonathan Cape released *Les Misérables: History in the Making*,[32] but Arcade Publishing and Little, Brown, and Co. retitled it *The Complete Book of Les Misérables*[33] when it was released in the United States. *The Complete Aspects of Love* continued the tradition.[34] Though published by different companies with text by different authors, each was similarly designed. The complete libretto was printed in small typeface and multiple columns on the last few pages of the book accompanied by black-and-white photographs. The rest of the books were dedicated to the history of their musicals, their source material, design documents, and sections of full-page color photographs showcasing the original productions. In 1991, Cape and Arcade Publishing followed their *Les Misérables* volume with *The Story of Miss Saigon*,[35] which abandoned the "Complete" formula for the title and did not include the libretto. Pavilion Books' 1993 follow up to their *Phantom* volume, *Sunset Blvd. From Movie to Musical* similarly eschewed the word "Complete" but did include the London version of the libretto.[36]

Although the libretti printed in these volumes filled in the lacuna of material left off the original cast recordings, the recordings were relatively comprehensible even in their abridged form. The production photographs, however, printed at a time before theatrical imagery was instantly and widely available on the internet, helped to establish the look of the costume and scenic designs that became iconic for these musicals. Further, the very presence of these books on the shelves of WaldenBooks, B. Dalton, or Barnes and Noble began to establish, for theatre fans, a new, transnational musical theatre repertory. For those living far from New York, the books served as a way to connect to what was happening on Broadway.

As discussed in the first chapter, by the mid-1990s at-home access to the internet had become a significant platform for the distribution of content. For those with a connection, access to the lyrics and libretti of many of the most popular musicals could be had for free. In an era when mass reproduction had become cheaper than ever, there emerged an aesthetic that preferred things that *appeared* to be more handmade and less polished (or at least less common). The 1996 musical *RENT*, with its minimal set, street clothes, and visible microphone headsets, appealed to this aesthetic. The companion book, the first to be designed by the New York–based Melcher Media, sought to be similarly distinctive. A faux-tape binding reflected the DIY aesthetic of the show and contrasted with the more staid and unremarkable bindings of the *The Complete* . . . books on shelves. Its unusual size (9.25 inches deep and 14 inches tall) further caused it to stand out next to standard-sized books, or, in some cases, to be featured in special displays that could accommodate the size.[37]

Unlike earlier coffee-table books, the libretto of *RENT* took center stage in the middle of the volume, and pull-quotes in large typeface, like those used in magazines of the era, highlighted selected lines. In some cases, the text is laid over the images, in others it is printed on a facing page next to a full page image. There are very few spreads without at least one page dedicated to an image. Melcher designed similarly unique companion books for *Wicked* (made to resemble a medieval spell book), *Avenue Q* (with a furry orange cover), *Jersey Boys* (with a cover textured to feel like an LP), and *Hamilton* (designed to look like an old history book). By 2003, though, the libretto was less essential to the souvenir book (early on the creators of *Wicked* were especially protective about "spoilers," and so the *Wicked* book contained only fragments of the book and lyrics). What was of interest, in addition to the photographs, was the detailed commentary on the process of creating the shows.

A competitor to Melcher Media, Roundtable Books, published companion books with libretti for *The Producers* (2001) and *Hairspray* (2003). Both of these included in-text annotations on the libretti, designed in a way that resembled the "pop-up video" bubbles made popular in music videos and for reruns of mid-twentieth-century television (e.g., *I Love Lucy*) in the 1990s and early 2000s. The editors of the *Hairspray* book, perhaps anticipating that the community of musical theatre fans may not significantly overlap with the audiences VH1 and Nickelodeon, used a slightly older metaphor, connecting the "marginal notes" to "the spoken commentary on DVDs." Annotated texts have, of course, been a familiar document almost since the beginning of writing. Annotated editions of works of literature (e.g., *Sherlock Holmes, Alice in Wonderland, The Wizard of Oz*) were popular in the 1960s and 1970s, and Issac Asimov edited the Annotated Gilbert and Sullivan in 1988.[38] However, until the twenty-first century, annotated musical theatre texts were uncommon. In 2010 and 2011, Stephen Sondheim published two volumes of his collected lyrics[39][40] that were rich in annotations by the author. Melcher media followed suit with a libretto for *Hamilton* annotated by Lin-Manuel Miranda[41] (who had already participated in the crowd-sourced annotation of his libretto on the open website, Genius.com).[42] Miranda followed the same template for the companion book for the *In the Heights* film adaptation and annotated the stage lyrics (sometimes with notes about changes made for the film).[43] Dave Malloy is also an active annotator of his own work on Genius.com,[44] and the companion book to his *Natasha, Pierre, and the Great Comet of 1812* similarly featured his annotations.[45]

By the twenty-first century, though, souvenir books were unlikely to be the primary way fans of a musical might encounter visual imagery connected to the show. Even by the late 1990s, the internet was quickly becoming the primary platform for promoting musicals, and so helped to shape both the repertory of the past thirty years and the way in which the texts of musicals were received. Laura MacDonald provides an early history of Broadway websites in her chapter for Jessica Hillman-McCord's *iBroadway* collection.[46] MacDonald describes the development of the web as both a site for fan communities (similar to a 1990s New York piano bar, to use an analogy MacDonald quotes from Ben Brantley) and as a place for producers to engage with potential ticket buyers, and in some cases, to sell tickets directly.[47] MacDonald notes that established theatrical organizations such as *Playbill*,

The Really Useful Group, the Shubert Organization, and the Rodgers and Hammerstein Organization were early pioneers in the space, creating websites as early as 1994 (a year after the release of the first widely distributed web browser), and also maintaining a presence on commercial dial-up services like Prodigy, America Online, and CompuServe. According to MacDonald, in 1997 *Les Misérables*, *Miss Saigon*, and the Rodgers and Hammerstein organization, among others, employed a design company, T3Media, to create a web presence for their brands.[48] In the first years of the World Wide Web, theatre publicists quickly identified the internet as an essential tool for making audiences aware of their products, and they worked to ensure a show's official internet presence did not erase fan enthusiasm but also did not rely entirely upon it.

Although many of these sites did include short sound clips (usually in a low-fidelity format), dial-up speeds and media compression were not yet suited for sharing large media files. Digital images, however, were integral to the design of the early web. Even text-heavy web pages often included a few low-resolution illustrations to distinguish the format from the entirely textual GOPHER, FTP, and TELNET sites that formed the basis of the internet prior to the invention of the web browser.

Musical theatre fans were interested in the imagery of their favorite shows, especially the iconic posters created for Cameron Mackintosh's musicals. On September 6, 1996, user "Pete in VA" asked in a poster on the USENET newsgroup rec.arts.theatre.musicals:

> Does anyone have any graphics files of the logos/clipart of musicals (especially ALW or Les Mis, Miss Saigon), or is there a site I've been unable to find?[49]

User Gary L. Sanders, who in his electronic signature identified himself as "V.P. of Engineering" at Sanders Media Adventures, Inc., responded:

> When you visit a website, you should find a lot of .gif files in your disk cache, if you don't delete your cache; as you should do occasionally. Often you can scan the files with a viewer and find what you need.[50]

Some websites offered easier ways for those seeking to download poster art to print on their new ink jet printer or save to their Windows background. The Harvard-based musical theatre group, "The Harvard-Radcliffe" notables, offered direct links to download several popular show logos including: *Candide, Cats, Evita, Hair, Jekyll & Hyde, Jesus Christ Superstar, Les Misérables, Miss Saigon,* and *The Phantom of the Opera.* A 1998 capture of the site by the Internet Archive's Wayback Machine includes an apology that "The Sondheim logos have been removed temporarily for legal reasons."[51] The rights holders, probably the poster artists, for the Sondheim logos (representing shows that had already closed) objected to unauthorized distribution of their intellectual property, whereas currently running shows may have seen the distribution as a form of free promotion.

Before T3Media launched the official *Les Misérables* or *Miss Saigon* pages, several fan pages served as the primary conduits online for content and news about the musicals. In the early 1990s, most with internet access were associated either with a government agency or an institution of higher education, and so a large number of relatively young adults were regularly joining the web each semester. These students also often had access to university servers and so, with minimal effort, could launch websites dedicated to their favorite subjects. By the late 1990s, subscription services like Prodigy and America Online had brought more users to the web, but the demographics of the internet continued to skew toward young adults. As a result, the most popular early pages dedicated to musical theatre were created by young amateurs. In 1994, William S. Kartalopoulos, a history major from Dartmouth, launched a *Les Misérables* webpage that was, for a time, the primary website most guides to theatre linked to on the early web. When the official website, *Les Misérables,* was launched, Kartalopoulos was given an "exclusive" link to a preview version of the site.[52] It was not until March 3, 1997, that *Playbill* reported that the official *Les Misérables* site had launched.[53]

Kartalopouls was by no means the only manager of a *Les Misérables* website, however. Steve A Taylor, a young man from the West Midlands in the United Kingdom, created what was then the de facto website for Alan Boublil and Claude-Michel Schönberg's musicals. In the "editorial" section of the page, Taylor thanked "the London office of Cameron Mackintosh for not interfering or objecting to these pages and for always being courteous when dealing with my persistent phone calls."[54] A notice on the bottom of the page warns visitors that "The copyrighted logos and photographs from the various shows [. . .] remain © Cameron Mackintosh (Overseas) Limited."[55] While the site was the creation of an amateur, it is clear it existed with the implicit permission and occasional support of the producers.

Visitors to Taylor's site could view images, listen to short audio clips (the site was one of the first to introduce audiences outside of London to the sounds of *Martin Guerre*), read synopses of the shows and recent news articles, or, in a relic of a more innocent age of the internet, sign a "Guestbook" with their email, name, location, and age with an invitation for other fans to write to them to discuss their mutual interests. Their entries were submitted to a Perl script, which seems to have automatically interpolated them into the Guestbook page in alphabetical order each day. The guestbook was divided into five geographical regions "UK and Europe," "USA and Canada," Australia, Asia, and the "Rest of the World." The majority of fans in the United States lived far from New York, and many of the fans in Europe did not live near London or any other open-ended run of these shows. The average disclosed age across the five regions was 19.6 (in the United States it was only 17.4).

In 1997, as a companion to the free website, Cameron Mackintosh's managing director, Martin McCallum, partnered with the German company EuroArts to create a two CD-ROM package called *Les Misérables Interactive*.[56] The two-disc set opened with a 360-degree panorama of the Palace Theatre in London (see Figure 2.2) and a short video by Cameron Macintosh, who appeared to walk out in front of the image to introduce the software. The interface, designed using Macromedia Director, allowed users to "explore" the theatre by clicking on different areas. A map on the wall allowed users to learn about areas in Western Europe featured in the story. Victor Hugo himself appears to be sitting in the mostly empty auditorium, and clicking on his image links to pages with details about his life (see Figure 2.3). Clicking a poster hanging in the box seats opens a window in which users could watch short video clips of productions from around the world.

One could also venture out into the "lobby" of the theatre, where there were three "tables" that served as links to the internet. In a piece in *Variety* in March of 1997, McCallum explained that a small cafe table with a sign that read "Internet Fan Club" (see Figure 2.4) connected "to an area on the [official] site called Le Cafe, where 'Les Miz' fans can post messages about the show."[57] Clicking on another table linked to a section that allowed users to book tickets for the live show. Finally, a virtual gift shop showcased souvenirs and compact discs available for purchase. These transactions could be completed by: (1) calling a toll-free phone number, (2) printing a form and faxing to another number, or (3) clicking an "Internet Link" (see Figure 2.5). However, in the late 1990s, the connection between the home computer and

Figure 2.2 View of the "stage" in the *Les Misérables Interactive* CD-ROM.

the internet was more tenuous than it would be a decade later in the days of nearly ubiquitous, always-on broadband. Clicking the links in the CD-ROM started a process that required the user to locate the web browser on their desktop and then connect to the internet. There were many ways this could go wrong, and for this reason, the *Les Misérables Interactive* featured more established mechanisms for remote purchases much more prominently.

The *Les Misérables* CD-ROM sits uncomfortably between a digital archive for the musical and a video game. McCallum described the "chief audience" as "educators," but it is not entirely clear how he imagined the disc being used in coursework. McCallum admits that he had some difficulty finding producers for the project. The people at EuroArts "were the only ones who didn't say I was crazy for wanting to do a CD-ROM."[58] Still, the CD-ROM captures the moment of transition when the World Wide Web was still new and marketers were learning how to use digital technology to connect with fans. In the days of dialup, video and audio were too large to be conveniently consumed online, and so a companion CD-ROM made a certain amount of sense. However, the cafe table in the lobby demonstrates that this

Figure 2.3 Victor Hugo is watching the show as well. Clicking on him will open a biographical section on the author.

Figure 2.4 Clicking on this table in the lobby linked users to the discussion page on the official website.

Figure 2.5 A ticket order form that featured the toll-free phone numbers and fax form much more prominently than the internet link.

self-contained experience could not do by itself what the internet of 1997 did best, connect individual fans to a fan community.

By the twenty-first century, though, digital video and audio could be easily distributed on both websites associated with a production and in ad campaigns on social media, and so the need for promotional books (or CD-ROMs) to provide a record of the visual elements of a production decreased. Although still images continue to capture iconic moments and often give a production with a recognizable visual brand, and souvenir books continue to be manufactured and sold, the "visual text" of musicals is now most fully fixed in other media, as will be discussed in later chapters.

3

Recording the Musical

In 1888, composer Arthur Sullivan, after listening to a wax-cylinder audio recording of one of his songs not written for the stage ("The Lost Chord"), famously made use of the newly invented technology to document his own response to it: "I am astonished and somewhat terrified at the result of this evening's experiments: astonished at the wonderful power you have developed, and terrified at the thought that so much hideous and bad music may be put on record forever."[1] It is unclear whether Sullivan, who aspired to be a "serious" composer and had a somewhat ambivalent opinion of the comic operas that made him wealthy and famous, would class his most famous work among the "hideous and bad music" that he feared the technology would preserve. Regardless, portions of his theatrical songs were among the first snatches of music fixed in the medium of the wax cylinder[2] and, in the early twentieth century, on 78 rpm discs. A 1906 recording of the Mikado on sixteen ten-inch discs and one twelve-inch disc represents one of the earliest near-complete recordings of an English musical theatre score (preceded by a complete recording of the opera *Ernani* in 1904 and several *Florodora* songs in 1901).[3]

Laurence Maslon's masterful book, *Broadway to Main Street: How Show Tunes Enchanted America*,[4] thoroughly explores the history of this particular form of documentation of the musical more thoroughly than the scope of this chapter allows. Here I will examine, in particular, how producers of cast recordings made use of the affordances of the particular technologies used to record and distribute their product, and how these records defined the "text" of the musicals they documented and shaped the form itself.

Maslon describes a "taxonomy for recordings of show tunes in the 1920s up through 1935" that includes "arrangement for dance orchestra," "medleys," or "gems" (a small selection of hit songs from a show, often covered by singers not part of the original cast).[5] Perhaps not coincidentally, these were the same genres in which musical theatre of the late nineteenth century was usually preserved in sheet music, and likely for the same reason. Documenting a full

Fixing the Musical. Douglas L. Reside, Oxford University Press. © Oxford University Press 2023.
DOI: 10.1093/oso/9780190073718.003.0004

score using either the technology of the printed book in the nineteenth century or the 78 rpm disc in the early twentieth was expensive and resulted in an unwieldy product that required significant physical effort to use. Playing a full piano score would have been exhausting, of course, but playing a stack of disks or cylinders would have also required the listener to regularly change the media and wind the player by hand.

The addition of the electric motor to the record player, and the invention of the record changer in 1927, made it possible to listen to a series of discs, each containing up to five-minute segments, in almost uninterrupted succession.[6] Producers of classical music, with movements that often lasted longer than the roughly three- to five-minute limitation imposed by the technology, were among the first to manufacture "albums" of multiple records that documented a full orchestral or operatic work. Musical theatre, though, still marketed as popular music, was mostly sold as single songs on single discs.

It is perhaps unsurprising that the musicals written during this period (e.g., *Show Boat* and *Anything Goes*) have a set of hit songs (or "gems") that are considered essential to the score and others that are little remembered and sometimes dropped in later productions. The "gems" were the songs recorded on disc. For instance, several of the songs from the 1903 Victor Herbert operetta *Babes in Toyland* were preserved on recordings in the early years of the twentieth century. The 1961 Disney film adaptation of the musical bears little resemblance to the original, but then, neither did many of the stage revivals produced in the intervening sixty years. All, however, include the "March of the Toys," a song that was recorded to disc in 1911 and so had become an essential part of the score.

Recording technologies also began to separate musical theatre performance practices from that of opera. Opera depends on stylized vocal techniques developed in the years before electric amplification helped the singer to be heard over an orchestra in a large performance venue. Musical theatre singers sometimes use this style, but the music, orchestrations, and (in the later part of the twentieth century) amplification allowed singers to adopt vocal styles that more closely resembled speech. In the 1910s, smaller venues, such as the Princess Theatre, also allowed singers to perform songs in a style that would allow audiences to more easily discern the wit of the lyrics of P. G. Wodehouse and Guy Bolton. Musical theatre performance had therefore begun to separate from opera even before the performances could be fully documented on record.

In the first two decades of the twentieth century, all who played, sung, or spoke for a recording did so into a large, tapered "horn" attached to the device. All of the sounds were recorded at the same time, and the operatic style was therefore required for the voice to be heard over the orchestra. The rise of the popularity of radio in the late 1920s and early 1930s led to improvements in microphone technology, however, and electrical microphones allowed full orchestras to be recorded in the same space, with different groups of instruments and singers recorded via separate devices. Lance Brunner explains how this allowed performers to employ more naturalistic emotional expression in their performance.[7] It took some time for this technology to be perfected, however, and recordings of musical theatre performances with full orchestras were not regularly recorded until the 1940s.

Porgy and Bess

The liminal status of the Gershwin's *Porgy and Bess* as work that sits somewhere between opera and musical theatre made it an ideal candidate for a recording in the 1930s. Eight songs from the score were recorded by Victor on Sunday, October 13, 1935,[8] four days after the show opened at the Alvin Theatre in New York. Sadly, the Black actors in the leading roles were not asked to record their performances and were replaced instead with white opera stars Lawrence Tibbett and Helen Jepson. The album was composed of four twelve-inch 78 rpm discs, each preserving less than five minutes of music. The order of the discs had no connection with the placement of the songs in the show, and Tibbett and Jepson divided up all of the solo songs, each portraying several characters on the album.

Five years later, Decca released an album of four twelve-inch discs with most of the same songs recorded by Victor but now performed by the original leading actors, Todd Duncan and Anne Brown. The label followed the precedent set by the previous recording, though, and had the two actors perform all of the solo parts for all but one of the same songs recorded by Victor ("A Woman in a Sometime Thing" was replaced with "Requiem"). Perhaps because the Victor album had been, as attested on the disc label, recorded "under the supervision of the composer," it had started to fix a performance tradition that defined the "essential" songs and an approach to recording them that required only two soloists.

Two years later, Decca released an album of three ten-inch discs featuring members of the 1942 revival singing their own solos as in the stage production. The album recorded "A Woman Is a Sometime Thing" and five other songs on ten-inch discs (with a maximum length per side of just under three minutes and thirty seconds). Decca attempted to unify the two recordings despite their different casts and the different physical dimensions of the discs by titling the second album "Volume 2." This provided an album of entirely new songs to customers while potentially reigniting interest in the first set. However, due to the practice introduced by Victor and continued by Decca on their 1940 release, there is no record of "Summertime," "My Man's Gone Now," or "It Ain't Necessarily So" performed by either the original cast or the actors in the 1942 revival. Re-recording the previously released songs might have seemed excessive (especially in an economy constrained by war). Further, while the ten-inch format used for "Volume 2" allowed Decca to save money and materials, it meant the four-minute-long "My Man's Gone Now" could not fit on a single side of a disc.

Today we think of a cast album as a document of most of the songs heard in the theatre as performed by the original cast. In the early days of commercial audio recordings, this was not assumed. Decca's halting and imperfect documentation of the original and 1942 casts of *Porgy and Bess* helped to set an expectation that the musical consists of a fixed score and that the songs are sung by actors performing roles rather than by singers who are simply providing diversions for a melodrama. If *Porgy and Bess* on stage was an important milestone in the history of a form that is not quite opera and not quite musical comedy, Decca, by the somewhat clumsy and fragmented release of the score, emphasized that this was a new form that demanded a new kind of recording.

The Cradle Will Rock

Although less broadly popular, Marc Blitzstein's 1937 musical *The Cradle Will Rock* became the first American musical to have most of its score recorded by the original cast. *The Cradle Will Rock* was, in many ways, perfectly suited for the recording technologies of the time. The score had been orchestrated by Blitzstein, but on opening night the cast and musicians were famously locked out of their intended theatre when the United States Congress decided to pull support for the show (likely due to its perceived radical message). The cast and the audience moved to a different theatre, but the score was performed by Blitzstein alone on stage with a piano as the actors performed their parts from the audience (due to a restriction from Actors Equity that prohibited their appearing on a different stage than originally contracted). Minimal staging and orchestration, a practical necessity in this improvised performance, became the standard practice for staging the show in following years.

In 1938 director Orson Welles was starring as the title character in the Mutual Broadcasting System's radio series *The Shadow*. He may have recognized that *The Cradle Will Rock* was uniquely suited for the affordances of the available recording technology, and so, in the spring of that year, the cast recorded the show much as originally performed, with Blitzstein narrating the action and playing the score on a piano. As Laurence Maslon notes, this recording, released on the tiny Musicraft label, was essentially "a radio program with music."[9]

For contemporary listeners accustomed to cast recordings that only preserve fragments of dialogue, Blitzstein's narrative summaries of unrecorded scenes can sometimes feel gratuitous. The amount of spoken text versus music on the album would have made the recording simpler, though, for the small studio that recorded it. The performances were recorded directly to disc (as magnetic tape recording was not available in the United States until after World War II), and the lathe that cut the record etched the sound waves into the disc as it turned while being pushed slowly toward the center (thus the groove of the sound recording forms a wavy spiral shape). Loud sounds would displace the needle further from its default spiral than softer sounds, and so speaking or quiet singing would displace the lathe less than orchestral music would.

Although today, the rate at which the lathe is pushed to the center during recording may be dynamically altered by digital technology, in 1938, it was almost always set at a constant speed. Pushing the lathe to the center at a faster speed was safer as it meant there would be a greater distance between each loop of the spiral and less of a chance of ruining a disc by a loud sound later in the recording bumping up and over an earlier part of the spiral. However, this also meant there was less time available on the disc.

The softer piano-only score with a great deal of spoken text made *The Cradle Will Rock* an ideal candidate for recording more grooves per inch. Even with the potential for somewhat denser recordings, though, the recording time of each side of each disc remained relatively short. The sound engineers played it relatively safe, staying below the five-minute maximum length for each side of a twelve-inch 78 rpm disc. The original cast recording of *The Cradle Will Rock* is roughly fifty-four minutes and thirty seconds split across seven discs (fourteen sides). The average duration per side is therefore three minutes and fifty-four seconds, though some discs are much longer.

The recording time permitted on each side was extremely limited by today's standards, and so, as Maslon notes, "The final product was unwieldy—one had to turn over records mid-scene."[10] The B-side of disc one ends in the middle of the courtroom scene, right after Reverend Salvation's preaches his moderate 1916 sermon but before the contrasting warmongering 1917 one. A disc change is required just when continuity might be especially advantageous. Disc five begins midway through scene seven with Blitzstein narrating the action, and then sets up the second side which jumps back to the beginning of the scene to capture Moll's song, "Nickel Under The Foot," in its entirety.

Perhaps because of the cumbersome nature of the album, the recording seems to have been mostly unnoticed by the mainstream American press. A syndicated column, "Dale Harrison's New York," discussed it in the May 18, 1938 edition, but focused on the use of the "cuss" words (the album begins with the name of "Jesus" used "in vain," a use of "damned" in scene six, and a reference to "whores" in scene seven). The review notes:

> There are good reasons, though, why "The Cradle Will Rock" is important. It may blaze a trail of transferring other Broadway productions to discs—a cultural contribution of great value, I should think, not because Broadway productions are mental manna to America's masses but because they are Broadway productions. In this particular case we have what the producers and the critics have referred to as a "new" form of entertainment which is neither opera nor musical comedy yet is a bit of both.[11]

Despite (or perhaps, because of) the "jolly old cuss words," Harrison believes even the "capitalistically minded [. . .] can still be happy listening to the songs" and notes that "in Boston [. . .] the sale of the records has been phenomenal."

The Cradle Will Rock was frequently revived in the twentieth and early twenty-first centuries by small, artistically minded companies and has produced a number of cast recordings. The early dissemination of the title on both paper and lacquer established it as "important" among the intelligentsia, and, as Dale Harrison of the delicate linguistic sensibilities predicted, it allowed inquisitive listeners from across the country to hear the kind of new musical theatre that was developing on Broadway.

Rodgers and Hammerstein

The reputation of Rodgers and Hammerstein's *Oklahoma!* as the first musical in which song and dance were tightly integrated into the story is, as many historians have observed, mostly unearned. If *Show Boat*'s score is too unstable to qualify, *The Cradle Will Rock* lacks sufficient dance, and *Porgy and Bess* is too operatic, then surely, as bruce mcclung convincingly argues, *Lady in the Dark* cannot be easily distinguished from *Oklahoma!* on the basis of form.[12] Unlike *Oklahoma!*, though, *Lady in the Dark* was never documented with a commercial recording of the original cast performing the original songs as they were sung in the theatre. Indeed, this was true of most of the musicals that opened between 1940 and 1943.

Maslon explains, starting in late 1940, ASCAP, concerned that their members were not receiving a fair share of the significant amount of money being made through the radio broadcast of music, attempted to force the National Association of Broadcasters to award songwriters higher royalties. The broadcasters refused and boycotted ASCAP's members' music. As most musical theatre songwriters were members of ASCAP (the organization had, after all, been largely created by the Tin Pan Alley theatre songwriters of the turn of the century), new Broadway music largely disappeared from the radio for most of 1941. Radio broadcast was the best way of selling records, and so music labels also turned away from recording musical theatre scores during this period.[13] Recordings of musical theatre music were further limited in 1942 when the head of the musicians union, John Petrillo, fearing recorded music was hurting the livelihood of their members, called for a musicians strike against playing on any album.[14] Thus, for the first three years of the 1940s, any musicals that might have staked a claim to being the "first formally integrated musical" struggled to enter the national consciousness because they could be neither recorded nor broadcast.

The enormous success of *Oklahoma!* in New York, though, raised considerable interest in recording the songs. Tim Carter reprints sections of letters from Oscar Hammerstein II to his son Bill in which the songwriter expressed a certain reluctance to "plug" songs for radio play (fearing they would wear out their welcome on the radio, and the live production was doing very well as it was).[15] Still, live and acapella covers of the songs on the radio became popular over the summer of 1943 (including an acapella arrangement of "People Will Say We're In Love" by Frank Sinatra),[16] and so in October of 1943, Decca contributed to the Musician Union's pension fund in order to garner an exception to record the show with the original cast and orchestra.[17] The album contained six ten-inch discs, each side playing less than three minutes and thirty seconds.

Three major songs were left out of the album: "Lonely Room," "It's a Scandal," and "The Farmer and the Cowman." Maslon notes that each introduces the idea of the outsider who struggles to be part of the community celebrated by the musical, and so, "listeners of the original album set might mistake *Oklahoma!* for a purely upbeat, optimistic story of romantic couples and their feudin', fightin', and making up in the end."[18] Maslon acknowledges, "To be fair, Decca made its decision based on commercial and technical issues rather than censorious ones; an album set of eight shellac disks would have been suitable only for stevedores."[19] The wartime economy and shellac rationing made even the use of twelve-inch discs, employed by *The Cradle Will Rock* five years earlier, impractical. On ten-inch discs the five-minute twenty-second recording of "The Farmer and The Cowman" would either have been divided over two sides (and thereby replace two other songs) or else have been severely truncated. The song "Lonely Room" had gone in and out of the show during previews largely, Alfred Drake believed, "because Howard Da Silva wasn't singing it too well [. . .]" and so was a natural choice for excision on the album.[20] Joseph Buloff speak-sings most of "It's a Scandal," and so it was perhaps selected to be cut for the same reason.

Although Decca eventually recorded these songs on a supplemental two-disc album released two years later (labeled, after the template of Decca's *Porgy and Bess*, "Volume 2"), their excision from the original album had a lasting impact on the text of *Oklahoma!* and, arguably, on the reputation of Rodgers and Hammerstein. The movie version in 1955 did not include "Lonely Room" or "It's a Scandal." When the album was re-released on long-playing record in 1949 there was time enough for at least two of the three songs to have been restored, but none were. The original Decca recording had defined the essential songs that make up *Oklahoma!* and in so doing helped to shape audience expectations that the title represented "an optimistic story of romantic couples"[21] Indeed, this is largely the reputation many Rodgers and Hammerstein musicals had until the revivals of the 1990s and beyond began to expose the dark subtext of these shows.

Unlike their recording of *Porgy and Bess*, Decca recorded and numbered the songs on the *Oklahoma!* album specifically for listeners with record changers. The sequence progressed from one side of a disc to the same side of the next disc. All of the A-sides could be played in sequence as the automatic changer dropped the next disc onto the platter when its predecessor had finished. The listener could then flip the entire stack and play the B-sides in sequence. The A-side of the first disc is labeled "Side 1," the B-side, "Side 12." This firmly fixed the songs as part of a single work to be listened to in a particular order. Even if a disc was found out of the album, the front and back numbering indicated there was more to this work than was recorded on a single disc.

Decca would do the same with Rodgers and Hammerstein's second hit musical, *Carousel*, but the length of Billy's "Soliloquy" posed a logistical problem. The song had already been made popular by Frank Sinatra in a radio broadcast of a 1945 Hollywood Bowl concert,[22] and so customers would expect it to be included in the album in its entirety. However, at seven minutes and twenty-eight seconds, it could not fit on one side of even a twelve-inch record. *The Cradle Will Rock* split scenes and songs across discs with reckless abandon, but Decca was apparently unwilling to split a single song over two physical objects. The only solution that respected both the record-changer order and the principle that "a-single-song-fits-on-one-disc" was to place the long song at the turning point in the sequence where the listener would turn over all of the discs and continue backward through the set. On the other hand, if a listener just wanted to listen to "Soliloquy," one only needed to pull out a single disc (see Figure 3.1). This meant, though, that, in this seemingly very intentionally ordered set, "Soliloquy" occurs earlier than it does on the stage: the songs "When the Children are Asleep" and "Blow High, Blow Low" seem to follow "Soliloquy" in the album but precede it in the show.

As with *Oklahoma!*, the choices made for the original-cast album release of *Carousel* had a lasting impact on the text of the musical. Like the original cast album, the film version of *Carousel* moved "When the Children Are Asleep" to follow "Soliloquy." Also, "Blow High, Blow Low," though dropped from the film, was included on the soundtrack recording positioned, following the original cast album ordering, after "Soliloquy." Enoch's song, "Geraniums in the Winder," left off the album, was cut from the film and also from the 2018 revival.

The 1949 LP release of *Carousel* likewise mostly follows the order of songs established by the first album. However, "Soliloquy" presented a problem

Figure 3.1 The fifth disc in the original *Carousel* album of 78 rpm discs, which split the song "Soliloquy" over two sides (author's collection).

yet again. In an effort to avoid splitting "Soliloquy" over the two sides of the disc, Decca moved it even earlier in the set, placing "June Is Busting Out All Over" on the second side. As a result, "Soliloquy" is heard immediately after "If I Loved You" (misleadingly suggesting, perhaps, that Julie is pregnant out of wedlock). In his plot synopsis in the liner notes, Louis Untermeyer seems to go out of its way to correct this possible misunderstanding. His summary does not use the name of any song except for "Soliloquy," and he places it in the position it occurs on stage (specifically noting that Billy is married when he learns Julie is pregnant).[23] The label seems to have recognized the limitations of the recording technology to alter the reception of the story and worked to ensure misunderstandings were corrected to avoid offending the moral sensibilities of record buyers and potential theatre goers across the country.

Long-Playing Records

The LP quickly became the default format for commercially released recorded music, and musical theatre cast recordings were well represented in the catalogs of the major labels. Cole Porter's *Kiss Me, Kate* was the first Broadway musical originally released on LP. However, as Maslon notes, the 1947 recording of *Finian's Rainbow* (originally released as a six-disc album of 78s), was re-released a few months before on the new format.[24] Before releasing *Kiss Me, Kate* in 1949, Columbia had also re-released its recording of the 1946 revival of *Show Boat*. Decca combined their two albums of songs from *Porgy and Bess* into a single LP release, thus emphasizing the integrity of the piece as a single work rather than a series of unconnected songs.

Not all musicals previously released as 78s were quickly re-released on LP, though. Although, in the early 1950s, Rodgers and Hammerstein were at the height of their popularity, and LPs of *Oklahoma*, *Carousel*, and *South Pacific* were all sold in 1949, Decca never did transfer their 1945 studio recording of songs from the Rodgers and Hammerstein movie musical *State Fair* to LP. RCA Victor, slow to adopt the LP format in general, did not re-release *Allegro* on LP until 1965 (eighteen years after the original release). Most musicals of the 1930s, even very popular musicals, were not immediately re-released on the new format (the original recording *The Cradle Will Rock* was not re-released on LP until 1964).

The introduction of the LP thus not only provided a new format for recording musicals, but also allowed record labels to establish their own repertory as they selected which earlier titles to prioritize for re-release on the new format. Books and scripts had been regularly reprinted in new editions since the rise of the commercial printing press, but the introduction of the LP was the first major format shift in commercial recording in which the industry had the opportunity to look at their back catalog and make choices about which titles were worth bringing forward into the next technological phase.

As LPs became popular, RCA Victor promoted the competing seven-inch, 45 rpm format, which became popular in jukeboxes. However, Maslon observes, at "less than four minutes of recorded music" per side, the 45 was "not much help for the commercial release of extended classical or Broadway material."[25] That is, it was "not much help" for the Broadway musical as defined by Rodgers and Hammerstein. The integrated musical, with songs intended to be heard in a particular order and as part of a single work, was ill served by the technology of the 45 rpm disc. However, not all musicals followed the Rodgers and Hammerstein format.

The original cast recording of *Kiss Me, Kate* may have been the first such recording of a musical to be released on LP in its first edition. However, the recording was virtually simultaneously released as an album of six 78s and in a set of four 45s (with a slightly abbreviated version of the overture). It is a musical well suited for each format as it stands with one foot in the 1930s and another in the Rodgers and Hammerstein era. *Kiss Me, Kate* may have been Porter's attempt to write a musical in the Rodgers and Hammerstein style,[26] but it remains a throw-back to the "pre-integrated" musicals of the 1930s. "Why Can't You Behave," "So in Love," "Always True to You," and, indeed, most of the songs not a part of the musical-within-a-musical are not especially specific to the characters or situation in which they appear.

Kiss Me, Kate was an enormous hit, and one can imagine an alternative history in which musical theatre after Rodgers and Hammerstein returned to a world of interpolated songs of the kind written by Cole Porter. However, by 1950, the LP had become the dominant format for commercially released albums of music.[27] Cast recordings were now largely consumed as a set of songs not easily separable from one another. Singles might be released on 45s, but when songs were gathered together, they were released on a single disc. The age of the LP supported and enforced the age of the "integrated musical" in the style made popular by Rodgers and Hammerstein.

Stereo

The repertory was again re-examined and further fixed by the invention of stereo recordings in late 1957. As a result of the ingenuity of engineers at Western Electric, stereo records were backward-compatible with old record players, and older records could be played on new stereo systems, so it was not necessary to re-release old recordings for the new format. However, customers did want to buy new stereo records. To meet this demand, some labels began to release new stereo studio cast recordings of popular musicals recorded before 1957. Maslon describes how Columbia recorded new, stereo studio cast recordings of *Oklahoma!* (1964), *The King and I* (1964), and *Annie*

Get Your Gun (1963) intended to be part of the subscription mail-order record club Columbia founded in 1955 once vinyl LPs proved to be durable enough to be shipped by mail.[28] These re-releases further demonstrated which titles were popular enough for a new release on yet another format.

Magnetic Tape

The emerging car culture of the 1950s increased the demand for portable, pre-recorded music. Although magnetic tape was used in the recording studio since the end of World War II, and open reel-to-reel tape had been used for dictation recording for about as long, the inconvenience of threading a reel through the machine and rewinding it when finished meant LPs remained the format of choice until closed-reel cassettes were introduced in the early 1960s. The 4-track, and then 8-track, cartridges were initially the most popular formats for this purpose. The latter could contain eighty minutes of music broken into four "programs" that roughly corresponded to the four sides of a two disc LP set. Unlike a disc in which a user could relatively easily skip from track to track by lifting the needle and setting it down in the area where the next song began, most 8-track players only allowed listeners to switch between programs (that usually contained all of the songs on one side of a record). Switching between these programs also meant jumping to the same relative position in each program (so jumping from program 1 to program 2 when halfway through program 1 would place the listener halfway through program 2). Later, the "compact cassette" tapes that became popular in the late 1970s and early 1980s only allowed listeners to skip tracks by the imprecise methods of "fast-forwarding" to the song they wanted. Repeating a song, likewise, required rewinding for the time the user had to blindly estimate was required (often while engaged in other activities like driving a car). All of this meant the technology encouraged the listener to experience the albums as a whole rather than jumping from song to song.

The small size of cassette tape, which made the format convenient for listening while traveling, also meant the size of the package could be greatly reduced. Liner notes, which might have included a plot summary and lyrics to accompany an LP release, were, if included at all, often printed with typefaces so small as to be virtually illegible. A few labels, realizing the problem, invited those who purchased a cassette the option of requesting a free copy of the full-size LP liner notes. However, cast recordings that preserved enough of the show that they could be understood without these contextualizing documents were especially well suited for this more compact format.

It is perhaps no coincidence, then, that the era of portable cassette tapes coincided with the popularity of mostly sung-through pieces like *Jesus Christ Superstar* (1970), *Evita* (1976), and *Sweeney Todd* (1979) that permitted the listener to hear a piece in (close to) its entirety and understand the plot without grabbing a magnifying glass to consult the liner notes. The format allowed longer recordings to be distributed on a few, easy-to-transport cassettes, rather than divided across large discs. These sung-through musicals were also well designed for those who wanted to listen from the beginning to the end of the album rather than replaying the "standards" from the score.

Compact Discs

When the compact disc emerged as a new, popular format in the mid-1980s, it was well suited to the trends in musical theatre that had started in the 1970s and led to the sung-through British pop-operas of the 1980s and 1990s. The compact disc could hold about seventy-four minutes of music, roughly fifteen to thirty minutes more than was usually recorded on LPs or commercial cassettes. While *Jesus Christ Superstar*, at around ninety minutes of music, could be fully recorded on two LPs, *Evita* and *Cats* could be trimmed to fit onto two LPs or cassettes, and *Les Misérables*, which runs at just under three hours on stage, had to be trimmed drastically for the original release on LP and cassette. Indeed, like *Kiss Me, Kate* in 1948, the British translation and adaptation of the French musical *Les Misérables* emerged at a moment of technological transition in 1985. The Original London Cast Recording was originally released on 2 LPs,[29] a "double play" cassette,[30] and compact disc in the same year. The LP and cassette versions cut the "Prologue," "Plumet Attack," "The Thénardier Waltz of Treachery," and "Turning"—songs and segments included on the double CD release.[31] The LP and cassette releases of the Original Broadway Cast Recording also cut the "Prologue" but restored "Plumet Attack," "The Thénardier Waltz of Treachery," and "Turning" to fill the space opened up by two songs cut from the London production: "I Saw Him Once" and "Little People."

Les Misérables is a long show (over three hours in its original London version), so cuts needed to be made (even on the double CD), but the decision to cut the entire ten-minute prologue on the shorter formats is, at first glance, a strange one. The segment introduces not only the characters but also many of the musical motifs used later in the piece. However, just as the original 78 releases of *Oklahoma!* and *Carousel* impacted recordings for years to come, the first recording of this show impacted the recordings that followed. The original French recording, released as a "concept album" in 1980, began with the French version of "At the End of the Day." Director John Caird described the original French production as "framed in a way that was comprehensible only to an audience that was intimately aware of the story, and the traditions of English story-telling were completely absent from it."[32] The first scene was added for the English version, but the very titling of the segment in the program and on the CD track listing as a "prologue" suggests the original creative team thought of it as supplementary. If cuts had to be made, they may have felt it could be easily excised without harm to the work as a whole.

Still, for the cassette release, it is unclear such cuts were entirely necessary. At around one hour and forty-four minutes, the CD version of the recording could easily have fit onto two sixty-minute cassettes. The musical was released on two LP discs and two CDs, and so a double cassette release would have seemed natural, but the musical was initially sold only as a single ninety-minute cassette. When the London recording was released and the marketability of the cast album might have been unclear, the single cassette may have been a wise business decision. However, by the time of the Original Broadway Cast Recording, the musical was a hit, and the success of the recording was virtually assured, but the cassette version still followed the LP edit and was released on one tape.

In 1987, CDs were still a relatively new format for commercial music. As music labels were trying to entice customers to buy on a new medium music they already owned, format-exclusive content was often added to make the new compact disc release more attractive. An expectation was created that CDs would offer a more complete experience than other formats. The additional tracks included on the CD were a kind of "bonus" for those who may have recently purchased a CD player.

For the original London cast recording of *Miss Saigon* in 1990, First Night Records and Geffen released four different versions of the original cast recording. The LP version, one of the last major recordings in this format until the vinyl revival of the 2010s, included two discs. The cassette version, released in this case on two tapes, included the short "Overture" that did not fit on the LP release, but otherwise mirrored the LP track lists side-for-side. The two-disc CD release, following the tradition established by

Les Misérables, included around sixteen minutes not available on the other formats. Further, the labels released a single CD "highlights" disc that included fourteen tracks.

Interestingly, the "highlights" release of *Miss Saigon* uniquely preserves Claire Moore's performance of the song "Now That I've Seen Her," which had replaced "Her or Me" as the show moved to Broadway. This practice of releasing cheaper, "highlights" reductions had been common for recordings of operas since the early twentieth century, and had been employed for the three-disc *Complete Symphonic Recording of Les Misérables* several years before. One might suppose that the inclusion of a song exclusively on this version was a marketing strategy to encourage completist collectors to buy the highlights album as well, were it not that the disc packaging makes no mention of the song (and, indeed, lists the earlier version "Her or Me" on the track list and includes the original lyrics in the liner notes). Oddly, the two-disc CD release incorrectly includes "Now That I've Seen Her" in the track list and prints lyrics for the new song in the liner notes (albeit in a slightly different typeface, as if it was inserted at the last minute, see Figure 3.2), but the song is not on the album.[33]

The fluidity of the show's texts across formats has, perhaps, made it easier for audiences to accept the occasional changes to the lyrics of these shows in production. Although the Cameron Mackintosh produced megamusicals of the 1980s (*Cats*, *Les Misérables*, *Phantom of the Opera*, and *Miss Saigon*) and earned a reputation for the supposed rigidity of the productions from city to city and tour to tour,[34] the writers have continued to adapt the music, lyrics, and dialogue over the last several decades. As will be discussed in the following chapter, the text of *Les Misérables* was modified after the tenth

> THERE ARE TIMES
> WHEN YOUR HEART CRIES THIS ISN'T HAPPENING
> BUT THE TRUTH IS COLD AND REAL
> AND I KNOW THIS STORM WON'T GO AWAY
>
> NOW THAT I'VE SEEN HER
> THERE'S NO WAY TO HIDE
> SHE IS NOT SOME FLING
> FROM LONG AGO

Figure 3.2 The lyrics for "Now That I've Seen Her" in the liner notes for the Original London Cast recording of *Miss Saigon*. Note that the typeface of lyrics changes slightly at the point where the lyrics differ from those in the earlier song, "It's Her or Me" (author's collection).

anniversary of the show on Broadway. The lyrics for *Miss Saigon* in the most recent revival are almost entirely rewritten.

By the 1990s, the compact disc had effectively replaced the LP as the format of choice for commercial music. Labels once again returned to their archives to select titles to re-release on the new format. The British label EMI released around forty titles under their Broadway Classic imprint between 1992 and 1997. These were titles originally released by Capitol Records that included the soundtracks of the film versions of the Rodgers and Hammerstein musicals and the cast recordings of many of the titles Harold Prince directed (e.g., *Zorba* and *Follies*). Sony Classical, likewise, re-released a selection of their back catalog including their Rodgers and Hammerstein and Sondheim recordings, along with a number of non-musical movie soundtracks. The apotheosis of Sondheim, if already well underway by the 1980s, was solidified by the transfer to CD in the 1990s. If the emergence of the LP in the 1940s ensured Rodgers and Hammerstein an incontrovertible place in the repertory, the CD re-releases of the 1990s, selected from the best-selling or most recognizable titles of the past twenty years, helped to raise Sondheim to the same level.

Less Tangible Media

In 1998, Audra McDonald, fresh from her Tony win for *Ragtime*, released her first album, *Way Back to Paradise*, which featured songs by emerging composers who were not then particularly well known outside of New York (e.g., Jenny Giering, Jason Robert Brown, Rick Ian Gordon, Michael John LaChiusa, and Adam Guettel). In the pre-internet days, a musical theatre fan might purchase McDonald's album out of an appreciation of her work in *Ragtime* and discover a new set of composers, but have little opportunity to hear more. Most brick-and-mortar stores far from New York would not have carried *Songs for a New World* or *Myths and Hymns*, and even if they did, purchasing a cast recording at a specialty store (often for between $17 and $25 a disc) was a relatively significant investment based only on a passing admiration of a single song.

In June of 1999, though, Shawn Fanning and Sean Parker founded the peer-to-peer file-sharing service Napster. When a computer with Napster connected to the internet, the music files on the hard drive were shared with others on the network. The Napster interface, which often displayed search results based on the idiosyncratic file organization of its users, made searching for individual songs easier than finding entire albums. McDonald's album was ideal for this system, and the composers on "Way Back to Paradise," particularly Jason Robert Brown, rose to prominence on college campuses (where access to high-speed internet was more common in the late 1990s).

In the following years as more and more households went online, digital music quickly replaced physical CDs as the most popular medium for consuming music. The release of the iTunes store in 2003 made it easier to acquire digital music legally and purchase a single song before buying an entire album. Many of the musicals that became popular between 1999 and 2005 were shows composed of a set of songs that could be appreciated both on their own and as part of the overall production; a form that had been mostly out-of-favor since the invention of the LP and the Rodgers and Hammerstein-style musical was once again becoming popular. Jason Robert Brown's *Songs for a New World* and *The Last Five Years* were perfectly suited for this format. *Avenue Q*, *Altar Boyz*, *Spring Awakening*, and many of the songs from *Wicked* ("Popular," "Defying Gravity," "What Is This Feeling," and "As Long As You're Mine") also had songs that, while integrated into the story and the score, could be enjoyed as a single download.

These songs could also be discovered on the various streaming internet radio stations that emerged in the first few years of the twenty-first century. In the late 1990s, RealNetworks developed the RealAudio format that permitted small bits of audio to be transferred quickly over even slow networks. The technology enabled a large number of internet radio stations focused on very specific topics to emerge. In the United States, the Digital Millennium Copyright Act somewhat slowed the growth of internet radio by imposing a requirement that internet broadcasters obtain performance rights for the music they played (something not required of traditional or "terrestrial" stations). Nonetheless, theatre websites with industry connections and some financial resources created their own radio stations that, unlike similarly themed stations on more mainstream platforms like satellite radio, played lesser-known (and even very obscure) recordings. Quirky musicals that might have quickly faded into obscurity after a short, off-Broadway run could now be discovered and celebrated by fans across the world.

In 2006 services like Grooveshark, Spotify, and eventually Amazon and YouTube Music made it possible to listen to the full catalog of most labels for a relatively low monthly subscription cost. Many streaming services also created personalized radio stations based on similarities either a trained algo- rithm or a human curator perceived among different tracks. Thus, the many fans of *Hamilton* could discover the cast recording of *Dear Evan Hansen*, and fans of both might discover *Be More Chill*. Audiences gained greater access to New York theatre music, and New York theatre-makers gained access to entirely new demographics of consumers including high school and college- age theatre kids outside of the city with a great deal of passion but limited financial resources.

Of course, since 2005, many audience members have discovered new musicals not only through legal audio recordings, but also through YouTube. Much of the canon of the late twentieth and early twenty-first centuries has not been defined by texts or cast recordings, but by the proliferation of video recordings both authorized and illicit. These video texts will be discussed in the following chapters.

4

The Musical as Moving Image

In December of 1966, Harold Prince, then president of the League of New York Theatres and Producers, wrote to the chairman of the National Foundation of Arts and Humanities, Roger Stevens, to encourage him to pursue "an arrangement with the theatre unions whereby all qualified plays and musicals can be recorded on film for history." Prince acknowledges that the "unions have been more than reluctant to permit [such a project] despite assurances that the material would not be used for commercial purposes and showings limited to a very small number of persons."[1] He notes, though, that he feels it "a terrible shame that unless Jerry Robbins decides to do WEST SIDE STORY again [. . .] that work is lost to posterity"[2] (Prince, Robert Griffith, and Stevens had originally co-produced the show on Broadway).[3]

Prince assumes that the essence of *West Side Story* is in the production rather than the score or script, and he clearly felt a kind of authorial ownership over many of the musicals he produced and directed. He was famously suspicious of revivals of his work staged by other directors. He wrote in his autobiography that revivals of *Cabaret* "disregard [. . .] the original metaphor which fueled [the original]"[4] (that is, that the Emcee as a character represents Germany as it descends into Nazism, an idea not explicit in the book or lyrics). Although Prince's argument that the full text of a musical includes the staging and design, this concept is not generally reflected in license agreements or royalty contracts. It is true that the text and score of a musical are generally designed not simply to be read and heard but also seen in a fully realized performance. Bruce Kirle's observation, quoted in the introduction of this book, that "Musicals are read by their audiences in theatres, not through scripts in a library,"[5] may be inaccurately binary, but it is certainly the case that, with the exception of a few concept albums, musicals are designed to be *seen*. Video recordings, both filmed stage productions and film adaptations, more fully capture at least one interpretation of the realized work, and these shape the textual history of the titles they represent. As with

Fixing the Musical. Douglas L. Reside, Oxford University Press. © Oxford University Press 2023.
DOI: 10.1093/oso/9780190073718.003.0005

the other forms of tangible media described in this book, they also help to define the musical theatre form and repertory.

After the invention of the motion picture in the late nineteenth century, stage performances were some of the first events documented on film. Initially most lacked sound, although there were some early attempts to synchronize wax cylinder recordings or discs with the events on the screen (Sarah Bernhardt's *Hamlet*[6] and early Walturdaw recordings of pieces of Gilbert and Sullivan[7] are early examples). This process was not unlike that used by the Vitaphone Corporation for the landmark 1927 film *The Jazz Singer*, in which the audio was recorded to a sixteen-inch disc capable of holding about eleven minutes of sound and synchronized to the action on film (the motor that spun the turntable was linked the with one that ran the film in an attempt to synchronize sound and image).

In the late 1920s, many musical films relegated dialogue to interstitial title cards. Even the smallest delay between the moment of the movement of the mouth and the sounds of speech can be distracting, and the Vitaphone sound-on-disc technology was not reliable enough to ensure an entire film could be presented with perfect synchronization. The audio in these early films was therefore limited to an instrumental score, sound effects, and often songs for which the mouth might naturally form words more slowly, and so slight variances between image and sound might be less noticeable. As a result, songs were increasingly fixed in the medium of musical film.

This is the period in which the musical *Show Boat* was launched, itself a transitional work sailing away from the shores of operetta but not yet docked in the port of formally integrated musicals. It was, however, one of the first Broadway hits to be released as a film with some of the songs from the original score included. Universal's 1929 film was not originally intended to be a musical, but the success of the stage version forced the director to license a few songs from the Hammerstein and Kern score that were added as a prologue to the otherwise silent film. The film was not particularly well received by critics, but as film historian Richard Barrios observes, "the box office returns were good [. . .] and in smaller towns it could not be compared [unfavorably] with its illustrious Broadway counterpart."[8] Like audio recordings on disc, the 1929 film introduced audiences across America to the title and the hit songs from *Show Boat*, but left the book on Broadway. The perceived importance of the title as a brand that must include a few (but not all) of Hammerstein and Kern's songs remains part of the textual tradition of *Show Boat* nearly a century later.

In the months after the film of *Show Boat* was released, the MGM film adaptation of *The Desert Song* brought the 1926 Romberg, Hammerstein, and Harbach operetta to audiences across the country. The piece harkened back to an earlier form of music theatre that was already starting to feel out of fashion in 1929. However, perhaps because of this and later film versions (1943 and 1953), *The Desert Song* held a place in the American musical repertory for much of the twentieth century. It has been revived twice on Broadway (most recently in 1976) and has been produced regularly in regional theatre (including thirteen times at the St. Louis Muny, even as recently as a 1996 concert version).

Not every one of the early musical film adaptations entered the repertory, however. Paramount's 1929 adaptation of the 1925 Marx Brothers musical, *The Cocoanuts*, was so dependent on the personalities and comedy of the original cast that the show has never enjoyed a Broadway revival. Remarkably for a 1925 musical, though, it has been produced regionally and off-Broadway at least three times in the last thirty years—at Arena Stage in Washington DC in 1988, at the Oregon Shakespeare Festival in 2014, and in a 1996 off-Broadway production by the American Jewish Theatre. These productions, it should be noted, were mounted in the era of home video when the film adaptation was easily accessible to producers and directors. Until home video players became ubiquitous in American homes in the 1980s, filmed and film musicals were fixed in a medium that was all but inaccessible for most home consumers. From 1930 to 1980, the cast recording, which could be played again and again, was more likely to shape the reception of a musical than a film, which was, for most audiences, almost as ephemeral as a live stage production.

There were a few exceptions, of course. If a film entered the repertory of revival screenings in cinemas and regular broadcasts on television, it might have become so familiar that it established the standard version of a musical text. The 1939 musical film adaptation of *The Wizard of Oz* was broadcast on network television annually from 1959 until the 1990s and became one of the best-known musicals of all time. Likewise, the regular Christmas broadcasts of the 1961 film adaptation of *Babes in Toyland* and rebroadcasts of the 1960 live studio production of *Peter Pan* made those recordings among the most familiar versions of those titles. The film version of Rodgers and Hammerstein's *The Sound of Music*, likewise, was regularly accessible across the United States from the moment it was released. The film was screened in cinemas for four and a half years in its initial run, and revived around the country for years after. Starting in 1979, NBC broadcast the film once a year for twenty years.[9] In 1977, it was one of the first three films to be commercially released on VHS in the United States.[10]

The ubiquity of the film version of *The Sound of Music* made the title one of Rodgers and Hammerstein's best-known musicals. It may, however, have created a kind of *Sound of Music* fatigue among theatre makers. Despite its enormous popularity, the musical was not revived on Broadway until 1998 (nearly forty years after it opened). In the same period, between 1960 and 1995, *Oklahoma!* was revived on Broadway once (in 1979) and *The King and I* twice (1977 and 1985). During the same decades, *Oklahoma!* was the most- (or the second most-)produced musical in American high schools, but *The Sound of Music* was never among the top five.[11]

Those who did license the show for educational or regional performance often wanted to perform the text of the film rather than the stage version. The Rodgers and Hammerstein Organization routinely approves some changes (amateur groups can request, for instance, to substitute "Something Good" for "Ordinary Couple"), but school groups are not generally permitted to move "My Favorite Things" from the opening scene in the Abbey to the storm scene in the bedroom. Until around 2021, the licensed libretto acknowledged the temptation to perform the film version and included a note after the list of songs:

IMPORTANT NOTICE

This script reflects the original award-winning Broadway production of *The Sound of Music*. There are certain differences between this script and the motion picture version of the musical. Those changes were made and authorized for the motion picture only and cannot be used in stage production. The License Agreement granting performance rights to *The Sound of Music* clearly provides that the musical must be presented as set forth in this script and we appreciate your respectful adherence to the Agreement.[12]

The licensed librettos of Rodgers and Hammerstein's other musicals, most also adapted into commercially available film versions, did not include this notice.

Still, the popularity and general availability of the movie version of *The Sound of Music* has replaced the published libretto and original cast recording as the canonical text of this musical. Even the 1998 Broadway revival and the 2006 London production used many of the changes made for the film (though both retained the Max and Elsa songs "No Way to Stop It" and "How Can Love Survive"). The two recent live television broadcasts of the musical on NBC and BBC, while hewing more closely to the Broadway book and score, still replaced "Ordinary Couple" with "Something Good."

Home Video

The VHS release of *The Sound of Music* in 1977 ushered in a new era in commercial distribution of movies for home use. While several studios had experimented with releasing movies on Super-8 film (a format for which many middle-class families already had playback equipment used to watch their own home movies), these were almost always cut down to less than twenty minutes (to fit onto home movie projectors) and were often released only as black-and-white, silent films. Sony's U-Matic video-cassette format, first commercially sold in 1971, was too expensive for most home users. It was not until 1975 when Sony's Betamax and JVC's VHS cassette formats emerged that it was feasible for most consumers to enjoy full-length recorded movies at home.

Cable Broadcasts and Off-Air Recordings

In *From Betamax to Blockbuster: Video Stores and the Invention of Movies on Video*, Joshua M. Greenberg chronicles the development of the VCR from a device primarily intended for "time shifting" television viewing (intended to enable users to record and watch broadcast television shows at a time most convenient for them) to a platform for watching commercially released films (often borrowed or rented from local stores or libraries). Even after the commercial market for home video was firmly established, though, most home users of video-cassette recorders had many more off-air recordings than commercial releases in their collection. The cost of purchasing a film on cassette was initially extremely high ($70–$90 on average). As studios began to understand that they did not need to fear the home-video market, the cost decreased, but it was still much cheaper to buy a blank cassette and record a program off the air. In the 1970s, the advent of largely unregulated, commercial, cable television also exponentially increased the amount of television available for home recording.

Luisa Lyons, in her online database "Filmed Live Musicals," describes a 1961 experiment in early pay television in Canada that broadcast a recording of the Carol Channing vehicle, *Show Girl*.[13] The restricted geographic area of the broadcast, and the general lack of commercially available video-recording equipment, meant the impact of this recording was very limited. In the 1970s, HBO and Cinemax had begun experimenting with offering pay channels, but a variety of open legal questions, including who had access to attach new wires to telephone poles and at what cost, limited the market for specialized stations. Nonetheless, producer Hillard Elkins arranged for the filming of *Oh! Calcutta!* in 1970 and broadcast it on pay-per-view in a few cities where technology and obscenity laws allowed (and some where only the former was fully secured).[14] Later in the decade, as Public Television grew after the Public Broadcasting Act of 1967, New York's WNET Channel 13 created *Live From Lincoln Center* and *Great Performances* and began to produce and present recorded performances (including, as theatre and television historian Kelly Kessler notes, the 1979 revival of *The Most Happy Fella*[15] recorded at Detroit's Michigan Opera Theatre before moving to Broadway).[16]

Pippin

In October of 1981, *Variety* reported that former CBS executive Arthur R. Taylor had finalized a deal between his Rockefeller Center TV (RCTV) and RCA to create "The Entertainment Channel" that planned to broadcast BBC television and Broadway shows.[17] Their first planned "Broadway" offering was a Canadian revival of *Pippin* produced, in the words of a July 1981 RCA release, "specifically for the cable and home video markets."[18] The musical had been closed on Broadway for almost three years, so it was not an immediately obvious first offering.

When I interviewed director David Sheehan in fall of 2020, he explained that the recording came about as a result of a conversation he had with Bob Fosse after interviewing him at the Cannes Film Festival in 1980 (where *All That Jazz* would win the Palme D'Or). After the interview, Sheehan remembers talking informally with Bob Fosse "in the bar of the Carlton hotel." Sheehan recounts his memory of the conversation as transcribed:

Sheehan: Of all the shows you've done, you know, *Sweet Charity, Lenny, Chicago,* what's nearest and dearest to your heart?

Fosse: Oh, *Pippin*! But *Pippin* is in a coma.

Sheehan: What!?

Fosse: It only exists in the hearts and minds of those who saw it on Broadway or in the road company.

Sheehan: Well, how would you like to immortalize it?

Fosse: What do you mean?"

Sheehan: You know, restage it, redo it. It's only been a few years. A lot of those people are probably still around.

Fosse: Rubenstein's too old, I can't use him . . . Vereen is around. I just saw him the other day. Well, what are you talking about?

Sheehan: Well, there's this new thing called "Box Office at Your Home."

Fosse: What's that?

Sheehan: I don't know, they call it, I think, TV for Pay or Pay TV or something like that.

Fosse Oh that's a bunch of shit, people are not going to put coin boxes in their bedrooms to watch TV!

Sheehan: Well, Bob I think they have a little bit more elaborate thing in mind, but it's still developing. [. . .]

Fosse: [. . .]Well, I would like that because I never got it quite right![19]

Sheehan found investors in the nascent Entertainment Channel and *Oh, Calcutta!* producer Hillard Elkins, and then, for the balance, mortgaged his California home as collateral for a deal with the Australian/New Zealand Bank to produce the show. The show was to be performed in a special three-evening engagement at the Minskoff Theater on Broadway and filmed with nine cameras over three performances. The Minskoff is built into One Astor Plaza, which also housed the offices and studios of many television companies, and the cameras were to be connected to a booth in a studio in the same building as the theatre.

Sheehan remembers the show was in rehearsals at the Minskoff when the Theatrical Unions informed the producers that they would require their members to be paid twice, once for their work on a live performance in front of a paying audience, and a second time for the use of that performance in a television production. Hillard Elkins suggested moving the company out of the States. Although the cost of moving the production was significant, the congeniality of the Canadian unions made the move worth it, and the production traveled to Hamilton, Ontario.

Unfortunately, the Canadian venue (the Hamilton Place Theater) lacked the Minskoff's unique proximity to a television studio, so they arranged with a local television station, CHCH-TV, to rent two trucks. These were parked outside the theatre, and feeds from microphones and the nine cameras were sent via cable out to the recording and editing equipment in the vehicles. The feed from each camera was recorded to the then-relatively-new one-inch videotape format, and a tenth recording, a "live edit," was simultaneously created by director Rick Bennewitz, who switched between cameras in real time as the performance played in the theatre. This "live edit" or "line cut" would have represented a fully edited, multi-camera version of the recording at the moment the curtain fell on that night's performance.

The team recorded three performances, two performances on Saturday, "pick up shots" in an empty theatre on Monday afternoon after reviewing the tapes on Sunday, and a final performance on Monday night. Sheehan remembers Fosse hated the first performance, and so none of the Saturday matinee footage was used. Sheehan therefore had eighteen camera feeds, two live edits, and a set of "pick up shots" to work with after the show closed.

In July of 1981, Fosse wrote to Sheehan and Elkins asking that they permit Rick Bennewitz and choreographer/director Kathyrn Doby (who restaged the show in Canada) to participate in the editing process. Fosse expressed his appreciation for Rick Bennewitz's live edits, writing, "Although none of the line cuts are exactly right (as Rick himself would admit), they got better and better. The last one was pretty damn good."[20] He concludes the letter, warning, with his famous disdain for Schwartz's score and Hirson's book, "PIPPIN is not the strongest of material and can be very easily 'screwed up.'"[21]

Sheehan does not seem to have taken this advice particularly seriously. He took the twenty recordings back to Burbank, California, where he edited them at a post-production studio called Compact Video Services. Using equipment at the studio, Sheehan could identify the start and stop times for each cut, and export a full edit to videocassette in either VHS or Beta format made from the original reels. Sheehan remembers exporting both formats and sending the copies by courier to Fosse, who lived in Montauk, Long Island. Fosse, Sheehan recalls, would review the copies and discuss changes with Sheehan over the phone. Sheehan remembers Fosse pushed for wider shots to avoid cutting off the dancer's feet, but Sheehan attempted to convince Fosse of the need for more intimate, closer shots designed for the "small screen" of television. Once the selections were made, the timecodes from the tape were submitted to a robotic system that would copy cuts from the original reels to the final "edit master."

The Entertainment Channel and the home-video producers had set guidelines for Sheehan. The show was initially planned for release on an RCA Selectavision disc[22] (see Figure 4.1) and on VHS[23] with a Laser Disc edition planned for the following year.[24] Both the Selectavision disc and VHS tapes (when recording at the highest quality) were limited to two hours of

Figure 4.1 The original SelectaVision disc of *Pippin* (author's collection).

recording time, so video director David Sheehan cut roughly twenty minutes from recording, including the song "I Guess I'll Miss The Man."

Fosse and Kathyrn Doby were not part of this final edit, and both were disappointed by the results. Doby remembers reviewing the exported video cassettes of the dance numbers at Sheehan's house and recalls that they tried to use the live edit wherever possible because of the difficulty of syncing the soundtrack for the dance numbers to multiple camera shots. Nonetheless, in certain cases she would suggest different cuts, which would be copied over from one cassette to the other.[25] Most of the editing, though, was done by Sheehan himself at the studio.

On November 23, 1981, Fosse wrote an angry letter to the cast and crew distancing himself from the final edit, writing, "I want to go on record with you that the deletions and cuts are *not mine*. As a matter of fact, for whatever reason, I only saw this foolishly butchered version of the show yesterday."[26] He adds:

> Although I have tried as hard as I possibly can to exert my influence and thoughts for the editing on Mr. Sheehan, my advice seems to have fallen on deaf ears. This experience has been even more frustrating for Kathyrn Doby who has given her time generously, or at least her availability—she was seldom called on—and most of the work she did do alone or in conjunction with me was not used.[27]

Doby herself speaks regretfully and angrily about the cuts made by Sheehan. "The Broadway show came in anywhere between two hours and two minutes and two hours and ten minutes. Now if we had known that the show cannot be more than two hours (even less because you need all the credits . . .) we could have cut it. Bob would have cut it."[28]

The recording was initially considered by many to be disappointing. Sheehan lost his house in California, which he had offered as collateral for the production. Fosse scholar Kevin Winkler writes, "Stephen Schwartz called [the video] 'frenetic' and 'terrible,' and Kathryn Doby said, 'It was such a mess, no wonder nobody likes it.' "[29] Whatever Fosse or the rest of the cast and creative team might have thought about the recording, though, it has come to represent *Pippin* for a generation of theatre fans who never saw the original production. Fosse's description of the show as uniquely "in a coma" in 1980 (despite the fact that the script and score were readily available for new productions) and his opinion of the work as "not the strongest of material," and that the show "can be very easily 'screwed up,'" suggest he remained conscious that his vision for *Pippin* differed in many ways from his collaborators, and that his contributions, which were not inscribed on paper, were ephemeral and might be forgotten with the next revival. This feeling was perhaps exacerbated by a 1973 Australian production that removed many of Fosse's thematic contributions, as well as the publication of the libretto in 1975 with many of Fosse's line changes removed.[30]

The videorecording, though, has helped to set *Pippin* in the musical theatre repertory and established Fosse's staging as part of the fabric of the show. Although the original production ran successfully for five years, its continuing popularity as compared to other commercially successful but now largely forgotten musicals of the early 1970s (e.g., *Shenandoah* or the Tony Award–winning *Two Gentlemen of Verona*) is at least partially due to the access offered by the video recording. The opening number ("Magic to Do") was used for comic effect in television episodes of both *The Gilmore Girls*[31] and *Big Bang Theory*[32] with gestures resembling Fosse's choreography. The 2013 revival, directed by Diane Paulus, employed a circus aesthetic in the costumes, sets, and new stage business, but Fosse's choreography was still very much present (particularly in the "Glory" tap number).

Interestingly, the ending line, a famously contested moment exposing the difference between Fosse and composer/lyricist Stephen Schwartz's competing visions for the show, remains surprisingly variable. The original script ended with Pippin's wife asking her husband how he feels. In Schwartz and book writer Roger O' Hirson's original text, he responds, "Trapped, but happy." Fosse hated "but happy," and he cut the final two words on Broadway. The published libretto and licensed text restored, "but happy," to Fosse's dismay. He felt that *Pippin* was the "the first celebration of nihilism"[33] in a musical, and "but happy" undermined this. For the video recording, Fosse eliminated "but happy" again, but added a somewhat inelegant tagline: "Trapped . . . Which isn't too bad for the end of a musical comedy, ta da!"

This video has proven to be less stable, though, than one might expect. In 2016, Sheehan and Schwartz agreed to license the recording to Amazon Prime for streaming. As part of this work, they returned to the original reels of *Pippin* and recut the show with a new ending in which the screen freezes after Pippin's wife asks the question. Pippin does not respond at all, but instead the song "Magic Shows and Miracles" plays as the credits roll by. What effect this version will have on the future reception of the musical is impossible to know, of course, but with the original edit available for nearly forty years and still available, if illicitly, online, it seems unlikely that the Amazon edit will entirely replace Fosse's original ending.

For all her reservations about the final product, Kathyrn Doby acknowledges the innovation of the filming technique used for the recording of *Pippin*. "We did it with nine cameras. It was shot like a sports event. They didn't shoot that way in those days. Maybe they have two cameras on television shows [. . .] but this kind of stuff, as far as I know, was only done for sports events."[34]

Pippin was followed by a wave of video-recorded musicals produced for the nascent cable and home-video markets in the early 1980s. The multi-camera shoot recorded to a mobile studio outside the theatre and edited in post-production is now common, but was only feasible starting in the late 1970s with the popularization of one-inch video tape and digital editing. Capturing live events to tape in locations far from a television studio required trucks with the capacity to record to multiple reels of film at once. Before one-inch film, most trucks could only hold and supply power to a single recording machine.

Prior to the development of electronic editing equipment, the earlier, two-inch videotape format was sometimes cut by hand. On this tape format, sound was recorded onto the tape a few inches ahead of where the video signal was recorded. As a result, editing was a difficult and time-consuming process that would have made compiling the eighteen or so recordings captured for *Pippin* prohibitively expensive. Post-production editing of the kind performed by Sheehan was impossible until the late 1960s and early 1970s when early computer technology permitted playback machines to use timecodes recorded on the tape itself to locate the precise edit points and copy audio and video to a destination device.

Sondheim

The Entertainment Channel would not last long after the initial broadcast of *Pippin*, but during the short time of their operation they pushed forward recordings of important Broadway shows of the 1970s and opened the door for later video documentation of live theatre. Some attempts were disappointing. In 1982, the Oak Media Development Corporation distributed a pay-per-view broadcast of the original Broadway production of the Duke Ellington revue, *Sophisticated Ladies*, but few watched it, and the recording was not commercially released for home video for over two decades (further limiting its influence).[35] The well-known video documentation of the work of Stephen Sondheim on television and video, on the other hand, helped to further extend the renown of the composer-lyricist across the country and establish performance traditions for his work that continue to the present day.

Sondheim had already had some experience with documenting his stage work on television. Just before closing on Broadway, the original production of *Pacific Overtures* was filmed by Academy Awards director Marty Pasetta for Japanese broadcast. The show was never licensed for television in the United States, nor has the recording been commercially released, but it perhaps prepared Sondheim and Harold Prince for a request that followed several years later.

Kelly Kessler describes how the Nederlanders decided to invest in television in part as a way to "outplay their rivals."[36] They were part owners of the Entertainment Channel, and in 1980, they decided to produce a television capture of *Sweeney Todd*. Television director Terry Hughes, who had previously directed television adaptations of *The Gin Game* and *Hughie*, was hired to lead the project. Hughes remembers that he went to New York to meet with Sondheim, where the composer told Hughes that

> he did not conceive [of Sweeney] as that vast epic set and that whole industrial revolution subtext that Hal [Prince] wove into it. He didn't see it as being that epic in size. And he was quite excited about doing the television version because it would refocus it on the way he had intended it as a chamber musical [...] It still had all the production values, but the cameras would focus on the characters and their intimacy and their interactions.[37]

Hughes said that this conversation gave him "insight" into how to direct the video recording, which, indeed, did focus closely on the actors rather than the set.

Hughes captured the Los Angeles run of the National Tour featuring many of the original Broadway cast including Angela Lansbury as Mrs. Lovett, Edmund Lyndeck as the Judge, and Ken Jennings as Toby. Hughes recorded the show over four days with five cameras, three stationary, one on a crane, and one handheld, all of which fed to a truck parked outside of the theatre.[38] Unlike David Sheehan, Hughes did not produce a "live" edit in the truck, but edited all of the recordings together after filming had concluded.[39] He remembers that the majority of the footage used came not from the two performances captured with live audiences, but from shots recorded in an empty house (moments in which it was much easier to film very close shots of the actors without interfering with the experience of a paying audience). Hughes remembers, "[Sondheim] came out for the whole of the shooting. He was there all the time [...] he was there sitting in the orchestra stalls or he was there in the truck with me not interfering in any way, but just observing."[40]

As with *Pippin*, the video recording helped to settle a difference of artistic opinion between collaborators, and the result affected the reception of the musical in the following decades. Today, when contemporary researchers watch the Broadway version of *Sweeney Todd* recorded by the Theatre on Film on Tape Archive at the New York Public Library for the Performing Arts, or review the set designs, the most frequent comment I hear is something like, "One forgets how enormous that set was." One forgets, I suspect, because the commercially available video recording captured Prince's direction, but often hid Eugene Lee's enormous set. Prince's vision of the musical as a comment on the industrial revolution and its effect on modern life is now more or less erased in new productions. The most successful revivals have been minimalist concert versions and the John Doyle production, which had almost no set and a cast that played their own instruments on stage.

Sweeney Todd was originally broadcast on the Entertainment Channel in September of 1982. Five months later, in February of 1983, channel's owners announced that they would cease operations in March.[41] Showtime and PBS both picked up *Sweeney Todd*, but the promise of cable television as a platform for Broadway shows was fading. A headline in a 1985 article in *Variety* summarized what many in the industry had decided, "Legit [Theatre] Cable Hopes Didn't Pan Out." The article quotes Broadway general manager Norman Rothstein's assessment, "There's not enough money from cable to make it worth our while [...] We'd rather wait and hope for a film sale."[42] The Broadway Unions hoping for Hollywood pay-offs for their labor could not come to an agreement on terms that would make the recordings profitable for producers. Curtis Davis, a vice president at the cable network A&E, acknowledged, "The licensing fees are modest—the kind of money I was paying in public television 20 years ago. It often comes as a considerable surprise to the creative theater people, it's so far below what they think their efforts are worth."[43]

Cable-television broadcasts may not have been profitable, but the home-video market that grew up at the same time allowed these recordings to be consumed and studied by fans (and directors of future productions), and so they began to shape the repertory. *Sweeney Todd* was released on VHS in 1984, and in 1985, producer Ellen Kass, who worked on the recording, noted it "just now showing a profit"[44] (perhaps due in part to repeat broadcasts on PBS and Showtime, but no doubt also due to sales directly to home viewers).

Throughout the rest of the 1980s, Sondheim's musicals were among the most frequently committed to videotape. Harry Haun, substituting for gossip columnist Liz Smith while she was on vacation in August of 1982, reported that Sondheim had been "delighted by what had been done to his show [*Sweeney Todd*] and immediately gave RKO/Nederlander carte blanche to any of his other shows they'd care to cable-ize."[45] The RKO/Nederlander television venture did not last long enough for the company to take advantage of Sondheim's offer, but in 1982 PBS had created a similarly intentioned series named *American Playhouse*. In 1985, producer Michael Brandman approached Terry Hughes again to direct a television recording of *Sunday in the Park with George*, which had won the Pulitzer Prize for Drama in April of that year.

Hughes recorded the show in the final days of the Broadway run, again with a mix of live performances and daytime shots in an empty house. Hughes remembers that this was especially difficult because Bernadette Peters was starring in Andrew Lloyd Webber's *Song and Dance* at the time, and the demands of that show combined with the long days of shooting *Sunday in the Park With George* followed by evening performances began to strain her voice and forced modifications of the shooting schedule. Hughes recalls, as with *Sweeney Todd*, the shots that made it to the final broadcast were largely those recorded in front of an empty house.

While Harold Prince appears to have largely left the editing of *Sweeney Todd* to Hughes (and was reportedly pleased with the result), Hughes remembers that *Sunday*'s director, James Lapine, was actively involved in the editing process. Like Fosse, Lapine seems to have preferred wide shots to close-ups and pushed for more of the stage to be seen in each shot. Hughes graciously deferred to Lapine, whose work as a librettist and stage director he respected, but he did not return to work on the final two American Playhouse recordings of Lapine and Sondheim's work, *Into the Woods* and *Passion* (both were both directed for television by Lapine himself). Later productions of these titles have generally hewed more closely to Lapine's original concept than revivals of *Sweeney Todd* have to Prince's.

In the introduction to the 1986 (second) edition of Craig Zadan's oft-revised history of Sondheim musicals, *Sondheim & Co.*, Zadan begins, "In the twelve years that have passed since the publication of the first edition of *Sondheim & Co.* [in 1974], Stephen Sondheim, in many respects, has changed quite a bit. [. . .] Until recently, Sondheim has been a cult figure, hardly a household name."[46] Eight years later, in the April 4, 1994, issue of *New York Magazine*, the table-of-contents page posed the tongue-in-cheek question, "Is Stephen Sondheim God?"[47] Rising from a cult figure to divinity in two short decades is a remarkable apotheosis, made possible, in part, by the access television and home-video recordings had provided to his work.

The financial realities that pushed the venue for these broadcasts from commercial cable television to PBS also had a valorizing effect on musical theatre. On American Playhouse, Sondheim's musicals were produced alongside Eugene O'Neill, Tina Howe, and Ntozake Shange, suggesting he was part of the new repertory of American theatre. The abridged video recording of a concert production of *Follies* in 1986 featured a cast of theatrical luminaries including Carol Burnett, Barbara Cook, Elaine Stritch, Adolph Green, and Betty Comden at the Philharmonic Hall at Lincoln Center, suggesting to audiences that *Follies* was about as high art as theatre could be. By the mid-1980s, Sondheim's place in the theatrical repertory had already been established, but these broadcasts helped to establish his work as the pinnacle of the form.

In the early 1990s, musical theatre, beginning with the works of Stephen Sondheim, began to be taken somewhat seriously in musicology and theatre departments. Southern Illinois University published California Theatre Professor Joanne Gordon's dissertation, *Art Isn't Easy: The Theatre of Stephen Sondheim*, in 1990, and the University of Michigan Press published Bristol University professor Stephen Banfield's *Sondheim's Broadway Musicals* in 1993. By the late 1990s, both Yale and Oxford University Presses started to publish scholarship in the field regularly. Regardless of the sophistication of Sondheim's work, had it not been for these PBS broadcasts and home-video recordings, he may well have remained a cult figure, and the chronically conservative aesthetic of the academy may have been much slower to adapt and make room for the musical.

The Megamusical

After the Sondheim broadcasts, PBS quickly became the home for musical theatre on television in the United States. In 1996, a tenth-anniversary concert of *Les Misérables* was broadcast on the *Great Performances* series during the spring season of "pledge breaks" in which programming was interrupted at regular intervals to allow for staff to make a plea for donations to support the station. Joseph McLellan, writing for *The Washington Post*, reported that he received a videotape to review "labeled, 'short pledge version'" with a running time of less than two hours and thirty minutes.[48] One of the "thank you" gifts sent to those who supported the station was the VHS copy of the recording with scenes not included in the broadcast (the front of the commercial VHS slipcover prominently advertised that the VHS featured "exclusive footage—never broadcast on television").[49] However, the broadcast version was likely recorded and rewatched more often than the official VHS and, so, came to represent an alternate text.

Even the full commercial release of the concert, though, ran only two hours and thirty-nine minutes, around thirty minutes less than the three-hour, twelve-minute Broadway running time (which, though it had an intermission, did not have the speeches or the encores included on the recording). The cuts made for the concert version were eventually introduced into the Broadway production in the year 2000 in order to cut the running time below three hours, the point at which union overtime rules would increase costs.[50] Before the concert version, the excision of around fifteen minutes of the show might have been deeply resented by audiences who knew and loved the Complete Symphonic Recording. Perhaps to assuage these fears, producer Cameron Mackintosh issued a statement, quoted by *Playbill*, reminding audiences, "We have already had happy experiences with cutting *Les Misérables* for the hugely successful concert version, which runs 2 hours and 21 minutes and has been one of the greatest successes ever in arenas throughout the world, on television and on video,"[51] The concert version helped to destabilize the text and accustom audiences to the slightly shorter version of the show.

In the late 1990s, the market for filmed performance on home video grew as entertainment corporations turned, once again, to releasing filmed performances for profit. In 1995, video recordings of Jean Butler and Michael Flaherty's Irish dance show, *Riverdance*, achieved enormous commercial success in Europe, and, later, on public television in the United States.

Back Stage reported that when Michael Flaherty created his own show, *Lord of the Dance*, PolyGram Video produced a video recording that sold over 100,000 copies.[52] PolyGram Video was a division of a PolyGram that, in 1991, had acquired a 30 percent share in Andrew Lloyd Webber's The Really Useful Group, and which had released many of the original cast recordings of Webber's shows under their Polydor label.[53] After the success of *Lord of the Dance*, Polygram looked to their own catalog and negotiated the television rights to six of Andrew Lloyd Webber's musicals.[54] The first, *Cats*, was filmed over three days in 1997 without an audience at the Adelphi Theatre in London. Andrew Lloyd Webber remembers that twelve cameras were used, and a "new [. . .] at the time" digital technology was used to synchronize the sound recording to different cuts from different days.[55]

Journalist Ken Mandelbaum mused in a 1998 column for *Playbill*, "One wonders, of course, whether the box office of the show in New York and London will be affected by having the show released on video and televised while it is still playing," but he conceded, "this video is an interesting experiment, and no one involved has much to lose, as *Cats* has already had a fairly good run."[56] Perhaps in light of these concerns, the creators of the recording attempted to make it clear that watching the video was different from watching the live show. Mister Mistoffelees disappears in a shower of digitally created stars at the end of his song, and there are several moments where the playback speed slows or repeats certain actions. These choices, combined with the lack of audience, caused *Cats* to sit somewhat uneasily between a music video and a film of stage production. For those rights holders uneasy about the effect filming a currently running show for commercial distribution might have on ticket sales, this odd liminality might have been somewhat reassuring. The digital effects, clearly different from stage magic, made it clear that this was not exactly what one might see on stage the next time the tour of *Cats* visited one's town.

It was also widely reported that the video recording cut forty minutes in order to fit neatly on a single VHS cassette (perhaps again signaling that audiences who loved the video should come to the theatre to see the *full* show). One of the most significant cuts was "Growltiger's Last Stand," a miniopera in which Gus, the Theatre Cat, re-lives in his memory the performance of a favorite role. The number could be problematic even on stage as it plays on early twentieth-century racist stereotypes of East Asians and uses a T. S. Eliot lyric with an ethnic slur. Further, the operatic style, particularly the lovers' last duet (which in the New York production included an Italian aria, and, in the United Kingdom, an unpublished T. S. Eliot poem), feels entirely separate from the pop-musical style of the rest of the show. With a running time of nearly twelve minutes, it was an obvious number to cut. This excision helped to establish a text of *Cats* that made the number optional and gave the producers of the 2015 London production (which transferred to Broadway in 2016) license to cut it altogether. Following the new tradition, it was also cut from the 2019 feature film.

The next recording, the 1999 television production of *Joseph and the Amazing Technicolor Dreamcoat*, was set in a children's school that magically transformed into a kind of digitally enhanced production of the musical. The 2001 American home video release of *Jesus Christ Superstar* closely documented the staging of a London revival that had transferred to Broadway the previous year with many of the same cast members. The revival had closed by the time the video was released in the United States and so the video would not compete with the live production. The final PolyGram/Andrew Lloyd Webber title, the 2001 recording of *By Jeeves*, was made in Canada and featured many of the same cast members who would appear later that year in a short-lived Broadway production a month after the September 11, 2001 terrorist attacks. However, unlike the earlier recordings, *By Jeeves* was never released on a format playable on American VCRs or DVDs. None of the PolyGram/Lloyd Webber video recordings were entirely successful, but they did suggest that such recordings of Broadway productions would not necessarily cannibalize the live market.

PBS stations began to look for other musicals with wider appeal than Sondheim. In the United States, they picked up the Andrew Lloyd Webber shows for their Great Performances series after the titles were released on VHS. Over the next few years an increasing number of musicals were broadcast on *Great Performances*, but these were often recorded in locations other than New York where union regulations were less onerous. A London transfer of the 1999 Broadway revival of *Kiss Me, Kate!* was broadcast in 2003 and released on DVD and VHS. The 1999 Paper Mill Playhouse production of *Crazy for You*, based on the original Broadway staging, was broadcast a few months after the run (though never commercially released on videotape or DVD). The 1998 London revival of *Oklahoma!* with Hugh Jackman was broadcast on PBS in 2003, several months after the Broadway transfer closed.

During the period of experimentation on not-for-profit PBS stations, there were new attempts to find a for-profit home for recorded Broadway musicals. In February of 2000, *Playbill* reported that two new companies, the Broadway Television Network and Broadway Digital Entertainment, were making plans to record Broadway shows and make them available on pay-per-view stations. Pay-per-view technology, wherein an encoded signal is decoded by a cable box given the correct key after purchase, had been used previously for both *Oh! Calcutta!* and *Sophisticated Ladies* but had not yet become a standard way of distributing Broadway recordings. The technology, however, had become increasingly popular for other live events (such as professional wrestling and boxing), and so, in those days before home internet bandwidth made digital streaming of full-length, high-definition video feasible, the technology proved seductive for Broadway producers.

Broadway Digital Entertainment was funded in part by the Shuberts and the Jujamcyn organizations, the Broadway Television Network by the Nederlanders. Broadway Digital Entertainment planned to record performances in a studio before a show moved to Broadway and would make these available with recordings captured earlier for PBS. They later decided to adopt a premium cable model, but never successfully launched.[57] The Broadway Television Network, which initially hoped to record the final performances of Broadway shows, was somewhat more successful and recorded *Smokey Joe's Cafe*, *Jekyll and Hyde*, and the Sondheim revue, *Putting It Together*. *Jekyll and Hyde* was shown in cinemas prior to the pay-per-view release, and all three titles were eventually released on VHS and DVD. After disappointing results from these three recordings, the company went dormant for nearly a decade. None of the Broadway Television Network recordings seem to have had a significant impact on the reception of these shows or their place in the repertory. The price the market was willing to pay for filmed theatre was below the cost many rights holders were willing to accept for their product, and so legal, for-profit distribution of videos of commercial Broadway theatre faltered for several years.

In 2007, a recording of *Legally Blonde: the Musical* was broadcast several times on MTV during the final months of the show's run. This was followed by a tongue-in-cheek reality show in which actors competed to replace star Laura Bell Bundy as the "next Elle Woods." The video was never released on DVD, but the recording helped to solidify *Legally Blonde* a somewhat unexpected place in the musical theatre repertory. The broadcast was digitally captured by many fans and redistributed via the new social-media video-sharing sites, most importantly YouTube, which had emerged only a few years before.

Five years later, digital video streaming was quickly becoming the most common medium for home-video consumption. Netflix, which had started streaming video in 2007 as a subsidiary benefit to their disc-by-mail service, announced in 2011 that they would no longer bundle the two services and would in fact separate disc-by-mail into a separate company. They ultimately reconsidered the spin-off idea, but digital streaming became a separate, and dominant, part of Netflix's business. In 2009, two British employees of Amnesty International, Robert Delamere and Tom Shaw, founded a video service dedicated to documenting British Theatre. Digital Theatre initially advertised themselves as following an "iTunes" model wherein consumers could purchase access to individual titles. Later, they shifted to the "Netflix" model and provided a catalog of recordings, all of which could be accessed by subscribing to the service. Around this time, the Broadway Television Network re-emerged under a new name, Broadway Worldwide and, in 2011, recorded *Memphis* for initial screenings in cinemas followed by distribution on Netflix and on DVD. In 2015, two of the producers of *Legally Blonde*, Bonnie Comley and Stewart Lane, founded a streaming service, BroadwayHD, dedicated to Broadway shows.

Also in 2015, producer Ken Davenport made an arrangement with the Broadway unions and guilds to broadcast a live stream of his production of the off-Broadway musical *Daddy Long Legs* for free online, the first off-Broadway musical to be so distributed. Davenport reported the broadcast was seen by over 150,000 viewers in its original stream and its subsequent three rebroadcasts over the next twenty-four hours.[58] The following year, BroadwayHD live-streamed the Broadway revival of *She Loves Me* at the Roundabout several weeks before the show closed. In both cases, the live stream allowed viewers across the world to watch the show together and discuss their reactions on social media.

This brought free attention to both productions (Davenport reportedly used only his own social media to promote broadcast[59]) and increased the value of both titles. Licensing agency Music Theatre International reported nearly thirty upcoming productions of the musical *She Loves Me* in the second half of July of 2018 (nearly as many as the perennial favorite, *Fiddler on the Roof*, by the same composer and lyricist). The live stream on BroadwayHD and later broadcast on PBS reintroduced the work to audiences around the country and made it an attractive choice to regional and educational theatres. *Daddy Long Legs*, which had enjoyed a few productions across the country in regional theatres, suddenly gained national attention as the unprecedented use of live-streaming technology for this purpose made the musical a national news story.

In 2016, the producers of *Hamilton* recorded the original cast with fifteen cameras over three performances. Although the recording was initially to be used as a source for clips in the PBS documentary *Hamilton's America*,[60] it was clear to cast member Leslie Odom Jr. that additional uses were being considered. He rallied his castmates to insist on a profit-sharing plan should the footage ever be fully released.[61] In February of 2020, Disney reportedly purchased the rights to the film for $75 million intending to distribute it to cinemas before streaming it on Disney+. The cost of the acquisition and the cast's profit-sharing agreement, while a well-deserved boon for the artists involved, portended difficult times for the streaming of less successful musicals in the future. By late February the rights holders of existing video recordings (e.g., the Sondheim videos) had already started to pull their content from streaming services like BroadwayHD, hoping to negotiate a better deal since *Hamilton* had established a high market value for these kinds of recordings.

Then, in March of 2020 the COVID-19 pandemic closed Broadway. Disney released *Hamilton* on Disney+ in July (over a year before the planned October 2021 theatrical release date). Theatre companies began to scramble to find previously recorded footage and negotiated with unions and rights holders to release their recordings (generally for free with a plea for donations). In the fall of 2020, the Screen Actors Guild and the American Federation of Television and Radio Artists (SAG-AFTRA) claimed authority over filmed theatre performances—work that the Actors Equity Association (AEA) also claimed to represent. Though SAG-AFTRA was willing to allow AEA to represent their members on screen during the pandemic, AEA was initially unwilling to accept this concession because both unions foresaw a lucrative market for filmed theatre in the coming years.[62] In November of 2020 an agreement was finally reached allowing AEA to represent actors in most filmed theatre until the end of 2021.

The resistance of American theatrical unions has continued to make it more profitable to record American-made productions in theatres outside of the country. BroadwayHD has continued to stream live theatre, but over the first five years of their existence they have shifted to filming more frequently in London (e.g., *Kinky Boots*, *42nd Street*) where the union regulations allow for less expensive recordings.[63] This practice of filming in international theatres was, of course, employed as early as Sheehan's recording of *Pippin*, but streaming has further loosened the regional restrictions that once were irrevocably encoded in physical media. Differences in the technologies of American televisions as compared to European, British, and Asian televisions meant

VHS recordings had to be encoded for the correct region. Most DVD players were theoretically capable of adjusting their output, but discs were coded to play only on devices manufactured for a particular region. Although legal agreements can limit which countries are able to receive a digital stream, the settings can be easily modified without manufacturing an entirely new edition of video cassette or optical disc when agreements change. Video recordings of international productions of American musicals are quickly becoming the standard video texts of the early twenty-first century.

Still, in the wake of the COVID-19 pandemic, changes are taking place, albeit slowly. The 2016 hit, *Come From Away*, was filmed for an invited audience in a Broadway theatre during the pandemic in 2021 and released on Apple TV+ on the occasion of the twentieth anniversary of the 9/11 terrorist attacks in September of that year (ten days before the show would reopen on Broadway). The musical *Diana*, slated to open on Broadway in the spring of 2020, announced their decision to film the show in an empty theatre and release the recording to Netflix several weeks before the show opened on Broadway in fall of 2021. The streaming release was roundly panned by critics and on social media, and the production closed quickly, but it is likely far more people had a chance to see and come to an opinion about the show than they might have in spring of 2020, when it might have closed relatively quietly like so many commercial flops.

The resistance that Harold Prince faced in the 1960s from rights holders opposed to permitting video recordings of stage performances seems to be diminishing in the wake of a nearly two-year forced experiment with streaming theatre. It is too early to predict the result of this shift with any confidence. However, earlier musicals, especially those that depend on visual storytelling (e.g., *Pippin*), have entered the repertory after video recordings were made. The medium has the power to shape both the repertory and audience expectations. It seems possible that in the coming years the video may become as ubiquitous and influential as the audio cast recordings that defined the musical theatre repertory of the twentieth century.

5

Bootlegging the Musical

At a panel at BroadwayCon 2018, a convention for fans of Broadway theatre, several staff members from regional theatres confessed, with relatively little shame, that as they programmed their own seasons they regularly viewed illicitly recorded videos of New York City productions to inform their selections and to gather ideas for staging. Although the ethics are complex and the illegality certain, for those who live outside of Manhattan, bootlegs are now one of the most common ways many initially engage with Broadway theatre. As a result, bootlegs are now helping to define the repertory.

Although the internet has made sharing of bootlegs much easier, theatrical bootlegging have existed almost as long as the commercial theatre. Some have argued, including the editors of the First Folio, that Shakespeare's work was originally published as bootlegs (or, in the words of those first authorized editors, "stolen, surreptitious copies, maimed, and deformed by the frauds and stealths of injurious imposters").[1] Musical theatre, too, was bootlegged at every stage of the development of the art form. The technologies used to make these "stolen, surreptitious copies," and the approaches used by rights holders to defend their property (or, at least, make bootlegging more difficult), had an enormous impact on the development of both the musical theatre canon and the shape of the form itself.

It is worth noting here that there are two different terms, "pirate" and "bootleg," that have historically been used interchangeably in the popular press to describe illicit copies of creative work. In recent years the terms have come to describe two distinct activities, and the distinction will be used in this discussion. Piracy is the unauthorized copying and distribution of official recordings. Bootlegging, on the other hand, refers to unauthorized recordings of live performances. The bootleg may represent a different recording of a work that is legally available through an official version, but it is not a simple duplicate of the official recording. A pirated copy may be the only available copy of a work that has long been out of print, or a copy of an official recording that was never made commercially available to a particular market, but if it is a copy of a recording that was made with the authorization

Fixing the Musical. Douglas L. Reside, Oxford University Press. © Oxford University Press 2023.
DOI: 10.1093/oso/9780190073718.003.0006

of the rights holders, it is a pirated recording rather than a bootleg. This chapter is mostly concerned with bootlegs.

Early Bootlegs

The script of *The Black Crook*,[2] one of the most popular musicals of the second half of the nineteenth century, was regularly dismissed not only by critics but even by those connected to the production. Joseph Whitton, the treasurer of the original production, considered Charles Barras' script nothing more than "a clothes-line onto which to hang the pretty dresses" of the ballet.[3] Charles Dickens, on a visit to America, was invited by one of the producers to see the show and claimed the script would only take up about "two pages" in his magazine *All The Year Round*, "the whole rest of it being ballets of all sorts, perfectly unaccountable processions, and the Donkey out of last year's Covent Garden pantomime."[4]

Nonetheless, Barras' text seems to have been a remarkably stable element of *The Black Crook* during the sixty or so years that the piece was regularly produced in America. Although the songs interpolated into the script regularly changed, sometimes even from month to month, all of the nineteenth-century prompt books and the two published American editions preserve a text with little variation from the version Barras deposited for copyright in 1863, and the cast lists in printed programs suggest that even the minor characters still appeared in all American revivals.

This consistency may have been due to the fact that the text, if relatively unimportant from a dramaturgical perspective, was considered essential for legal ownership of the piece. Joseph Whitton, the aforementioned treasurer, recounts that when producers Henry Jarrett and Harry Palmer approached the owner of Niblo's Garden, William Wheatley, with the possibility of joining with them to produce "A Grand Ballet." Wheatley naturally asked, "What shall the piece be?" They proposed the *Naiad Queen*, which was in the public domain. Wheatley rejected the idea, saying, "Should we make a success of it, every concert saloon in New York will be playing the 'Naiad Queen.'"[5] If the script was to be a clothesline, Wheatley wanted it to be a clothesline that he could own.

When Barras offered his script to Wheatley, Joseph Whitton remembers advising his boss to purchase the rights for the play, even at an exorbitant price, because, "the title alone is worth all [the author] asks."[6] He may have been right, for by the time the musical opened at London's Alhambra Theater in 1872, the title was, in fact, the only real connection to the show that so enchanted audiences at Niblo's Garden in New York City. The New York production was an original (albeit in the loosest sense of the term) melodrama heavily influenced by the Faustian German opera *Der Freischütz*. The British production was a new adaptation of the French fairytale *La Biche Au Bois* (best known today as a version of *Sleeping Beauty*). None of the text and likely none of the music from the American production crossed the Atlantic to the Alhambra. The title alone was, by this point, sufficient to attract audiences.

Unfortunately for the licensors of *The Black Crook*, though, the copyrighted script was not always sufficient to protect production rights. In October of 1866, an unscrupulous theatre manager, Julian Martinetti, employed an early theatre bootlegger "to attend [a performance of the Black Crook] and take down the parts in short-hand as they were spoken and acted by the players."[7] Martinetti produced the piece in San Francisco under the title *The Black Rook* and had the audacity to sue the producers of a licensed production of *The Black Crook* when it was produced at another theatre in town. The licensed production counter-sued and, remarkably, lost the case, because, the judge argued, "A play like this has no value except as it is appreciated by the theatre-going public. It cannot be *read*—it is mere spectacle, and must be seen to be appreciated."[8] He concludes it is not, for that reason, "a dramatic composition" and cannot be protected by laws designed to guard the intellectual property of the authors of such works.[9]

The judge, it is interesting to note, seems to have made his decision based purely on the witness of those who had seen both productions, as the official script had not arrived from New York at the time of trial. The legal licensees had purchased a copy of the pirated version and were using that text until the original could be procured. The script was commercially published by Rockwell, Baker, & Hill in Buffalo in 1866[10] and by Rounds & James in Chicago in 1867,[11] but it appears these were not readily available in California. Today, in fact, these printed copies are even more rare than the manuscript promptbooks. To my knowledge, the Chicago edition is preserved only in the rare books collection of the Library of Congress, and no complete version of the Buffalo edition is extant (though copies of the title page are pasted into manuscript promptbooks at the New York Public Library and the Players Club). Later musicals (*Florodora*, *The Wizard of Oz*, *Babes in Toyland*) rarely published their libretti at all, and it seems possible that the published editions of *The Black Crook* exist mostly because Barras himself valued his text and did not consider it a musical libretto but rather a work of dramatic literature.

It is tempting to consider the lack of integration of story and song in *The Black Crook* and other musicals of this period as representative of an early stage of a developing form—the first release of a technology with bugs that would be worked out by later innovators like Rodgers and Hammerstein and Stephen Sondheim. To tell the history of musical theatre as a story of continuous formal integration from *The Black Crook* to, say, *Hamilton* is to ignore the fact that opera and operetta already offered fully integrated scores, and that many of these scores were popular favorites in the 1860s (Jarrett and Palmer had, after all, proposed the opera *Undine* as the clothesline for their "pretty dresses"). Formally integrated music theatre existed, but the innovation of the creators of *The Black Crook*, if they made one at all, was in its remarkable lack of integration. The "unintegrated" musical was perfectly designed for the technologies used to fix and reproduce the elements that could be commercially marketed in the 1860s and 1870s.

In this age before commercially available, mass-manufactured recordings of music, the easiest way to enjoy theatre music was to play it at home oneself (or have a musically talented friend or family member do so). Many middle-class families at the turn of the twentieth century had a piano in the house and at least one family member who could play it.[12] Proficiency would have varied, of course, and the limited time that could be devoted to live performance meant that simpler, shorter songs would have been more likely to be learned and performed than the full scores of an opera. If a musical ran for a long time, the production could sell more sheet music if the songs changed frequently so new publications of music associated with the production could be released at regular intervals.

Compared to the libretto, sheet music for songs used in the nineteenth-century productions of *The Black Crook* survive in many libraries and private collections. Only two months after the production opened in September of 1866, the music printer William A. Pond and Company (located on the same block as the theatre) released a series of sheet music titled *Gems from the Black Crook* that included the music director Thomas Baker's arrangements of "Waltzes" and "Galops" [*sic*] from the show.[13] Harvey B. Dodworth, conductor of the original production, also published the vocal music for the hit song, Kennick and Bickwell's "You Naughty, Naughty Men"[14] and an arrangement of "The March of the Amazons" by Emil Stigler.[15] The following year, Pond published Baker's "Transformation Polka."[16] Some of the songs were more popular than others. Carline's song, "You Naughty, Naughty Men," is mentioned in many early retrospectives about the show. Still, none seems to have been thought essential to the piece, as programs suggest new music was interpolated over time and even "You Naughty, Naughty Men" quickly cycled out of the piece.

The songs would not even need to be originally composed for the theatre. The sheet music of a song interpolated into a musical could be sold in a new edition that made reference to its inclusion in a popular show. Likewise, a show could benefit by advertising the interpolation of a popular song. This practice was common in both London and New York throughout the latter half of the nineteenth century, but annoyed some composers who felt it to be a misuse of their intellectual property. Biographer Andrew Lamb notes that Leslie Stuart, the composer of the popular musical *Florodora*, published an open letter in two of the important entertainment journals of the time (*The Era* and *Entr'acte*) warning directors not to interpolate his songs without permission, and advising that he would never give permission for fewer than two verses to be used in any production.[17]

Performance fees had become the most reliable source of income for popular composers as sheet music was no longer a profitable commodity due to new printing technologies that had led to rampant piracy. Like the photocopiers of the twentieth century, the invention of lithography (as discussed in Chapter 1) made it possible for music pirates to cheaply and quickly create unlicensed copies of sheet music to sell on the street. Andrew Lamb writes, "Printed music [in England] was covered by the same copyright law as books; but, whereas the process of setting up type, printing, and binding books was an expensive one, popular music of two or three pages could readily be photographed or lithographed in any old shed or barn."[18] Like books, even a short libretto would have required more resources than the average private bootlegger could invest, but, as Lamb notes, single songs could be cheaply copied and sold at a profit.

In 1903, American composer John Philip Sousa wrote a letter to the British *Musical News* in which he expressed "astonishment [. . .] on arriving in London to find that pirated editions of my compositions were being sold [. . .] in the streets of your city."[19] The editors of *Musical News* follow the letter with a note, tinged with a bit of ruffled nationalism, observing that "English songs have before now been appropriated by American pirates and printed in cheap, one dollar books."[20] They specifically cite Arthur Sullivan as one who, as a result of the lack of international copyright law in the late nineteenth century, was famously forced to stage simultaneous productions of *The Pirates of Penzance* in both England and the United States to secure simultaneous copyright. If a writer or composer depended entirely on sales of printed music, piracy would be crippling. Indeed it was a source of major losses for Leslie Stuart, who went bankrupt later in life.

Nevertheless, the fact that authors could cross the Atlantic and find that their work had so prolifically, if illegally, preceded them meant there was an audience ready and eager to see their work on stage. The stage, then, as Stuart concluded, was where money was to be made for composers of popular songs. Lamb suggests that Stuart's move from writing popular and patriotic songs to musical theatre "may have been in part a reaction to the piracy he was suffering, because royalties for theatre performances were so much easier to collect and protect."[21] Public performances must widely advertise their location and times with plenty of notice, giving defenders of copyright the ability to shut down illicit productions. Printed sheet music, however, could be manufactured and sold quickly, and when the law came near, the pirates could easily flee. Lamb describes the particular difficulty of enforcing copyright law in England, even after some of the reforms supported by Stuart had passed:

> The new Copyright bill [passed in 1902, several years after the first production of *Florodora*] required a publisher to go through a wholly unrealistic rigamarole. His agent carried around printed forms, claiming copyright in specified songs. When he found pirated copies on sale in the streets, he was required to find a police constable and hand the signed form to him to authorize seizure. By the time this was done, the pirate had probably made his way to another location.[22]

Shutting down pirated productions staged in immovable buildings was much easier.

Even on the stage, though, enforcement of copyright was difficult if the use of particular songs was not advertised. Interpolated songs might not be listed in the publicity for a show. An advertisement for a full musical like *Florodora* would clearly indicate Stuart was owed royalties, but if one of his songs was interpolated into a new piece without permission, Stuart or his friends would have to see the production to identify the infringement. Productions that "secretly" used unauthorized music in this way might close before the rights holder noticed. The key to fighting illegal interpolation turned out to be tighter integration of music and text.

Composers whose work was tightly integrated into the play would be less likely to be interpolated into other situations (and if they were, the audience might recognize the song as a piece from *Florodora*), and so word of mouth might bring the violation to the notice of the rights holder. It is probably not coincidental that the composers who did the most to create musicals in which the songs were tightly linked to the title of the show were those who also were most concerned with protecting music copyright: in England Leslie Stuart and Arthur Sullivan, and in the United States, most of the founders of ASCAP: Victor Herbert, Irving Berlin, Jerome Kern, and John Philip Sousa.

Audio Bootlegs

Even as legal protections strengthened, new technologies made bootlegging easier. The invention of audio-recording technology in particular allowed the work of the performers as well as the writers to be captured and shared. Though not exactly illicit, some of the earliest such audio recordings (of music theatre or otherwise) are the famous Mapleson Cylinders. Recorded from the prompter's box and, later, the flies over the stage by the company's librarian, Lionel Mapleson, these wax cylinders document performances of New York's Metropolitan Opera company from 1900 to 1904. Mapelson used two of Edison's spring-powered phonographs, the "Home" Model A and, later, the "Triumph" Model A.[23] Both models would have been especially well suited to the task of recording from various spots in the theatre as they were powered by a spring-driven motor that was wound by hand. Although the Metropolitan Opera had electrical wiring by at least 1884,[24] finding the appropriate power source for the phonograph would have severely limited possible locations for recording.

Around three decades after Mapleson created his audio bootlegs, someone, likely associated with the production, recorded the tour of *The Ziegfeld Follies of 1934* at the Shubert Theater in New Haven, CT. David Hummel's indispensable *Collector's Guide to the American Musical* notes, "Recording was done on approximately 50–78 rpm discs on a home disc recording machine. They were edited together to form a complete performance tape [. . .] This is the oldest live performance tape the author has been able to trace."[25] If Hummel's provenance is correct, this recording demanded that the bootlegger change discs every three minutes or so, a herculean effort that, nonetheless, seems to be exactly in line with the kind of obsessive dedication to documentation bootleggers have displayed in the century that followed. Portions of the recording were released on compact disc by AEI in 1997, but until then it was known mostly through the trading and bootlegging community.

At the same time, Ray Knight, a teenager from a wealthy Florida family, began recording some of the earliest film bootlegs of Broadway theatre. Born in 1914, Knight was given a home movie camera for his sixteenth birthday in December of 1930. The following summer he traveled to New York City, where he captured Fred and Adele Astaire in *The Band Wagon*. This began a forty-two-year career of recording theatre on his regular trips to Broadway. The home movie cameras of the 1930s were mostly powered by clockwork; the user would turn a crank to compress a spring that would slowly turn the mechanism that fed the film past the lens. Filming was usually limited to around three minutes per shot.

The noise from the operation of the camera would have been noticeable to neighboring audience members, and so Knight would typically capture either a loud moment in the production, or else the applause during the curtain call. Knight's filming could not have gone unnoticed by ushers, but he never seems to have faced serious consequences for his bootlegging. A friend of Knight's told *Washington Post* reporter Megan Rosenfeld in 1989, "Sometimes he'd get kicked out, or his camera would be confiscated, but he'd just go back the next day and try again."[26] Rosenfeld notes, "in the clip of *By Jupiter* [recorded by Knight], Ray Bolger can be seen during the curtain call, spying Knight and pursing his lips in playful disapproval."[27] Bootlegging was illicit from the earliest days of recording technology, but prevention was lax.

In the first half of the twentieth century, reproducing recordings was extremely difficult, and so bootlegs were rarely sold. Indeed, although any product for which there is sufficient demand will eventually be monetized, financial gain has rarely been a significant motivation among theatrical bootleggers. Most seem initially driven to capture and document work that might otherwise be lost and are then compelled by a human impulse to share what one enjoys with others who appreciate it. Mapleson reportedly would play back his cylinders for the cast the next day—wanting not just to capture performances but also to replay them for others.[28]

Bootlegging is, in its own way, a kind of performance that requires an audience to be satisfying. This satisfaction, though, requires that the bootlegger be recognized as the source of the recording, the producer behind the performance. A 1935 New Yorker article described the then-septuagenarian Mapelson as a "pink-cheeked old party with a testy disposition."[29] He "locks his door and plays the records on his phonograph once in a while, but he has consistently refused all sorts of fat offers from phonograph companies for the privilege of re-recording the old cylinders. 'They're much too personal' [he would say]."[30] Commercial release would have removed Mapleson from the performance and decreased the scarcity that made his recordings so valuable.

Knight likewise "performed" his film bootlegs. His friends remember he would host parties that would involve either outings to the baseball stadium or else evenings "spent watching the musical movies, with original cast recordings providing the sound."[31] Like Mapelson, part of Knight's pleasure in his collection was "performing" his recordings with an interested (or at least accommodating) live audience. These recordings were eventually acquired by Miles Kreuger, a collector and Broadway historian who, as of this writing, lives in the Hollywood area in a house that he has designated the home of the "Institute of the American Musical." Like Mapelson and Knight before him, Kreuger is generally happy to screen the films for those who come to visit. He has, like Mapleson, also declined most offers to make them more broadly available. Over the years, he has talked about his desire to sync the video with audio recordings and provide accompanying commentary about the shows documented. This has not yet happened (though a few clips have appeared in documentaries). One gets the sense that for Kreuger, as for Mapleson, these recordings are "much too personal" to publish in a medium that would separate the collector from the performance of the collection.

Knight's recordings, then, have had relatively little effect on the musical theatre repertory or the established texts of the shows he documented. They were created using a technology that produced a medium that, at the time, did not allow for quick, inexpensive reproduction by amateurs. Knight's geographical isolation in Florida from the Broadway theatre community followed by Kreuger's tight control of the recordings have minimized whatever impact they may have otherwise had on musical theatre history.

Bootlegging in the Age of Sharing

Later bootleg recordings on magnetic and then digital media were more influential. As discussed in Chapter 3, magnetic tape was not commercially available in the United States until after World War II, and the quality of recordings made on it were unsuitable for music until the 1950s. However, in November of 1951, *Der Spiegel* reported that a West German engineer, Willi Draheim, had invented a "wallet-sized" device, powered by batteries, that could record over two hours to a spool of wire.[32] The minifon, as it was called, could be attached to a microphone hidden in a fake wristwatch, making it appealing for surreptitious recording (see Figure 5.1). Actor Beatrice Lillie's manager made a recording of her performance in the 1958 London production of *Auntie Mame* using such a device, and the recording (and secret microphone wristwatch) are preserved in the Beatrice Lillie Papers at the New York Public Library for the Performing Arts.[33] The technology of the minifon did not lend itself to reproduction, nor to musical recording (it could not record in stereo), but it did introduce a popular market for portable, and concealable, audio-recording devices. The columnist for *Der Spiegel* reported, "confidential 'one-to-one conversations' will theoretically soon be over."[34] While this may have been an overstatement, it was certainly the case that soon after the release of the minifon, unauthorized full audio recordings of professional theatre began to proliferate.

Advertisements for tape machines in the 1950s openly anticipated recording of live performances as a primary use of the technology. In the April 1954 issue of *Magnetic Film & Tape Recording*, the ability of the Webcor line of reel-to-reel tape recorders to change recording directions and so achieve "TWO FULL HOURS ON THE SAME REEL" without turning over the tape is promoted explicitly for recording "a symphony, opera, play or speech recording."[35] However, aside from the minifon, battery-operated recorders were rare until the late 1960s, and so bootleggers would have needed access to the electrical outlets in the theatre. While it would have been difficult for an audience member to make use of these outlets without notice, those with access to the backstage could sometimes find a secret place to conceal a device. Therefore, most bootleg recordings made in the 1950s and 1960s were "inside jobs."

One of the earliest of these is a full recording of the 1954 musical *The Golden Apple* and a 1955 Boston tryout of Marc Blitzstein's ill-fated opera, *Reuben, Reuben*, possibly recorded from the monitor in Kaye Ballard's

Figure 5.1 The minifon watch microphone used to record Bea Lillie's performance in *Auntie Mame* is preserved in the Rodgers and Hammerstein Archive of Recorded Sound in the New York Public Library for the Performing Arts (photograph by the author).

dressing room. In 1956, someone involved with the production of *My Fair Lady* (likely stage manager Biff Liff, whose estate gave what appears to be the original recording to the New York Public Library) recorded the sitzprobe (the first rehearsal with the orchestra) on reel-to-reel tape. Ethel Merman's final performance as Rose in *Gypsy* was famously recorded to an often duplicated and shared reel-to-reel tape in 1961. Those familiar with the re-cording believe it was made by music director Milton Rosenstock from a speaker in the orchestra pit at the request of Jule Styne as a present for Ethel Merman. Robert Schear, a stage manager for many Broadway musicals be-tween 1958 and 1980, was not involved in the recording, but claims to have heard the story from Rosenstock himself. He recalls, though:

> Oddly enough, Merman had no equipment to listen to these things. I used to send her copies of big shows, and she'd say "I don't have anything to play it on! I don't have that stuff!" And she never did. [. . .] Not into that. The only thing she ever heard was her recording sessions played back at the studio.[36]

Both creating and consuming bootlegs in the early 1960s required access to technologies that were, if not uncommon, at least not entirely ubiqui-tous. However, justifying one's bootlegging activities as a service to the ac-tors (whether or not they desired such documentation) seems to have been common throughout the past century.

Writers, though, do seem generally pleased to have copies of their work. Jule Styne was apparently happy enough with the results of the *Gypsy* re-cording that he decided to try again with *Funny Girl*. In this case, Schear was enlisted to do the deed. When asked about the recording, he responded:

> I'm the one that did that. Myself, and Dorothy and Charlotte Dicker. Dorothy was Jule's assistant for years, and she was like his right and left hand. Her sister, Charlotte, was an assistant to Joe Kipness. And they lived together. [. . .] They were almost like twins, but they weren't. They just did everything together. [. . .] Dorothy more than anyone is the one who instigated this through Jule. She got me to schlep my 40 pound machine over to the Winter Garden. I can't even remember what the machine was, but it was one of those early reel-to-reel recording machines in a heavy case with a handle. Of course I had to be the first kid on the block to have it. So she said "Could you please bring it over? I'll pay for your cab fare. Come over early [you know, way before half hour]."
>
> So I think I got to the theater at around 6:00. Dorothy was very instru-mental in helping me [find] where to hook up. We found a dressing room that no one was in. It was at the very top of the Winter Garden. I don't know why it was empty. The cast was quite large, but it wasn't a very large room.[37]

The audio tape reels, which Schear remembers purchasing himself, could only capture about thirty minutes each, and so had to be changed frequently. Schear remembers:

> I changed the tapes every half-hour, and some of the changes were made during major applause [moments]. I worked as fast as a magician could. I wanted to watch the performance from out front, but I was sitting in this utility closet with a recorder while the Dicker sisters were out front having a wonderful time.[38]

He recalls feeling guilt-stricken at the end of the evening:

> As soon as it was over, the machine was unhooked. And I got out of there as fast as I could. I took a cab and got home. And I really felt that I was stealing something. I felt awful. It's a terrible feeling to do something like that, for me, because it was the first time . . . and the last time.[39]

Still, he admits, "I am, in a way, glad that it's preserved because it is a wonderful treasure to have that."[40]

It seems most bootleg recordings through the mid-1960s were made in a similar way. The difficulty of sneaking a reel-to-reel recorder into the theatre and changing and re-threading the tape during the show without being stopped all but demanded a connection to the production. By the mid-1960s battery-operated portable recorders became more common, and by the 1970s bootleg audio recordings exist for most Broadway and many off-Broadway musicals. As audience recordings proliferated, a small community, and then a market, developed to share, trade, and in some cases sell recordings. A 1971 piece in the *New York Times* on opera fan culture briefly notes an almost comic scene observed in the foyer of the Philharmonic Hall after a performance by soprano Magda Olivero:

> five men in bulky raincoats (no rain was predicted that night) and carrying bulging briefcases chat conspiratorially. A friend passes and asks, "Did you get it in stereo?" Silence from the group. They are professional recordists who run lively bootleg operations, releasing illegal recordings of live performances of certain singers. Olivero is a hot bootleg item.[41]

These recordings were sold in several music stores in New York City. A particularly notorious hub of this underground economy was Music Masters at 25 W 42 street (just north of Bryant Park). The staff there would purchase these recordings from bootleggers, reproduce them, and sell them to customers who knew how to ask.

In 1990, in an article about the closing of Music Masters, the *New York Times* quoted playwright Albert Innaurato's memory of the shibboleths used to ferret out law enforcement. When Innaurato asked for a bootleg of Olivero singing Medea, the clerk asked, "'How many times did she sing it before Dallas?' [Innaurato] quickly answered, 'It was her first time,' and he said, 'O.K., you can have it.'"[42] One gets the sense that the password was not so much a way of avoiding legal prosecution as a way of filtering out the true fan from the interloper.

With the infrastructure of a market like Music Masters, bootleg recordings began to have an economic value. Naturally, better-quality recordings could fetch higher prices. Many of the most prolific bootleggers, though, seemed to maintain a kind of ethical rule of only *trading* recordings for others they wanted (something that could also be done at Music Masters).

As part of my research for this chapter, I was introduced to a small community of men (the activity seems to have been a predominantly masculine one) who regularly bootlegged musical theatre from the 1970s until the dawn of the YouTube era. A man now in his sixties, who I will refer to as "Frank," recalls visiting Music Masters as a young teenager and discovering their backroom selection of bootlegs.

> [They] had a little backroom. If you went into the store there was a register on your left and there were these bookshelves like being in a library. And if you went behind the books where the workers would go [there would be] all these bootleg tapes in this area.[43]

Most of the illicit business of Music Masters, though, seems to have been opera recordings and gray-market pressing of out-of-print or never-released material from decades before. Frank recalls:

> They used to make bootleg LPs. They would take archival stuff from the 30s or 40s. They would go out and get tapes of this really rare Gershwin stuff or Jerome Kern or Sigmund Romberg. They would have live tapes or radio broadcasts or stuff that was done on acetate. [Store owner] Willy Werner

would actually make labels for it. An orange label or a yellow label for whatever it was and he would put it on the album cover and sell it for $25 or $50.
[. . .] No covers. Just a black sleeve with a label. A yellow label or an orange
label with a list of what was on it, what the name of the album was, what
the years were, and who sang it. This went on for years. The Broadway stuff
wasn't as much. But the operas and these LPs [were] huge for him.

He had cancer, and he died. It was him, and [competing stores] Nappy
and Colony. [. . .] And Music Masters was much more successful at it because they were reasonable about it.[44]

Despite Frank's perception that Music Masters was more reasonable, the
prices of the bootlegs were still too high for his teenage budget:

I didn't have money to pay. . . . I was 12 . . . 13 . . . 14 years old. So I started
doing them myself. So I was given a lecture [on how to produce the best
recordings]. The idea was that people would go in with a huge tape recorder, called a Uher, and most of them would have two microphones so
they were stereo, and they would record these shows live. And that's why
today we have the whole show of *Follies*, *A Little Night Music* (in stereo) that
were done in New York on previews or opening night. I was fascinated by
all of this.[45]

The Uher recorder Frank mentions was a German-made reel-to-reel device
marketed to law enforcement for the purpose of recording statements. The
Uher 4000 series, introduced in 1961, was approximately 11×8×3 inches in
size (about the size of a thick notebook) and weighed roughly twelve pounds.
Higher-end models could record around four hours of four-track audio (that
is, stereo recording on both sides of the tape). The recorders could switch
to recording directions without removing the reel, which increased uninterrupted recording time. Frank was not able to afford a Uher, but this did not
stop him from recording:

I didn't have the money, but I did get a hold of this reel-to-reel machine, and
I did this one show, *Frank Merriwell*, which ran one night. It was supposed
to be opening night, but they had postponed the opening. So I went with
my father and his girlfriend and my brother and my sister. And we sat front
row mezzanine. And I put the microphone on the ledge of the mezzanine.

The reel to reel tapes were not big. [. . .] They maybe lasted an hour, maybe 45 minutes. It was 7.5 [inches (of tape) per second] which was the standard speed. There was a slower speed that was good for talking, not for music recording that was . . . maybe half of the 7.5 . . . and there was a third speed that was even slower.

So I used to do these at 7.5 which was the best sound. And that came out terrific. There was nobody sitting in the mezzanine, and there was nobody really looking at me. So I was able to get away with it. And of course I was so young that no one would ever suspect what I was doing, you know.[46]

Frank recalls that after this first foray into bootlegging he quickly moved to cassettes for their price and convenience. He continued to experiment with methods to capture the best sound:

As I got older and got a little bit more gutsy ('cause very few people would stop me from doing it) I started using microphones. In 1973, I went to the very first preview of *Chicago* at the Forrest Theatre in Philadelphia. And *Chicago* was 3 hours long. And it was a stereo machine. And basically I put the microphone down the light box cause I was sitting in the front row mezzanine. And after the first act they took them away. I was caught. I only have the first act. And I never got the microphones back.[47]

Like many bootleggers from this period, Frank took special pride in the quality of his work.

Some of the bootleg tapes that were done at the time were not done very well. [. . .] Some of these people would move around . . . the microphones were very sensitive . . . so when they'd move you'd hear the mic moving. Or they would be too close to somebody and you would hear them laughing or applauding or coughing or whatever. But with me I was very sensitive to all of that stuff, so I would make sure I was either sitting away from somebody . . . and if I was using a condenser microphone I was very circumspect about it and made sure it had clear access to the stage. I never really wanted to sit in the orchestra. I always wanted to be in the mezzanine. Front mezzanine preferably because the sound was so great up there.[48]

This attention to quality naturally meant that Frank's recordings could command a higher value in the market of the time, especially at Music Masters.

Willy Lerner was particular. He wouldn't take things that sounded bad because [he had] to justify the price tag of $40, $50, $60. (I think sometimes
they were $25 depending on if they were stereo or not.) He would listen
to them to decide whether he wanted to take them or not. My stuff was always good, so I used trade them. [. . .] Lerner was amazed that I had such
a collection.[49]

Frank recalls that stores like Music Masters were also gathering places
where bootleggers could meet one another and go on to trade copies of their
collections. He recalls a day in January of 1972 when he met a lifelong friend
at such a store after the first Broadway revival of Lorraine Hansberry's *The
Sign in Sidney Brustein's Window.*

I went to see the *Sign in Sidney Brustein's Window.* It was play with music
with Zohra Lampert and Hal Linden. It played the Longacre Theatre. [. . .]
Music by Gary William Friedman Lyrics by Ray Errol Fox[50]. I was thirteen
years old. The subject matter was way above my head. After the matinee
I went to this record store called Nappy's. They were on Broadway next to
the famous Rivoli Theater which is long gone now. They were the sister store
to Colony Records. There was a guy in there named Ellie. I was showing
him my list of all my live tapes. I'm not sure why I was talking to him but
I was. He was a clerk behind the counter.

And I showed him all my live tapes and I thought I could make trades
with him or whatever. And as I'm doing this [another well-known boot-
legger] is looking over my shoulder and he said, "Oh I have this and this
and this!"

And we became friends that way. [. . .] He is 10 years older than I am. He
started the same time I did.[51]

This bootlegger, who I will call "Jim," lived outside of New York City and became a source of recordings from places like Philadelphia or Washington
DC. His recording technique became legendary in the community. Frank
remembers:

He had a briefcase. And [. . .] he would cut out part of the briefcase in the
top right hand corner. It was a black briefcase, and he would get a microphone and tape it into the side [. . .] and cover all of the surrounding [area]
with black electrical tape so that the mic would stay up. So he would have

the briefcase on his lap so nobody knew what he was doing. And he would open it up to change the cassette if it was an hour or 60 minutes or whatever. Or if he was in the mezzanine he would stand his briefcase up and face it towards the stage.[52]

Jim confirms that the briefcase was cheap and made of "cardboard" allowing for easy modification.[53] Perhaps because of this unique device and the rarity of his out-of-town recordings, he became well known. He recalls feeling both embarrassed and concerned when he was once recognized on a subway and approached by a collector who he did not know but who wanted to request one of his recordings.[54]

By the 1970s, small cassette recorders easily concealable in a pocket or bag became widely commercially available, and many less "professional" bootleggers began making their own recordings. Tapes typically could hold only about forty-five to sixty minutes per side, so audible clicks would be heard in the middle of a long act as the devices either stopped recording or else switched direction to record on the "other side" of the cassette. Several bootleggers recalled this tape-changing moment at the opening of *Sweeney Todd* and *Merrily We Roll Along*. Sondheim, in fact, was especially well documented by such recordings, and many of Sondheim's colleagues seem to have taken a relatively supportive approach to the production of these recordings. Frank remembers,

> On the closing night of *Pacific Overtures*, I remember . . . [Scenic designer] Boris Aronson was in a wheelchair [. . .] And I was in the back of the theatre, and [choreographer] Pat Birch and [librettist] Hugh Wheeler[55] were standing in the back with me. I had an extension microphone and I was holding the machine up and Boris Aronson tapped me on the back and asks "what kind of camera are you using?" [Frank laughs because it wasn't a camera, but a tape recorder]
>
> So I'm taping the show. It's a closing performance. And Ruth Mitchell, who was Hal Prince's assistant, tries to stop me from doing it. Hugh Wheeler and Pat Birch jumped out from behind me and said "Let him alone, let him alone, he's doing it. Let him go!" and she did.[56]

Another bootlegger, "Max," recalls that help sometimes even came from the stage:

When I went to see *Wise Guys* the early version of *Bounce* or *Road Show* at New York Theatre Workshop [. . .] I was in the front row right in the center with two friends on either side. And I had a new kind of recorder that actually automatically turned over to the other side so you could set up a 90 [minute] cassette and it would go the whole show. [Cast member] Nancy Opal was a friend and she saw me. And she was on stage and kind of mimed "[Max], cover your hand over the microphone. Everybody can see the tape recorder."[57]

Not everyone was so supportive, of course. Frank remembers that Goodspeed Opera House was particularly vigilant in stopping bootleggers (perhaps especially motivated as the shows that opened there were often works in progress and not meant to be consumed broadly). Still, even there, Frank had his defenders.

There was a show trying out called *Bodo*, book by Hugh Wheeler, music by Lee Pockriss (who wrote *Tovarich*), and lyrics by Anne Croswell. I went to see the show, and I was talking with Hugh Wheeler outside the show, and [casting director] Warren Pincus comes up behind both of us and he says "OK, [Frank] give me the tape." Hugh Wheeler said, "Leave him alone. I want it."

And he turned and started having a fight with Hugh Wheeler about it. And I thought, "My God!" And Warren was like a dog with a bone, he was relentless. And Hugh Wheeler finally said, "Listen Warren, that's it, he's got the tape, I told him he could do it, and that's it!"

There were people who really took my side in all of this, who really felt I was doing a service.

But even so, some people felt they had to be the bad cop, even as harmless as it may seem. I wasn't doing it for profit or whatever, [but] they felt it was their obligation to make sure that none of this existed. All I can say to these people, most of whom aren't around anymore, [is] "God bless them! Good luck!"[58]

Nonetheless, like stage manager Robert Schear of the *Funny Girl* recording, Frank confesses to feeling a twinge of ambiguity about his actions: "On one hand I'm not proud I did it, but on the other I am, because this is the only thing that exists."[59] Frank, like Schear, seems glad that the history has been preserved, but a little uncomfortable that laws had to be bent or broken to do it.

Sometimes bootleggers found semi-official ways of releasing recordings for which there was never a sanctioned edition. The musical version of *Breakfast at Tiffanys* played only four previews on Broadway, but was bootlegged and given to Bruce Yeko, who released it on LP under his private label, S. P. M. (Society for the Preservation of Musicals). Yeko similarly released the otherwise unrecorded original casts of *Foxy* and *Her First Roman*. Yeko went on to develop the fully legally sanctioned Take Home Tunes, which partially recorded Stephen Schwartz's musical *The Baker's Wife* with only the three principal cast members. The musical has since enjoyed multiple regional and international revivals, and a full recording of a London production was released by Jay Records in 1990.

A similar label, Blue Pear records, emerged in the 1970s, initially with a release of bloopers recorded on the set of the original *Star Trek* television series (the name, "Blue Pear," was, it seems, a pun on the word "blooper"). After the initial album, though, the label exclusively released musical theatre material from bootleg recordings or private demos. The record jacket claimed the company was based in Longwood, FL, but it was in fact founded, funded, and operated out of Los Angeles by an accountant named Harry Friedenberg, who, according to those who knew him, had little interest in theatre music, but saw a money-making opportunity. His friend Brad Bennett would receive cassettes from friends in New York or demos from producers and agents and would edit them to fit onto a single disc and lay out the art for the album jackets. Another friend, Los Angeles theatre critic Rick Talcove, would write liner notes under the pseudonym Niles Marsh (a name shared with an early twentieth-century "female impersonator"). Friedenberg would pay for the pressing of several hundred discs, which he would then distribute to record stores in Los Angeles.[60]

Bennett remembers that "on three instances" someone complained about copyright infringement, but Friedenberg would plead ignorance saying that since the show was "such an old thing, they didn't know they would have to pay." If the rights holder continued to protest, Bennett remembers that Friedenberg would send them a box of all of the releases, and they "never heard any more from them." The one exception was a live recording of Bernstein's *1600 Pennsylvania Avenue*, which the label did not release after the Bernstein office threatened legal action.[61]

Other bootleggers used recordings they made to inform their work on legitimate commercial recordings they later produced. Several in the community told me that, in his early twenties, music director and record producer John McGlinn was commissioned by his friends to travel to Boston to bootleg the tryout of Sondheim's *Pacific Overtures*. His large and indiscreetly concealed reel-to-reel recorder was noticed by the house staff and confiscated at intermission. Several of those I interviewed independently remembered the moment and McGlinn's extraordinary distress, compounded by the fact that his train ticket had been paid for by those at home expecting to hear a recording of the new Sondheim show. At least two bootleggers claim they supplied McGlinn with the second act from their own recordings, which they had made with greater discretion. McGlinn's dedication to audio preservation of musicals did not diminish but found more-legal outlets. Working with EMI he produced a critically praised a three-CD album of *Show Boat* along with several other detailed reconstructions of early twentieth-century musicals.

Record producer Robert Sher acknowledges that access to live recordings is beneficial for his work:

> Those tapes are invaluable [. . .] Right now I'm doing *Peter Pan*. I'm doing the '79 revival which has never been recorded. [. . .] And there's lots of audio on that show because it ran for two years and they made changes after the show left Broadway and went on tour. And I have all of that, and I'm going to be able to reconstruct everything. We included all of these cut songs written by Comden and Green. It's going to be the most definitive recording of *Peter Pan* ever.[62]

As with Shakespeare's quartos, bootlegs move from illegal contraband to invaluable historical documents relatively quickly.

Video Bootlegs

As audio bootlegs became more common, the prestige (and economic value) of audio recordings diminished, and video recordings created with the newly emerging technology of portable videotape recorders became the new coin of the bootlegging realm. In a 1977 article in the *New York Times* on the personal video-cassette recorders that were then becoming widely commercially available, Dorothy Rodgers expresses reservations about the new technology:

> "I love it, but it's a very dangerous machine," Mrs. Rodgers said in her Fifth Avenue apartment. "It's going to make it very easy to steal material and to bootleg it. That's what's happening already with [audio] cassettes in music, and Xerox machines, which are copying entire books."
>
> "My husband just won a class-action suit to stop unscrupulous people from taping live performances of his musicals and then selling the recordings on the black market."[63]

Dorothy Rodgers was referring to a lawsuit Richard Rodgers filed against the aforementioned William Lerner, the proprietor of Music Masters. Music Masters, however, continued to operate for another decade, finally put out of business not by the copyright police but by the big-box stores like Tower Records and Best Buy. Despite Rodgers' efforts, video bootlegging became more and more common.

While the first devices to have a recording apparatus built into a camera did not emerge until 1982,[64] portable, battery-operated video-cassette recorders that could be attached by wires to external cameras existed for some years prior to that. In 1971, a bootlegger who goes by the pseudonym "Uncle Louie" managed to capture about forty minutes of the closing night of the short-lived musical *Lovely Ladies, Kind Gentlemen* on what would have been an open-reel two-inch quadruplex tape. The reels he used were larger than could be accommodated under the device's flip-top lid, and so the recording was made with the lid open. As a result, the device required nearly twice the space it occupied with the lid closed.

Uncle Louie remembers the difficulty of recording the show with the technology of the time:

> You can't even imagine. This was a huge camera, and of course it was silver so it reflected everything in the theater. The lens alone was about 12 inches. Any zooming that you did (and I did a lot of it) had to be done manually.
>
> [. . .] The battery pack was [made by] a different company. You got one battery that fit in the machine. It went dead in 12 minutes. So I wasn't going to go through all that agony only to have the battery go dead. So I found this battery pack which you wore around your waist which was equivalent

to . . . let's say 8 of the large batteries. You had to be strapped in to do this. It was all built into the leather belt that was, let's say, 6-7 inches high. So I mean, you had to be able to cover it. You had to have a loose fitting jacket. [. . .]

[The] microphone . . . plugged into the camcorder . . . the recording part of it clipped onto my tie. [. . .]

How did I get all the equipment in? I had to go with a friend. We were always very well dressed. You know, the London Fog raincoat which was over half of my equipment. The other person took half of the equipment in. It all had to be assembled. Cables . . . it was a bitch to thread the tape then. It wasn't like a regular audio recorder. It all had to down through a million loops. I don't know where I got the balls to do it. [. . .]

The people sitting next to you saw you take out that mic and camera [. . .] and usually they would ask questions. [But they would see how quiet the machine was and say] "Oh that's not making any noise." And the video cameras didn't make any noise! And I would always say, "I'm doing this as a favor for . . . [whoever's singing that night]." That would always just kinda quiet them down. [. . .]

The camera [. . .] the only viewfinder it had was on top. You had to hold your eye up to it. And it was a little screen inside the camera that lit up. Now in a dark theater if you have the tiniest bit of light coming out, you know, that's like putting on a spotlight. So I had to press that camera so close to my eye that not a drop of light came up, to the point that my eye was just tearing. Tears were coming down. I couldn't really see what I was doing once I got things in focus. I could zoom, but then that was done [. . .] not really being able to see. When I finished and took the camera away from my eye I couldn't see for like a half hour because everything got so dark from staring at that little screen.[65]

It was hardly a technology designed for surreptitious recording, and its utility for bootlegging probably required the laissez faire attitude of a front-of-house team on the closing night of a flop musical. Until the late 1970s, few would have technology to play back video recordings at home, so the technology initially kept these early video recordings limited to the private use of the one who made them.

However, Uncle Louie recently has started to upload his old recordings to the internet and has found some gratification in the response.

Nobody else in the world has a lot of the stuff that I have. And one day I just decided I'm gonna put everything on YouTube because I don't want all this to go to waste. [. . .]

I've looked on the web and I've looked at a million things. There's no one that recorded video in the days that I did.

And I have thousands of hits from all over the world. But it's fun to read some of these things like:

"God bless you for doing this, I never knew this existed."

"How in the Hell did you ever do that"

"Am I dreaming?"

And it's kind of fun to look at that. [. . .] It's good to know that when I croak that all this shit isn't going to be thrown into a dumpster like it usually is. So I put everything I could online.[66]

The sense of preserving a part of history for posterity (and the praise such activity elicits from internet strangers) seems to be a primary motivation for many bootleggers.

With the exception of *Lovely Ladies, Kind Gentlemen*, Uncle Louie stuck mostly to recording opera. Around a decade later, though, another bootlegger, "Lester," recorded over thirty years of live theatre using the new technology of battery-operated video cameras.

I had the recorder in one of those carry-on bags that had a sort of flat top. But it had some depth. It wasn't like a briefcase, it was thicker than that. I would put that on my lap. It was just too big to put at my feet cause you're sitting in a theatre seat. So I would put it on my lap. And I would take that little camera that was with it and put it on top of that. [. . .] I never used the viewfinder because with that you'd get caught. If you used the viewfinder it'd put out too much light, so I would have a little TV . . . a little one-inch monitor in a bag [. . .] in the "briefcase" and that's how I viewed what I was doing.

The camera ran off the VCR. They used to have these long-[life] batteries you could buy for these VCRs. Like car batteries almost. They were like 8–12 hour battery things.

[The television] was a Sony Watchman [. . .] ran on 4 double A batteries. I would always put new ones in every show to make sure it didn't run out. [. . .] It was black and white, and I would put a [lighting] gel over the TV [. . .] A blue . . . a gray . . . so it would diminish the light that came out of it.

I would still be able to look in and see what I was doing but it wouldn't show to anybody else.

And I always came with people on either side of me to make it harder for anyone to catch me. [. . .] I had to put stuff on top of the VHS machine which was at the bottom to make it high enough so I could use it as my stand which was on my lap.

So I would put . . . just stuff in it to make it look like I was going on a trip. So they could open it and thumb through it and they wouldn't find anything because it was really covered with so much stuff. And that was how it got in.[67]

Lester worked in the theatre industry for a time, and so he felt honor-bound by a loyalty to his colleagues not to share his recordings with anyone aside from a few cast members who appeared in the shows he taped. Some of these cast members, however, have shared their copies, and so a few of Lester's recordings have become widely available on the internet. Lester emphasizes, though, that there were relatively few people video recording Broadway shows in the 1980s and 1990s:

There were only a few people back then, maybe 3, in the world that were doing it. So when I took over I only really knew one other person who was doing it at the time. And then they stopped, and then I was the only one. And I don't know anybody but me [who] did it for about 10 years. [. . .] It wasn't until really the last 10 years that you started getting multiple people.[68]

Lester, like the audio bootleggers before him, took great pride in his work:

I remember seeing the tapes that were being done that were very shaky [. . .] What I really strived for was making mine as good or better than seeing the show live. Other people were just capturing the show. And that's a different thing.

Another bootlegger attests to the quality of Lester's work and notes that he was often hired by people in the industry to record their performances for their own collection:

He would be hired by someone involved with the [show]. He would get 3 seats in the front mezzanine just off center. One of us held a microphone which was wired through our shirts down around him up his shirt to the camera. If we saw people we knew, we did not want to talk to them. His video tapes are amazing.

He would only give it to the member of the team, that was his rule. But he has a video screen in his house that's like a movie screen, that's like 50 feet.[69]

Like Miles Kreuger and Ray Knight, part of Lester's pleasure in making the recordings is to play them back for those he knows.

Still, the impulse to share often pushed bootleggers beyond their immediate circles. Before the World Wide Web, some in the bootlegging community recall that magazines like *After Dark* or *Cue: The Weekly Magazine of New York Life* would occasionally feature classified ads inviting readers to write for a catalog of bootleg recordings. Readers of David Hummel's *Collectors Guide to the American Musical Theatre*, which noted the existence of "non-commercial recordings," would sometimes write to Hummel asking about these bootlegs and would usually be connected with the source. Still, until the internet provided anyone with access the ability to quickly broadcast offers and requests on message boards, listservs, and, later, social media, the bootlegging community remained small and largely limited to relatively wealthy or well-connected people who lived in or frequently visited Manhattan.

In the late 1980s and early 1990s, USENET newsgroups like rec.arts.theatre.musicals and listservs dedicated to the topic often officially banned discussion of bootlegs, but the communities became places where fans of musicals could find one another and then discuss offline what was forbidden in the public forum. By the late 1990s, peer-to-peer music-sharing services like Napster, Audiogalaxy, and Limewire provided a platform for the instant trading of audio bootlegs, and, in 2005, YouTube and its then-competitor, Google Video, were quickly populated with bootlegs of then new and popular shows like *Wicked*, *Avenue Q*, and *Hairspray*.

The ability to rapidly reproduce and anonymously share bootlegs meant, though, that sharing a bootleg no longer satisfied the desire to "perform" the recording by either playing it for a live audience (as Mapleson and Knight did decades before), or by earning social or economic capital by trading something rare. Once a bootleg is shared with one person on the internet, it can very quickly propagate to a large community, and so the value of the recording based on its rarity quickly diminishes.

Many bootleggers are especially protective of the ownership of recordings (ironically, given that bootlegging is, by its very nature, sharing the work of others without permission). A newly made bootleg recording gives one a certain amount of capital among collectors. If access is doled out in a limited way, the bootlegger or collector remains a kind of folk hero or aristocrat, but if a bootleg becomes too widely available and from multiple access points that do not include the original source, the collector's stock may plummet. Thus, the collector of bootlegs must struggle to earn social capital by making their wealth known, but cannot share it so broadly that abundance decreases its value.

As the law will not protect bootleg ownership, some bootlegging communities have developed ethical codes to maintain the "wealth" of those who take on the greatest risk in creating and disseminating the content. The owner of a Weebly site with the subdomain "freebroadwaymusicaltrades" puts an all-caps notice at the top of the site: "**NONE OF THESE ARE MY MASTERS** [that is, recordings made by the one sharing]. **TO MASTERS: IF I AM NOT SUPPOSED TO LIST THEM, I AM SORRY. UNLESS I AM TOLD OTHERWISE, I AM NOT SURE WHAT IS OKAY TO LIST AND WHAT IS NOT. I TRY MY BEST TO NOT STEAL FROM OTHERS. IF YOU WANT SOMETHING TAKEN DOWN, PLEASE PLEASE LET ME KNOW POLITELY. THANKS:)**"[70] Another Weebly site that does include "masters" lists both the owner's own and those of their "trading partner Zach." The site owner assures visitors that "You can trade for his audios either here or with him[,] either is fine."[71]

Some "masters" also set "not for trade" dates on their collections, asking those with whom they trade not to further share their collections until a particular date—perhaps a time after which the creator feels they will have squeezed out whatever financial or social capital might be gained from the bootleg. The creator of a recording may also wish to restrict access until it will no longer competes with the live production (e.g., the date after which a show will close or a major cast change will take place).

These rules are, of course, enforced inconsistently by the limited power of a dispersed and largely anonymous community. Some sites include lists of "good" and "bad" traders. One Weebly site notes that "Euphorianger" is a "really nice trader! Willing to make a deal. Quick responses, trades playbills too!," but that another is "An older woman who is very rude. She was speaking very harshly, and even after refusing a trade, she continued to email me to the point where I had to filter her messages to the trash."[72] Indeed, given its illicit nature, bootlegging is somewhat counter-intuitively a very social activity. Many in the community simply post copies for "free" (or, in the language of bootlegging sites, as "gifts"). Of course, the more one becomes known as a creator and sharer of bootlegs, the greater is the legal risk one incurs for doing so. Still, by sharing copies, bootleg collectors establish their own devotion to the art and their own importance within the fan community.

Some sites also have rules as to who has the "right" to offer "gifts." The "theatertrades" Weebly on "how to start trading" warns against sharing via YouTube links that "might attract attention to the trading community, and that's the last thing we want" (because law enforcement might crack down on the community).[73] A separate FAQ section notes that such links make videos "easily available and kind of defeats the point of trading."[74] Concern over the economy of bootleg trading seems to be, in many ways, of more concern than potential legal repercussions. Abundance decreases value, scarcity increases it. Every takedown notice sent to YouTube to remove a bootleg video increases the scarcity, and therefore the value, of that bootleg.

Though publicly, the unions, guilds, and producers oppose bootlegs, in many cases videos remain on YouTube for months or years. In part, the lack of zealous policing may be an admission of the futility of such efforts. In a 2008 piece for the *Washington Post*, Nelson Pressley quoted Actors Equity representative Maria Sommers, saying, "We're there to protect the actors and their images, [. . .] the problem is, it goes back up."[75] Policing efforts seem to be currently focused on currently running shows with powerful corporate backers. Videos of *The Lion King* are now quickly taken down by request of Disney, but as of this writing full-length bootleg videos of various Broadway casts of *Les Misérables* and the short-run musical *In Transit* are among the first results returned when their titles are searched for on YouTube.

Some in the industry have even expressed a certain amount of appreciation for bootlegs. In an interview with Medium.com's video news magazine, *FFWD*, playwright Jeremy O. Harris is quoted as saying in praise of internet videos:

> I grew up in a town where I had no access to any of the types of theater I wanted to see outside of YouTube and Tumblr [. . .] I honestly feel like if those things hadn't been there, I wouldn't have had as rich a theatrical database to pull from when I got to my undergraduate degree.[76]

Similarly, Stephen Sondheim, in the second edition of Mark Horowitz's *Sondheim on Music*, said in response to a question about YouTube videos:

> As far as I'm concerned, I'd be in favor of those things being sold [officially by the rights holders.] The unions of course would have none of it. I think this kind of thing should be available to everybody. Everybody should be able to see a tape of *Pacific Overtures* who never saw *Pacific Overtures*.[77] They should just be able to see it if they want to see it. [...] On the other hand if everybody takes my stuff and puts it on YouTube I'm going to have to sell my house. So I have very mixed feelings on it.[78]

Sondheim and Harris represent a minority voice among those in the industry who have spoken or written publicly about bootlegs, though. Lin-Manuel Miranda famously responded to a request on Twitter for a *Hamilton* bootleg before the cast recording or professionally filmed version was available:

> We're going to make a really good recording of the show this summer and I want you to hear that. I'm thrilled you haven't heard a shitty [bootleg] version yet, because I spent 6 years writing this and when you hear it, I want you to hear what I intended. I'm sorry theater only exists in one place at a time but that is also its magic. A bootleg cannot capture it. I'm grateful and glad you want to hear it, and I want you to hear it RIGHT. I ask your patience.[79]

In a chapter for Jessica Hillman-McCord's anthology, *iBroadway: Musical Theatre in the Digital Age*,[80] I note that these concerns strikingly echo the language of the editors of the First Folio of Shakespeare's plays cited at the start of this chapter. The unauthorized printings arguably led to money rightly owed to Shakespeare's company passing instead to those with mechanical rather than artistic skill, but they also seem to have created (or at least identified) a market for an authorized version. The friends of Shakespeare attempted to crush the bootlegs with an official edition, presenting the plays "cur'd, and perfect of their limbs."

The early unauthorized printings of Shakespeare, though, textual scholars will insist, may represent important textual witnesses, which some believe are more faithful representations of the original performance than the official Folio. Likewise, the early video bootleg recordings of *Hamilton* capture moments and choices not documented by the Disney+ recording. For instance, some bootleg videos of *Hamilton* document the performances of original cast members Betsy Struxness and Emmy Raver-Lampman, who had left the production before the official filming and did not return for it.

Still, the Folio, in most cases, represents the established text of Shakespeare's plays, and while bootleg videos of early performances of *Hamilton* still exist, the majority of the world now knows the show via the original cast recording and the professionally shot and edited video on Disney+. Indeed, publishing the script, the score, the cast recording, and the official professionally shot video is perhaps the best way to ensure that bootlegs are not the version of a musical best known by the public. On the other hand, when an official text is not released commercially, bootlegs begin to define both a received text and an alternative repertory.

Rare bootlegs become signifiers of true fandom, separating the simple aficionado from the true devotee. Few texts are rarer than live recordings of short-lived shows. In his influential analysis of twentieth-century flops, *Not Since Carrie*, Ken Mandelbaum writes:

> How can any intelligent person wish to collect catastrophes like *Legs Diamond* and *Kelly* or camp disasters like *Home Sweet Homer* and *Whoop-Up?* [...] Fans of flops know about these shows, can sing songs from them, and love the kinship they feel with others who know them. Casual followers of the musical have some idea about why *Oklahoma!*, *West Side Story*, and *A Chorus Line* are important, but the world of *Breakfast at Tiffany's* and *Into the Light* is a private world, and those who are a part of it can't wait for each new Broadway season to make, as it inevitably does, its contribution.[81]

There is, of course, no simple binary distinction between "casual followers of musicals" and the "kinship of flops," but rather a continuum across which knowledge of rare musicals is slowly communicated. "Super fans" may mention their own acquisition of a particularly rare and valuable recording to a simple "aficionado" who may then mention the title to a "casual follower." The obscure recording begins to accrete notoriety. The economy of bootlegs results in an alternative repertory established not by commercial or artistic success but because of the value of the recordings in the bootleg market.

As with Shakespeare's plays, the notoriety of these bootlegs sometimes leads to official recordings. The score of the musical *Carrie* was once tightly controlled by the creators after its infamous failure on Broadway. New productions were forbidden. However, bootlegs were widely shared among fans and became readily available on the internet in the days of Napster. As awareness of the musical grew, desire for a new production intensified, and in 2012, the creators were finally convinced to permit an off-Broadway revival at Manhattan Theatre Club (both Patrick Healy in *The New York Times*[82] and David Rooney in the *Hollywood Reporter*[83] mentioned bootlegs in their reviews). The score was also finally legally recorded by Ghostlight Records that year.

Likewise, the original production of Stephen Sondheim's *Follies* was much bootlegged, both on audio tape and on silent film. The commercially released original cast album, released on a single, fifty-minute LP, had almost none of the dialogue and only a confusing abridgement of the score. Columbia record producer Thomas Z. Shepard told Laurence Maslon, "If you didn't see the show, you would have no idea what it was about."[84] The original production ran for just over a year. The Lincoln Center concert was not recorded until 1985, and the London production did not open until 1987. Nonetheless, the show quickly passed into the musical theatre repertory and along with *Company* and *Sweeney Todd* was considered one of the Sondheim-Prince masterpieces. The full-length audio bootlegs, broadly shared among Sondheim fans, surely helped to establish its reputation in a way the original cast recording could not.

Today, bootlegs on YouTube help to establish new audiences for musicals among those who may visit New York only rarely. The musical *RENT* was actively bootlegged, and the bootlegs arguably helped create national interest in the piece, which led to the infamous rush lines camped outside the theatre. As I have noted in other venues, the musical *Wicked* opened on Broadway just before the founding of YouTube and became one of the most bootlegged shows on Broadway. It found an audience among young people who came to know the show not only through the original cast album but also through the many performances documented online.

Although the original production of *Spring Awakening* won eight Tony Awards (including Best Musical), it ran for only two years—a respectable, though hardly a record-breaking, run. Nonetheless, bootleg videos of the original production have become some of the most shared bootlegs on YouTube, and the musical is now part of the high school and college repertory (the title was featured in the recent television series, *Rise*, which tracked the drama around rehearsals for a high school musical). *Spring Awakening* was revived on Broadway in 2015, less than seven years after the original production closed, and bootlegs of the new production are also easily available on YouTube.

In the age of the internet, inventorying and cataloging every known bootleg is an impossible task with a finish line that changes every evening that theatres are open. Still, the managers of the website Encora.it (previously Encora.one) are making a valiant effort. As David Hummel's *Collectors Guide to the American Musical* did in the early 1980s, the site documents the existence of live theatre recordings with some annotations about the quality and source. Before a redesign in December of 2020, the site listed the number of recordings known for each title in the database. Table 5.1 lists the top forty titles, each representing shows with more than 150 more known

Table 5.1 The top forty most bootlegged shows in Encora.one's database in 2020[a]

Wicked	3068	Anastasia	275
The Phantom of the Opera (Andrew Lloyd Webber)	1622	Billy Elliot: The Musical	264
Les Misérables	1418	Mamma Mia!	251
Matilda the Musical	788	Legally Blonde	245
Waitress	655	Elisabeth	240
Hamilton	614	Evita	227
Dear Evan Hansen	561	Jersey Boys	224
Six	546	American Idiot	213
Mean Girls	461	We Will Rock You	207
The Book of Mormon	428	Miss Saigon	204
Tanz der Vampire	373	9 to 5: The Musical	199
RENT	319	Hairspray	198
Kinky Boots	319	Hadestown	184
Jesus Christ Superstar	314	The Rocky Horror Show	176
Bat Out of Hell	313	Beauty and the Beast (Disney)	174
Spring Awakening	301	Avenue Q	166
Cats	298	Beetlejuice	160
Come From Away	297	Heathers: The Musical	158
Next to Normal	289	Frozen	153
Grease	288	Chicago	152

[a] "Everything Broadway, Everything Musical—Encora," accessed July 3, 2022, https://encora-archive.github.io/encora.one/index.html.

bootleg recordings, suggest a fascinating alternative repertory among online collectors.

The website is based in Europe, and the site's contents consequently skew somewhat European (it is especially well populated with titles like *Tanz der Vampire*, *Elisabeth*, and *We Will Rock You* that enjoy far greater popularity outside of New York). Still, the list suggests that some of the most documented titles of the early twenty-first century are not necessarily those that might initially seem to be most influential or important. *Heathers*, *Beetlejuice*, *Mean Girls*, *Legally Blonde*, and *American Idiot* all appeal to younger audiences whose tastes may differ from those of professional journalists and who may lack the resources to buy tickets in sufficient numbers to keep the original productions afloat. Yet, as bootlegs become increasingly important texts in the community archive of musical theatre, these titles may, as generations shift, soon join the repertory.

The history of musical theatre is still developing, of course. The form has only received serious scholarly attention in the last three decades. However, it seems likely that future scholars studying the musical of the first years of the twenty-first century will find that their primary texts are found not only in renowned institutional archives but also in digital repositories assembled by amateurs who collect and preserve the illicit, but invaluable, bootlegs that for many served as the important texts of this generation.

6

Licensing the Musical

Most of the media described in the previous chapters—commercially published libretti, cast recordings, photographs, and home video—are texts designed for the enjoyment of an individual consumer outside of the theatre. Each is designed to serve as a memento of the experience in the theatre, or perhaps a partial substitute for it, rather than to provide the foundation on which a new production might be built. Since the late nineteenth century, however, several commercial enterprises have emerged that manage the legal licensing of musicals for new amateur and regional productions. These companies work with the artists they represent to create materials designed to support new productions in environments that may be very unlike the stage on which the musical first premiered.

As American and international copyright law developed in the nineteenth century, the exclusive right to print a musical is not necessarily linked to the right to license new performances. A legally purchased printed script or score does not convey to the purchaser the right to perform the work it documents. Indeed, it was not until a revision to the copyright law in 1856 that public performance of such texts was explicitly protected by copyright law at all. Brent Salter[1] details the emergence of copyright protection for theatrical texts, and Anthea Kraut[2] examines the protection explicitly offered (and initially denied) to choreography and dance performance, and what is notable in both studies is how long it took for intellectual property in performance to be as clearly protected. When the primary commercial value of a work was found in performance, then, it was not necessarily in the interest of the authors to provide broad, legal access to the production materials. If the exclusive right to profit from the finished work could not be protected, the "source code" must be tightly controlled.

An alternative to broad publication emerged when licensing companies began to collect the performance rights to plays and musicals. These companies could rent production materials to customers for the period

Fixing the Musical. Douglas L. Reside, Oxford University Press. © Oxford University Press 2023.
DOI: 10.1093/oso/9780190073718.003.0007

for which they had a license to perform them. Over the past two centuries, the materials offered to licensed productions have varied from company to company and have changed as technologies and copyright laws developed. These materials, though, represent an influential set of tangible media that have shaped the understanding of the repertory and its texts. In this chapter I will examine the materials offered by what were, until very recently, the five major musical theatrical licensing companies–Samuel French, Dramatist Play Service, Tams-Witmark, Rodgers and Hammerstein, and Music Theatre International, and how these materials shaped the reception of the titles they represented.

Samuel French

One of the first licensors of plays in both the United States and the United Kingdom was Samuel French. Although the company frequently dated its founding to 1830, Salter notes that this date refers to the start of one of the companies acquired by French (Thomas Hailes Lacy).[3] In *Truly Yours: One Hundred and Fifty Years of Play Publishing and Service to the Theatre* (a history of the company published in 1980 by its own London office), the authors note that a better starting date for the company might be 1854, when French "began to publish his own *French's American Drama*."[4] As his new company grew, French "bought up every set of printing plates that he could lay his hands on, thus absorbing his competitors."[5] In addition to the texts, the company also provided "everything the budding amateur dramatic group might need–make-up, wigs, costumes, lights and even sets [. . .] everything, in fact, apart from acting ability, and [they] even tried to supply that in the form of how-to-act books!"[6]

Likely due to the company's origins as a publisher, Samuel French, more frequently than any other licensor of musicals, often sold copies of scripts in addition to licensing the texts for production. However, lax enforcement of the 1856 copyright protection for dramatic presentation led French to keep some texts carefully guarded. The authors of *Truly Yours* note that initially, most of the plays published by French "were reprints" though after 1856 "French did publish first editions of several American plays important to the professional theatre [. . .] such as *Uncle Tom's Cabin* by George L Aiken and *The Poor of New York* by Dion Boucicault."[7] The authors note, however,

that "it was not until many years later that French was able to claim performance royalties for his authors."[8]

Derek Miller notes that the difficulty in claiming royalties led to a period in the nineteenth century in which "Manuscripts—or, in later decades,
scripts printed for private use–remained important for controlling uncertain rights, particularly for playwrights whose work was valuable on both
sides of the Atlantic."[9] Miller notes "from the early 1840s to 1891, plays in
finely bound, carefully printed reading volumes all but disappeared from the
market, replaced by cheaply furnished, poorly printed, inexpensive acting
editions. The high-quality printed play vanished for fifty years."[10] Miller's
end date to this period is bounded by the passing of the Chance Act in 1891,
which protected international copyright in the United States if the work was
published.[11]

In *Truly Yours*, the authors reprint a portion of an interview with Samuel
French himself from the June 19, 1895, issue of the London theatrical magazine *The Sketch*.[12] French gives the journalist a tour of his London offices.
At this point, the Chance Act had only passed several years ago, and there
remained a "safe" in the London offices that contained, as French tells his
interlocutor, "manuscripts of some two thousand plays and operas which
are not printed or published, and of which the rights are protected only
by the equity law of stage rights."[13] French's tour also includes a visit to the
company's "well-known fit-up proscenium and set of stock scenery for the
use of amateurs, in full working order."[14] At the end of the interview, French
notes, with seeming frustration, that many amateur companies attempt to
evade paying royalties ("generally over 'charity' performances"), and that
"People are willing to pay for scenery, wigs, &c., but they have a strange desire to avoid paying the author."[15] French's comments suggest that his cos-
tume- and scene-rental business seems to have been at least as healthy as his
play licensing, suggesting that the design elements of French's catalog were
likely at least as well known as the scripts for which they were created.

Notably, neither French nor the authors of *Truly Yours* seem terribly
concerned about the intellectual property of the designers of the sets and
costumes or of the original directors. Direction and design are described
as mere technical necessities rather than independent creative works that
should command royalty payments to the creators. In a section on the "Acting
Edition" in *Truly Yours*, the authors further describe the ways in which the
company strove to include most elements of the original production in the
licensed copy of the text. They describe how the earliest acting editions

included detailed blocking notes, telling the actor "where to put his feet, if not his hands."[16] The editing of these texts required the careful curation of the often conflicting stage directions recorded in the original production's "Prompt Copy," which served as the source text. Instructions as to how to reproduce sound effects (even those that originally required "the exertions of fifteen men") and the "full professional Lighting Plot" were also included "until sometime in the 1950s."[17] By 1980, though, the staging and technical details included in the acting editions had been reduced to "only a skeleton structure" and "a simple description of the effects as the audience is expected to see or hear them."[18] The reason given for this reduction in description is not an increased respect for the intellectual property of designers and directors, but a recognition that those involved in amateur productions "have become increasingly adventurous and competent" and that "some people read plays for pleasure, and they must not find their enjoyment spoiled by unnecessary stage directions that hold up the action."[19]

Samuel French came to musical theatre relatively late and never invested in the form as a primary market. In *Truly Yours* the authors claim the first musical French published was *The Belle of New York*, thirty years after its 1897 Broadway premiere. *Truly Yours* notes that "a close relationship was later built up between French's and the librettist Eric Maschwitz and the composers George Ponsford and Bernard Grun," whose works including *Balalaika*, *Goodnight Vienna*, and *Waltz Without End* were added to the catalog.[20] Later in the chapter they note, "Today it is usually only the larger amateur societies who can put on the older musicals, with their heavy demands on chorus, orchestra, and scenery. [. . .] But tastes are changing all the time and more and more drama groups are making forays into the musical theatre. For such groups the successes of the 1950s such as *The Boy Friend, Fings Ain't Wot They Used T' Be, Lock Up Your Daughters*, and *Salad Days* [all British shows] have now been joined by the more recent, small cast, easy-to-stage, plays such as *Grease, Godspell, Jack the Ripper*, and *Something's Afoot*."[21] The British office of Samuel French, it seems, had felt early twentieth-century musicals were not as marketable since the production demands were so much greater than plays, but began investing in the form more seriously in the 1970s.

Nonetheless, French did attempt to make their limited early catalog as attractive as possible. The authors of *Truly Yours* note:

After 1956 it became apparent that some of the earlier Musicals were showing signs of wear. The music was still excellent, but audiences had acquired more sophisticated senses of humour and the comedy had long been outgrown. Eric Maschwitz and others were invaluable in bringing some of these other books up to date and giving the scores a new lease on life.[22]

The reason for 1956 as a milestone date is not cited, though it may refer to the opening of *My Fair Lady* in New York. The title proved that American musical adaptations of British playwrights like George Bernard Shaw that told very British stories could be incredibly successful, and that the form could no longer be considered only an American phenomenon.

The American Acting Editions of French's musicals, like their non-musical counterparts, feature various production aids in addition to the libretto itself. Many include prop and costume lists and schematics of designs for a scene or two. However, French's acting editions were usually cheaply printed in small 5.5 x 8.25–inch editions, and so detailed schematics are often all but unreadable. Moreover, any single scene would be unlikely to give more than the barest suggestion of the original staging (and less information than might be gathered from original production photographs in souvenir programs or in annual publications like *Theatre World*).

In 2015, French introduced a mobile app, the Abbott Reader, that allowed users to either subscribe to gain access to a set number of plays each month, or else purchase individual copies from the company's library. In 2018, Samuel French was acquired by Concord Theatricals as part of a massive acquisition of many of the major theatrical licensors. The Abbott reader was transformed into ConcordReader+, which now provides access to these eBooks. The text and formatting in ConcordReader+ is generally identical to that found in the printed Acting Editions of the same plays. As a result, these acting editions are now much more easily obtained by anyone interested in the titles. While the app is still very much a niche product marketed to theatre makers, easier access to these editions may eventually begin to develop popular familiarity with the text of these titles. Audiences who have seen a local production might, for instance, be inspired to find and purchase a digital copy to read the text for themselves.

Musical scores were not sold by French, but rented to those who had licensed the plays. One of the first pages in the acting editions sold by French included instructions for requesting a quote to license the piece for performance. Applicants were asked to specify whether the production would "use an orchestration or simply a piano." At the end of these instructions was a note that listed the instrumentation for the available orchestration and informed the reader that these could be "loaned two months prior to the production ONLY on receipt of the royalty quoted for all performances, the rental fee and a refundable deposit [for the musical parts]."[23] Printing full musical scores would have been expensive, and, aside from the rare musical theatre scholar, few would want them unless they planned to use them in performance. Controlling the orchestrations as rental properties both reduced costs and helped to prevent unlicensed productions. Providing companies with the option to license the available orchestration or simply to use a piano made French's properties more accessible to small companies with few musicians, but it suggested that the orchestration was not part of the work itself, but, similar to costumes or sets, a feature of a particular production— inevitably ephemeral and easily shaped to the practical needs of the company. This reflects and perhaps informs the approach to orchestrations in new First Class productions. Very few musical revivals use the original orchestrations in their entirety.

Dramatist Play Service

In 1936, approximately a century after the founding of Samuel French, the Dramatist Guild founded their own licensing agency in an attempt to provide a way for playwrights to increase their share of royalties from amateur licensing. In George Middleton's primer on the Dramatist Guild, the stated "policy of the Play Service" was:

> Primarily to stimulate competition among amateur agencies [such as French]; to charge the same commission—20 per cent—on every Broadway play and off-Broadway play handled; never to favor one play over another; and to stimulate the whole non-professional theatre in the country through publicity and personal contacts, with particular attention to the needs of individual producing groups.[24]

The company quickly began to acquire the rights to major playwrights and musicals.

Dramatist Play Service (often known as DPS) also published acting editions that closely resembled those of Samuel French (paperback, cheaply bound volumes with a cover printed on colored paper of a heavier stock than the pages within). The DPS editions also often featured prop and costume lists and technical schematics of scenic designs. The DPS editions of musicals, however, were often at least an inch longer and wider (6.5 by 9.5 inches) than those published by Samuel French, and so the technical designs were somewhat more legible in these books. In 2013, the catalog announced that a selection of the company's plays would be available as "ePlays" in the ePub format (an open eBook format supported by nearly every reader with the notable exception of Amazon's popular Kindle) and, as of this writing, continues to sell non-musical plays in this format.

Like French, DPS only makes scores available as rental properties (though they do allow companies to request "perusal scores" after supplying a refundable deposit). However, the company's "Catalogue of new plays" informed potential customers that "Complete sets of scores are required for all musical productions" (though the catalog is not explicit that these orchestrations must actually be used, the requirement to rent them at least suggests that the score is an integral part of the work).

In April of 2021, DPS was acquired by the relatively new agency, Broadway Licensing. DPS would be the imprint for plays, but the Broadway Licensing name would be used for musicals. Broadway Licensing does not, as of this writing, sell acting editions, but since the COVID-19 pandemic, they do provide free access to read the libretti they license on their website. Unlike DPS, musical materials (scores and orchestral parts) provided by Broadway Licensing as part of a license package need not be returned to the company.

Tams-Witmark

Over the first two decades of the twentieth century, the texts and scores of music theatre (including opera and operetta) were largely controlled by two companies, the Arthur W. Tams Music Library and the Witmark Music Library. In 1925, *The New York Times* reported:

> The Metropolitan Opera in New York and the Chicago Civic Opera Company are the only two institutions maintaining libraries containing material for all the operas of their repertoires. All other operatic organizations, professional or amateur, when presenting grand or comic opera or musical comedies not originating with them had to go to either Tams or Witmark for orchestrations, scores and other material.[25]

The subject of the article was the consolidation of the two companies, after years of bitter rivalry, into a single entity, Tams-Witmark. The *Times* notes that the Tams assets "also includes complete furnishings such as costumes, properties, wigs, &c., for all the operas in the music library."[26] As with Samuel French, Tams built a business on providing amateur and regional companies with all that they needed to stage their own production.

However, unlike Samuel French or Dramatist Play Service, which both served as publishers as well as licensors, Tams-Witmark had no publishing history and so tightly restricted access to their materials. Even into the 1990s, Tams-Witmark rental materials sometimes included only mimeographed "sides" (character lines with cue line) for small roles. This practice not only reduced printing costs, but also reduced the likelihood that a cast member would copy the entire work before returning the rental book.

The orchestral parts provided with a rental package could also be fragmentary. On the "News" section of the company's webpage captured by the Internet Archive's Wayback Machine in 2010, there was an announcement that a "computer-engraved" edition of the score for *Oliver!* was newly available in which "all parts follow the music, measure for measure, in the published Vocal Score, which is also Tams-Witmark's Piano-Conductor's Score."[27] They further note that "a dedicated orchestra piano part" is available, "eliminating the cumbersome practice of playing the part ab libitum, using the Vocal Score." Finally, the new offering also includes "Full Scores (Partiturs) for both the full orchestration and the combo instrumentation" (licensors could select which version best matched their resources), though these full scores were "not a part of the regular rental package for either arrangement and must be requested as a separate rental item."[28] Around the same time, the company had cleaned up and "computer-engraved" the score for *A Chorus Line*.

While this news of the improved quality of the materials would clearly have been of interest to those renting them, it is in hindsight remarkable that one of the country's foremost licensing companies was still in the process of "computer engraving" their most popular offerings in the second decade of the twenty-first century. Moreover, one might have assumed the reconciliation of the various musical parts would have seemed an essential part of the work of preparing the initial rental product for such frequently licensed titles as *Oliver!* and *A Chorus Line*. That this was not the case speaks both to the way in which orchestrations were (and to a large extent still are) viewed as ephemeral and linked to a particular production rather than a part of the work itself. In some cases, fully reconciled editions of scores documenting the original orchestrations sat somewhere between the (supposedly) inviolable book and lyrics and the production elements of staging and design that are expected, even legally required, to be newly created with each license.

Rodgers and Hammerstein Theatre Library

After the success of *Oklahoma!* on Broadway, Richard Rodgers and Oscar Hammerstein joined with the publishers Max and Louis Dreyfus (whose Chappell Music had published Gilbert and Sullivan and many other musicals) to form a new publishing company, Williamson Music. This was part of a larger business partnership that produced plays and musicals and, eventually, started to license their own catalog through the Rodgers and Hammerstein Theatre Library. The dialogue and plots of many of Rodgers and Hammerstein's musicals were generally inoffensive to the sensibilities of many across the United States in the mid- to late twentieth century, and so they were safe for schools to perform. Further, the titles were familiar and popular due to regular tours and, perhaps even more importantly, successful movie adaptations. As a result, the Rodgers and Hammerstein Theatre Library quickly became one of the leading licensors of musicals in the United States. Over time, the library acquired the rights to many musicals not written or produced by Rodgers and Hammerstein (including Lin-Manuel Miranda's *In the Heights* and Joe Iconis' *Be More Chill*).

Rodgers and Hammerstein required licensees to rent all of the printed materials, including a full set of scripts from the company. In a Frequently Asked Questions section of the company's website in 1999, the site editors respond to the question, "We purchased our scripts years ago. Do we still need to rent yours?" as follows:

> Yes. When you apply to The R&H; Theatre Library for a License to present one of our musicals, we are obligated to license only the version the copyright holders want licensed. We fulfill this obligation by providing you with the exact materials approved by the copyright holders we represent.[29]

When a theatre company licensed the musical, they were automatically rented a set of libretti and scores. This insistence on the use of the authorized version also potentially increased the profits of the company, as licensing a work from the library required payment not only for a new license but also for new materials *every time* a company performed the work, and it also suggests that Rodgers and Hammerstein Organization, as a company founded by two authors to license their own work, were especially interested in avoiding unauthorized variants from the licensed text. In fact, as a way of further limiting variant versions, the published reader's editions of Rodgers and Hammerstein were kept largely out of print from at least 1980 until the company was acquired by Imagem Music Group in 2009 and began publishing new readers' editions.[30] Ted Chapin recalls:

> When I got to Rodgers and Hammerstein and discovered the readers' editions were out of print, I thought it was a smart idea to keep them that way so that if anybody really wanted a copy of the script in those pre-internet days, they had to contact us. I would make them available for classroom study, but classes had to sign them out so we knew where they are. [. . .] Then, when Applause came to me about printing copies to sell, I figured the world had changed, so we proceeded.[31]

The Rodgers and Hammerstein Organization commissioned renowned Broadway poster artist Frank Verlizzo (creator of the famous designs for *Sunday in the Park with George* and *The Lion King*) to create "the logos that you always thought were there" to give the musicals a distinctive and consistent visual branding (since, as Chapin notes, "since these shows didn't have brilliant original artwork"[32]).

The texts of the Applause editions were based on those first printed by Random House. The texts that the Rodgers and Hammerstein Organization licensed, though, were not always entirely consistent with these editions. Chapin recalls that when he started at the company most of the libretti that were licensed were based on the London version of the text:

> Most were based on the London stage manager's script [. . .] so there were all these cues and stage directions. [. . .] "Light cue 4a goes here."
>
> In the back of the books there was a lot of information about costumes . . . about the sets . . . about lighting . . . to a certain extent sound. The scripts included some Britishisms. "DiMaggio's glove" was "a leather glove" [in the song "Bloody Mary"] I wasn't convinced they were the correct scripts to begin with.

[. . .] The *Sound of Music* was different–it seemed very carefully crafted which may very be because Lindsay and Crouse had a fifty percent say in it. It's very readable and clear. There are certain stage directions. In the back there are some very good choreographic notes. Also there are the scenic and costume plots.

In an upcoming book on London musicals, Arianne Johnson Quinn explains how the London productions of Rodgers and Hammerstein's *Oklahoma!* and *Carousel* mostly replicated the Broadway productions (with a fidelity that would have been unusual for the period).[33] In the years after Oscar Hammerstein's death, the materials gathered for these re-stagings seems to have come to represent the "official" text that could then be rented out to amateurs.

Chapin, upon assuming leadership of the company, attempted to restore the Broadway texts and adapt the stage directions for amateur use.

Under my watch we went through and cleaned them up. Certainly took out a lot of the stage manager cues which I felt had no meaning. [. . .] In the case of *South Pacific* [. . .] I got a hold of Oscar Hammerstein's script annotated for the Random House for the published edition. It was very interesting that he rewrote stage directions, sometimes to say less, "Move stage right" and more explaining the action—"Exits to go off to war," for example.

I gathered the brothers Hammerstein (both of whom had directed *South Pacific*) and I took chunks of scenes where I had gone through and crafted stage directions. Then we would hash them out [. . .] Sometimes what was there didn't make any sense to me, so I would guess what the action was and they'd say, "No, no he's moving to the bench."

We spent a lot of time on the *South Pacific* script. I'd also sit with Bill Hammerstein at productions of *South Pacific* where nobody understood the military rankings . . . people would salute the wrong people. So I made Bill write [. . .] a note on the military which I put at the beginning of *South Pacific* so at least people would know Captain Brackett's at the top [. . .] and who would salute and who wouldn't. My goal was to give the customer enough tools so if they follow the directions, they mount a good production.[34]

For a generation, these are the scripts amateur actors and their audiences would have encountered when Rodgers and Hammerstein was performed.

The authorship, and licensing rights, for stage directions can be compli-cated, though. In some cases they are written by the librettist, but in others they record the work of the director or choreographer. "Nowadays, the copy-right in the direction is a lot clearer," says Chapin, "but I figured since Rodgers and Hammerstein wrote and produced the shows they had the rights to the direction and choreography. Some of the directions in the scripts came right from the very first drafts."

In other cases, Chapin explained that he recommended reaching out to the original choreographers and directors to document and officially license their work. Agnes de Mille biographer Kara Anne Gardner writes:

> Chapin [. . .] approached de Mille for her help in creating a record of the original dances of both *Carousel* and *Oklahoma!*. Documentary films were made for both shows, with the aim of helping future directors and choreographers recreate the steps and emotional content of de Mille's choreography.[35] De Mille Productions, the entity created to receive the royalties for de Mille's work, now receives payment from the Rodgers and Hammerstein Organization whenever *Oklahoma!* and *Carousel* are leased out for performance.[36]

Via the technology of video recording, the choreography became part of the licensed text of these two dance-dependent musicals.

Since Rodgers and Hammerstein, like Tams-Witmark, considered them-selves a "library" rather than a publisher, they did not publish acting editions for sale, but still needed to reproduce popular titles in volumes large enough to supply companies and schools across the nation with rental copies. Chapin remembers:

> When I got there, the scripts were printed by a place called Chernay which is out in Pennsylvania. They were a printing house, and they knew how to smyth-sew scripts instead of "perfect binding." [Which would not lie flat on the directors table.] We did not want perfect binding. We used Chernay for the shows that needed lots of scripts; it wasn't worth doing a print run unless you were going to do thousands of copies. And that would be *Oklahoma!* And the *Sound of Music*. *Show Boat* was borderline. What you didn't want was a warehouse full of boxes of scripts that went unused.
>
> Then we started to print them in house, especially if we only needed a few copies. [. . .] If it was *Me & Juliet*, we'd need twenty a year tops.[37]

Thus, the more popular titles had higher-quality rental materials than less commonly produced shows.

In 2017, Concord Music Group purchased Imagem and with it the Rodgers and Hammerstein properties. The company then produced new acting editions that could be purchased apart from licenses and viewed in the new Concord+ reader adapted from Samuel French's Abbott Reader. In the twenty-first century, the libretti of Rodgers and Hammerstein's musicals are again easily accessible, though in several different versions that vary most in layout and stage directions. These variations emphasize the licensor's legal definition of the work as a text and score that require a reader (or a director) to collaborate with the author in a Barthesian act of interpretation to complete them and "make them go."

Music Theatre International

Rodgers and Hammerstein were not the only writers to recognize the appeal of publishing, licensing, and producing one's own work without a third party to collect a percentage. In 1952, composer/lyricist Frank Loesser and orchestrator Don Walker founded Music Theatre International (MTI) to license both their work and those of their fellow writers.[38] Like Rodgers and Hammerstein and Tams-Witmark, the company was not a publisher but only rented materials to those licensing their shows. Although they were one of the last of the major licensing companies to emerge in the twentieth century, they established practices for printing and distribution that were emulated by their competitors. Ted Chapin remembers:

> By the time I got there, the Rodgers and Hammerstein Theatre Library, which is what it was called then, was very much modeled on MTI. We had warehouses one floor above the other in Long Island City. MTI was the best organized of the houses. What both of us did was to create a standard package which gave you enough scripts to do the show and enough musical materials to do it. [. . .] We created combined scripts with a melody line for all the songs in the back.[39]

Especially for titles that were less likely to be licensed, these books were printed in relatively small batches, and so the licensing companies used a variety of inexpensive technologies to produce them.

Karl Gallmeyer, the Director of the library at MTI, recalls that when he was hired in 1993 the company was in the very earliest stage of converting their rental materials into digital files. The materials in the library at that time, he remembers, had often come directly from the producers at the end of the original Broadway run.[40] Early copies of MTI material do suggest that the scripts and scores that were licensed were often reproduced from the same masters used to make copies for the cast and musicians.

Reproducing Scores

Rental scores that reference MTI's early home at 119 West 57th Street (which they occupied from the 1950s until around 1980) often include copies of manuscript music with the words "Diaz-tec 500" at the bottom. "Diaz-tec" was the product name for the onion-skin paper sold by the New York–based company Associated Music Copy Service for reproductions using an early photocopying technology called Diazo printing. Diazo printing refers to a set of processes whereby a document is copied by overlaying a blank, chemically treated page with an original document on a thin, translucent paper (sometimes called "onion skin"). The one copying the document would shine light through the onion skin onto the chemically treated page to start a reaction that, when finalized by exposure to ammonia vapors, causes the areas not exposed to the light to become dark, thus creating a new copy.[41]

Associated Music Copy Services, which produced the Diaz-tec onion skin paper, was an essential fixture in the process of music reproduction in the latter half of the twentieth century. Founded by pianist and singer Judy Haring and her husband Robert in the 1950s, the company offered copyist services,[42] sold music materials like pencils and staff paper, and reproduced musical books using technologies like diazo printing. The company also seems to have been a kind of community hub where musicians could learn how to be copyists, meet fellow artists, and find support and encouragement from Judy Haring, who seems to have served as a kind of mentor to many of the young musicians who passed through her shop.[43]

MTI received materials generated at Associated (both parts generated by their copyists and materials reproduced by their equipment). I own a copy of an MTI vocal book of *Ain't Misbehavin'* (purchased from a thrift shop) with an MTI address that suggests it was created in the late 1970s or very early 1980s. The book seems to consist of Xerox copies of the diazo print masters—the "Diaz-tec 500" brand mark is reproduced at the bottom of most pages (see Figure 6.1), and a portion of a stamp from orchestrator Luther Henderson's copyist, Brick Fleagle, is occasionally visible (see Figure 6.2).[44] These markings suggest the licensed book was copied directly from materials supplied by the production.

Gallmeyer of MTI remembers that before he joined the company, some scores were reproduced by copying "the music [. . .] onto these translucent sheets which were then placed on a light table to cast the shadow onto the sheets below [. . .] And they would turn that into a plate for printing." Gallmeyer cautions he "never saw this" process, but it is an excellent description of diazo printing.[45] By the late 1970s, though, the instability of the diazo print, combined with the relatively slow and unpleasant process of creating multiple copies in the presence of ammonia fumes, naturally led MTI to abandon the technology as soon as faster and better methods of reproduction became available. Rental materials for less popular titles were produced by photocopying using the company's own machines. What was photocopied, though, was often the prints from the earlier reprographic processes like diazo print. Gallmeyer recalls that as MTI worked to digitize their library, "there were [diazo prints] that were filed incorrectly and we had to peel them apart and they had so much noise on the page from the image it got stuck to [that staff would] put the image into photoshop to erase [the imperfections]."[46]

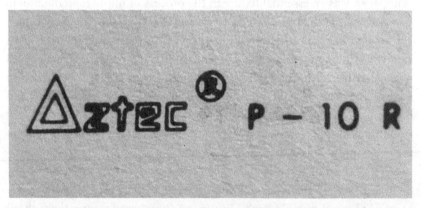

Figure 6.1 The logo for the Diaz-tec paper produced by Associated Music Copy Services (as it appears in an early rental score for *Ain't Misbehavin'* in the author's collection).

Figure 6.2 Music copyist Brick Fleagle's stamp in an early rental copy of *Ain't Misbehavin'* (from the author's collection).

Throughout most of the late twentieth century, amateurs would have received exact copies of the materials used to learn and perform the music on Broadway, and so the music (including the physical appearance of the parts) would have been fixed by these photocopies of the original documents. If a musical part was poorly copied or somehow rendered illegible on the Broadway sheet music, amateur musicians might need to improvise in the same places as those who might have subbed into a part in the Broadway orchestra.

Reproducing Scripts

Scripts, too, often were reproduced from master documents that came from the production. Sometimes copies were even generated by the same company that made copies for the cast and crew. Before photocopiers could store an image of the original document in digital memory, the original page had to be scanned each time it was duplicated. Mimeographs, which used a stencil of all of the text on the page wrapped over a drum of ink, could print multiple copies more quickly. There emerged an industry of mimeograph services that would type up mimeograph stencils and then produce copies on demand.

The most popular of these in New York was Studio Duplicating Service, a company founded by Jean M. Shepard in 1957.[47] The scripts, bound with faux leather and embossed with the name of the company, are familiar to collectors and those who have worked in performing-arts archives (see Figure 6.3 for an example). Shepard's son, Grey, remembers:

> [My mother] started it down in the Village with George C. Scott's first wife, Pat Scott. After a couple years, Pat didn't want to do it any more so my mother just bought her out and said she'd go on doing it. [. . .] The only advertising she did was she went to Tennessee Williams and said "I will do your scripts for free if you tell people."[48]

Manuscript or typescript drafts would be delivered to the office by the writers. According to Grey:

> They would bring in the script. They would either send it in or they would bring it in themselves. It had markings on it. And they would give it to my mother or one of the managers to briefly go over. Then it would go to the proofreader, and the proofreader would read it over right off the bat to see if things were correct: syntax and spelling. Then it would go to the typist who would type it onto the stencils. And [then] it would go back to the proofreader.[49]

One of the regular employees, Joseph Sicari, recalls that proofing would be done by placing the stencil on a light table and correcting any mistakes by filling the holes with liquid wax brushed on with "a nail polish brush."[50] Grey recalls that after the proofing was completed,

> it would go to the mimeographer who mimeographed it. And either the mimeographer or someone else would sort [the individual pages] into scripts. At the same time that's going on, someone is printing and embossing the covers for the scripts with the gold stamp that we had. [. . .] Heated letters that would push gold ink into the covers. When the sorting was finished, the covers were done, [. . .] all the holes would be punched

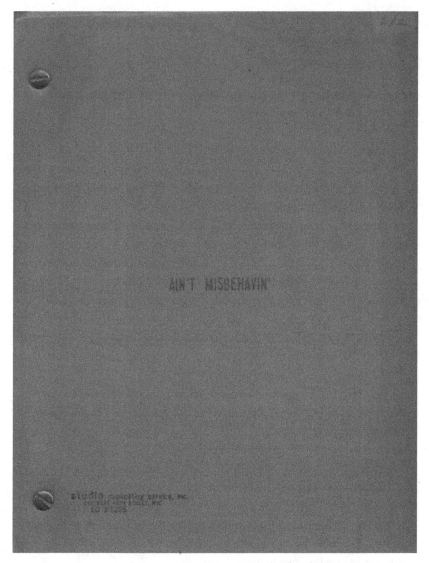

Figure 6.3 The cover of an MTI rental libretto for *Ain't Misbehavin'* produced by Studio Duplicating (from the author's collection).

and then the covers were put on [. . .] My mother would keep the stencils and a copy of the script.

The stencils were kept in the basement because once the play was in rehearsal they may decide to rewrite a scene. So then Tennessee Williams would come back and say "Here's my rewrite for scene two, act two. They had to go down, pull the stencils [. . .] replace them with new ones, and print up a whole new script again."[51]

Like Associated Music, the service quickly became a fixture in the theatre industry, with a large staff working in the office twenty-four hours a day, seven days a week. Shepard remembers:

> It was all pretty much actors that worked for her. All people in the theatre. They were all people who were "going to make it some point but were now just typing until then." Some actually made it. We had Marcia Wallace the voice for [Mrs. Crabapple] on *The Simpsons*. Most people would go off and do summer stock or do something and then come back. My Mother was really good about that. People could come and go as they wanted. She was just trying to support the theatre. She did it by the work she did, but also by allowing people to come and go and work as they pleased and still have a job when they came back after the run of a play or something like that.

Sicari recalls that the fact that the employees were all associated with the theatre industry was part of the attraction for clients of the company.

> We all were in the business. We were fledgling actors or directors. We might get an off-Broadway show, and we would be typing during the day to supplement our income. With our knowledge [. . .] we would be able to pick up a lot of errors that a normal layperson wouldn't catch. We'd be able to call the author. "You know this speech . . ." and they might say "oh yeah."
>
> I worked for a month with Tennessee Williams for a month in his apartment, and I would catch things. I was working on a script, and I went to him to type it, but basically I ended up being his editor. I would go to him and I'd say "You know there's a speech here that has information that really was previously [used] somewhere else."
>
> And he'd say, "Oh yes, yes, yes. Oh Joe, when I was going through the script, I decided to put the information down here in this lady's speech. I forgot to take it out there."
>
> By the third time I went to him I remember him saying, "Joe listen, [. . .] when you see something like that you just correct it yourself." Which was amazing!
> [. . .]

But we would be able to do that. So that's why a lot of writers trusted Studio Duplicating. I would say [we printed] probably about 90% of the scripts that were produced on Broadway.[52]

The company would keep the master mimeograph stencils and revise them as requested by the writers. Sicari recalls:

When someone came back with revisions, but not every page was revised, [...] we'd take [the last draft's stencils] down from the shelf. Then you'd deal with each one. You'd have to look up against a light and then you could see, "Hmmm ... I think I can save this page." If it's a slight change. [...] And then of course [...] they'd get charged less money. [...]

It was very messy work when you did revisions because you had all these inked sheets, and they were almost stuck to each other because we didn't have the backing to separate each sheet—we had torn them off.[53]

Sicari recalls the efforts used to simplify version control:

So your first rewrites are yellow. Your second rewrites are blue. So if you see a script that has blue pages in it, you know that's the latest rewrite. Now when we add pink for the third rewrite then you have to look for a script that has pink pages in it.[54]

Once a company reaches something they'd "pretty well [...] settled on," Sicari recalls they would "type another script and the front page will say 'Revised such-and-such a date.' so that nobody will ever pick up the wrong script."[55]

Initially, MTI, at least, would purchase new copies of the script printed from the stencils created by Studio Duplicating Service (some early licensed librettos are embossed with the company's signature gold imprint on the cover). Thus, while the materials produced by companies like Associated Copy Services and Studio Duplicating Service were originally intended for use only by the original production, they became, for a time, the materials (or the source of the materials) licensed by MTI to productions around the world. Eventually, Gallmeyer remembers, MTI moved away from mimeographs and created a paper repository of scripts that served as masters for photocopying: "We used to keep file cabinets of paper copies that we would have to drop into the printer to rescan. There was a limited amount of memory [so scanned files were not kept]."[56] Eventually, around 1994, the company moved to a digital repository of scanned materials kept on digital tape (with the files stored in a proprietary format designed by Xerox). Nonetheless, these master copies, whether paper or digital, were often made from the mimeographs created for the original production.

In 1998 the company moved to Adobe Acrobat, which, Gallmeyer remembers, significantly improved the consistency of the materials.

> Acrobat came along and allowed [us] to have a fixed format and [eliminate] the font problems and the reflow problems [. . .] [It also allowed] all of the files to live in one place [. . .] so that basically you can have these servers that contain all of these files. [. . .] Just the fact that we can keep them filed like that goes a long way to being able to say "What else needs to be updated?" [. . .] it's all here. Here's the whole list of things. [. . .] So that we can get rid of the whole problem [. . . of only part of the materials getting updated.[57]

This change meant, though, that the licensed text was now at least a significant generation removed from the materials used on Broadway. This new edition of the text and score meant amateur performers no longer saw the same physical presentation of the text and score as was used in the original production. It also meant revisions could be introduced much more easily. In the 1970s or 1980s, a writer or composer might, of course, request that the script and score be revised before the rental copies were produced, but the inconvenience (if not the cost) of requesting such changes likely kept revisions between the Broadway production and the licensed version to a minimum. With the advent of digital scripts and music, it was much easier for writers and composers to create a final revision before submitting their materials to the licensing agencies. Gallmeyer explains:

> [The production materials] won't necessarily come over unchanged anymore. [. . .] What the authors want to put out in release [is different from the Broadway version]. [. . .] They want to restore things that got cut, or they want to cut things that they didn't like or didn't think worked. Or after the first national tour they say, "Oh well you know we made these changes, we want to make those the licensed version of the show." So then either that will be assigned, for the music materials, to the original copyist and they'll

make the edits and deliver the final files to us, or if it's not something significant we will make the changes ourselves to the files.[58]

The text and score performed on the opening night of a Broadway show, if not commercially published in an unrevised form or else captured by a recording, is therefore likely to be different from any text heard by audiences after the original production closes.

Digital Musical Resources

Music Theater International, earlier than most other licensing houses, also experimented with new digital technologies to support their customers' productions. A 2005 iteration of the MTI's website notes a conscious corporate strategy over "the last decade" to create "support products [. . .] beginning in 1989 with RehearScore®, the MIDI Rehearsal Pianist."[59] The printed 1994 MTI catalog advertised "RehearScore" as "a computerized player-piano, programmed with sensitive phrasing to play every musical number in a show, including scene change, dance, and underscore music, and recorded by a top Broadway pianist."[60] The 1994 version allowed users to adjust the volume for (or silence altogether) each character's vocal part as well as the "piano," the "drums," and the "orchestra." The tempo could also be adjusted to allow the choreographer to "gradually increase the tempos (without changing the pitch)."[61]

Later advertisements clarified that RehearScore was composed of two parts, the MIDI file (essentially the piano roll for the "digital player piano") and, for the Macintosh, "the RehearScore sequencer program," a program that allowed the user to control how the MIDI file was processed and played back. MIDI sequencers were common in the 1990s, but MTI created their own interface especially designed for use in theatre rehearsals. Initially this program only ran on Macintosh machines, but PC users could purchase or download their own sequencer to use the files. Because the sound quality produced by early 1990s computers was not adequate for use in rehearsals, the program required a MIDI interface (a kind of dedicated sound card) to connect the computer to an electronic keyboard that would actually produce the sound. MTI rented a Macintosh-compatible interface device to customers, but PC users were expected to source their own.[62]

The name of the app (RehearScore) suggested that the program was meant to be exclusively used for rehearsals rather than live performance. Advertising copy for the software warned: "Please keep in mind that the RehearScore™ is a rehearsal tool and IS NOT to be used for performance under any circumstances. To do so violates your performance agreement with MTI and U.S. copyright law."[63] The creators of the musicals licensed by MTI clearly felt some ambivalence about the use of these electronic musicians and did not wish their scores to be heard by an audience as synthesized sounds. Nonetheless, in 2003, the company began offering orchestra supplements they called "OrchEXTRA," which, according to the website of the time, was created for "organizations" who are "interested in producing musicals" but "don't have access to enough musicians to make up an orchestra."[64] The "How it Works" section of the site explained:

> For each musical, every part of the orchestration is recorded by a trained musician, then put together with the other parts to create a "sequence." Each sequence can then be played back "beat by beat" using the OrchEXTRA™ system. Since each orchestra part is on a separate track, they can be turned "on" or "off" depending upon the musicians you have available. Your musicians play, as usual, while the instruments missing from your ensemble but required in the score are played by OrchEXTRA™.[65]

In 2008, the company added a "fine print" note to their website, clarifying: "OrchEXTRA® is not intended to be used as the sole source of music for your production. It is recommended that OrchEXTRA® be used in addition to at least 3–4 live musicians in order to maximize the sound quality of the score."[66] However, language of "intention" and "recommendation" suggests MTI was not actively enforcing a minimum of "3–4 live musicians" in their licensed productions.

OrchEXTRA was a branded version of a product called Sinfonia created by a company called Realtime Music Solutions (RMS). The company also licensed a version to the Rodgers and Hammerstein Organization branded as "Instrumentalese." Music Theatre International still offers the product today, though Concord and Broadway Licensing now use similar competing product, Fill|Harmonic created by Right on Cue Services that uses a "wireless handheld device" to control playback through the motions of an orchestra conductor holding it rather than by tapping keys on a computer.[67] For those without access to any musicians, both MTI and Right on Cue Services now offer pre-recorded "Performance Accompaniment Recordings" that can be played in different keys and tempos through specially created apps.

These programs have the potential to stabilize musical theatre orchestrations far more firmly than they have been in the past. In earlier eras, a small community or educational theatre may, out of necessity, re-orchestrate a score for the needs of their production. These products allow the original, authorized orchestral parts to be used (and more theoretically required) by the rights holders. Although professional companies with un-ionized musicians in the United States have been reluctant to adopt these programs,[68] the stabilizing effect these programs have on the orchestrations for amateur performance may eventually create audience expectations that a particular title is inextricably connected with a particular orchestral sound.

Further, orchestrators have, over the last several decades, started to inte-grate both instrumental and non-instrumental sounds into the keyboard part. Alex Lacamoire told *Salon* in 2015 that the harp part in the Broadway production of *Hamilton* is entirely synthesized (on the keyboard) along with musical sound effects like the "hip-hop horse."[69] These synthesized sounds may now be licensed from a company called KeyboardTEK that partners with most of the major licensing houses. At present, using these sounds come at an optional and additional cost to licensees, and so are not legally a part of the work itself. However, as synthesized sound is more regularly integrated in contemporary musical scores, it may soon be difficult to meet audience expectations without them.

Design Resources

Although none of the major licensing companies maintain the kinds of scenic or costume shops once maintained by early licensing houses like Samuel French, most now provide some level of support for the physical elements of productions. MTI offers, as an optional rental, the puppets used in *Avenue Q* and *Little Shop of Horrors*. They also manage a "Community Marketplace" where those who have created scenic and costume elements for a popular production may sell or rent them to others.

As early as 1998, the MTI website began offering "Production Slides" for some shows. In a 2000 iteration of the MTI website, the company suggested the slides, which were "created by some of Broadway's top scenic and pro-jection designers," could be used as "an additional scenic element," "a replacement for cumbersome scenery (especially effective for 'concert' or fund-raising performances)," or as "a guide (almost like 'painting-by-numbers' for backdrop or scrim designs)."[70] As with their initial ventures into pre-recorded music, the company seemed reluctant to suggest that the slides *replace* locally made sets altogether (except perhaps in "concert" versions), but suggested the product might be used to "enhance" the work of existing talent onsite.

The slides licensed by MTI were newly created for licensed productions, but by the second decade of the twenty-first century, digital productions were regularly featured in Broadway designs. By 2014, Samuel French offered digital projections from "pre-existing Projection Images from the original production" where available. This offer seems to have been discontinued after Concord purchased the company, and it is unclear how useful they ever might have been as digital projections often depend on precise placement of specific hardware that projects on specific physical surfaces in the theatre.

MTI, in collaboration with a company called Broadway Media, now offers two levels of digital projection, one that uses custom-made software designed to be used by amateur productions with little projection design experience, and a "Pro License" that works with projection-mapping software to provide something closer to the technologies used in professional productions. The advertising copy for the projections on the Broadway Media page notes "Directors and educators are choosing Broadway Media's Scenic Projections for their theatrical digital scenery to spend less time and money on building sets (or hanging those dusty old backdrops), and more time on what matters: *creating amazing theatre.*"[71] "Creating theatre," in the minds of the publicists for the software at least, is limited to the work done by the actors on stage. The rest, by implication, is merely part of the infrastructure.

Staging Resources

Choreography and staging have, for the last century, existed in something of a gray area for licensed texts. Some productions, like *Fiddler on the Roof,* have included very specific instructions for staging that were always part of the production package and considered part of the text itself. In other cases, few staging notes were provided, and directors were expected to create their own staging. Amateurs who had seen a professional production (or who had been involved in one) might attempt to reuse the staging in their own work. The original creators (directors and choreographers), without the legal resources of a licensing corporation like MTI, would be forced to pursue damages on their own. Choreography was not clearly protected under the US copyright law until 1976, and what is truly protected remains somewhat ambiguous,[72] and so unlicensed reproduction of staging and choreography in amateur productions rarely results in legal action.

Still, there have been occasions when professional productions are stopped for adhering *too* closely to the original design or staging. In 2006, for instance, the designers, choreographers, and directors of the Broadway production of the musical *Urinetown* sued the Carousel Dinner Theater in Akron, OH, for borrowing too heavily from their work without a license (possibly using either archival or bootleg video recordings as a source). The case was settled out of court,[73] but a message was clearly sent that while regional productions are expected to use the book, lyrics, and score without any changes, they may not replicate any other elements of the original production (at least without seeking additional permissions not usually provided by the licensing agency).

Even so, some directorial innovations, even when the text and score remain intact, have been challenged by rights holders. Jessica Hillman chronicles one of these cases in her essay "Tradition or Travesty? Radical Reinterpretations of the Musical Theatre Canon," recounting the story of a 2003 production of *Annie* at the Trinity Repertory Company in Providence, RI, in which the title character awakens at the end to realize her adoption had been a dream. Although the spoken libretto and score were not changed, lyricist Martin Charnin and representatives from Music Theatre International argued that the staging "could lead audience members to believe that the dream concept was part of the original libretto."[74] Amanda Denhert, in an interview with Hillman, explained that Charnin felt Denhert's production would "irreparably damage the material."[75] The production, which had hoped for a future life in New York, never left Rhode Island.

The amateur or regional director, then, must walk a fine line between respecting the intentions of the original creators without replicating the original production work too closely. Today, though, new technologies are simplifying this challenge. Until video could be shared as easily as cheaply as text, officially licensing staging and design elements of a production involved significant practical concerns. Creating, manufacturing, and shipping video cassettes (or, in still early eras, films) was complicated and expensive. Today a link to a streaming video may be sent as part of an email confirming a license.

In April of 2022, Broadway Media announced that they had acquired choreographer Jerry Mitchell and dancer Paul Canaan's company, "The Original Production," which aims to license and teach original choreography to dancers working in amateur and educational productions. Much like the prerecorded music offered by Real Music Solutions and Right on Cue Services, Broadway Media is reluctant to suggest that their product should be used to entirely replace local creative work. The promotional video for the guides suggests that guides can be used to "easily adapt and integrate the top notch choreography with your own vision." Still, the resource is clearly designed to provide tools to reproduce at least parts of a choreographic text created by Broadway professionals.

Professional directors and choreographers, are, thus far, adopting this product slowly. At present, only fourteen titles (along with a few junior versions) have choreographic guides available through Broadway Media, and three were choreographed by Jerry Mitchell and three by Sergio Trujillo. Still, as of this writing this product is still very new, and some choreographers and directors may be convinced to allow their work to be documented and officially licensed rather than pirated.

The Future

As new technologies begin to make other elements of the musical more easily reproducible and available to audiences, more of the original production is quickly becoming part of the expected text. As more work becomes fixed, the opportunities for interpretation in each new production narrow to performance choices made by the actors (the kind of variability expected within a long-running original production). Even if licensed First Class productions continue to exercise creative freedom to reconceive everything from staging and orchestration to the dialogue in the original book, it may soon be the case that the text licensed by regional and educational theatres will be a set of instructions to re-create the most recent First Class production. As strange and possibly uncomfortable as this may seem to some now, many theatre teachers and community-theatre directors may already assume that the work of "creating amazing theatre" is the work of actors bringing a fixed text to life for a new audience.

7

Fixing the Future

I began work on this book in spring of 2019. At that time, the liveness of theatre and the fixity of media technologies felt like an interesting overlap of seemingly contradictory subjects. In January of 2020 I presented an early draft of some of the first chapter of this book at a conference in Switzerland, little knowing it would be the last time that I would perform this text live and unmediated before an audience for over two years. By March of 2020, Broadway was closed and I was "sheltering in place" as the COVID-19 virus began to ravage New York City.

Over the next twelve months theatre artists experimented with making work in the new, "socially distanced" digital environment. As I write this in late 2021, Broadway has only just started to reopen, and it is too early to truly understand the impact these new forms of performance will have on the musical theatre repertory going forward. Still, the relevance of the years of the pandemic to the topic of this book feels too strong to simply ignore. I am fully aware this chapter is the least likely part of this book to age well, but it nonetheless feels necessary to include. Later work will provide better context to the observations and musings chronicled here.

Pandemic theatre was largely, by necessity, internet theatre. But internet performances already existed and had been influencing live musical theatre for some time. In 2003, *Wicked* lost the Tony Award for Best Musical to *Avenue Q*, another youth-oriented show written for the digital age (with songs like "The Internet Is for Porn"). Publicist team, Spotco, famously produced a mock political campaign for the latter with a newly written song encouraging voters to "Vote their heart" (rather than for *Wicked*, which might have had greater appeal to the more conservative audiences, who are likely to buy tickets at touring venues). The campaign likely contributed to the unexpected victory of *Avenue Q* over *Wicked*.

Still, both shows quickly built internet fan communities of largely younger audiences. *Wicked* was often discovered through online bootlegs. *Avenue*

Fixing the Musical. Douglas L. Reside, Oxford University Press. © Oxford University Press 2023.
DOI: 10.1093/oso/9780190073718.003.0008

Q, though also widely bootlegged, seems to have been discovered by many young fans through a music video. The video was part of the genre of "machinima," popular in the middle of the first decade of the twenty-first century, in which often humorous songs were played from a pre-existing recording while the creator captured video of characters in a video game "performing" the song. This digital puppetry increased the popularity of the novelty songs of singer-songwriter, Jonathan Coulton, whose songs about evil scientists and office zombies released weekly as part of his podcast were regularly adapted as machinima using characters from World of Warcraft. In 2006, the World of Warcraft player (or perhaps players) with the username "Evil Hoof & Flayed" released a machinima video of "The Internet Is For Porn," which was viewed thousands of times, was frequently reposted, and won Gamesradar's 2007 video contest for best World of Warcraft video.[1]

By the second decade of the twenty-first century, the basis of the joke "The Internet Is for Porn" no longer rang quite as true. Of course, internet pornography was still popular, but the technology had come to permeate every part of daily American life. The once-scrappy social-media platforms like Twitter and Facebook had become platforms for politicians and corporate marketing. Slick, professionally produced content dominated the web. In 2019, it might have seemed that the internet content had become too professionalized for the kind of scrappy fan-produced work that had become popular and influenced theatre makers in the 1990s and early 2000s.

Then, in March of 2020, the COVID-19 pandemic forced everyone, from late-night talk-show hosts to high school teachers to reinvent their daily work with whatever technologies they knew or could quickly learn. The pandemic hit the United States just as many high school theatre programs were gearing up for their spring show. Most were canceled, there being no time to sort out the technical and legal implications of producing an online musical. Some held online cabarets as the school year wrapped up.

In April of 2020, a video recording of a teenage girl dressed as Elphaba lip-synching to the original cast recording of *Wicked* went viral. The girl, Isabel Perry, was hoisted into the air by a crane in the back of a rented truck as part of a drive-by costume parade for her friend's socially distanced birthday.[2] Although the flying apparatus rented by Perry's parents was impressive, it was an early and relatively crude example of the technologies of pandemic theatre that would become more and more sophisticated as the weeks and months of quarantine rolled on.

Later in April of 2020, a nine-year-old girl from Jacksonville, FL named Aubrey was interviewed on the video-conferencing platform Zoom by actor John Krasinski and his wife Emily Blunt for their short-lived pandemic-inspired YouTube series "Some Good News." Aubrey had tickets to see the tour of the *Hamilton* before the pandemic forced the suspension of the tour. In the middle of Krasinki's show, the original cast of *Hamilton* "dropped in" to surprise her and sing the musical's opening number.[3]

Like a lot of live television in the early days of the pandemic, Krasinki's show was transparent about the slap-dash production values necessitated by the moment. The logo for the show was designed by Krasinki's young daughters and seems to be taped to the wall of his home office. Krasinki begins by acknowledging he "has absolutely no idea what [he's] doing." Still, the amateurish style belies the relatively complicated technical work required to make the *Hamilton* performance work. Many musical artists quickly discovered that singing together on Zoom was frustrating and often impossible because differing internet speeds meant each participant on a call would receive the audio stream at slightly different times. While this was not especially noticeable in most meetings (when, ideally, each participant waits to take their turn to speak), when singing or playing instruments together, the delay made synchronization almost impossible.

The opening song of *Hamilton* is, within the context of Krasinki's show, presented as if it were performed live for Aubrey, a feat that would have been virtually impossible given the number of times the cast sings in unison. However, on close examination of the recording, it is clear that the number was pre-recorded prior to showing it to Aubrey. Though Aubrey talks with Miranda at the beginning of the number, the states of the rooms where it happens change when the song begins. When Miranda talks to Aubrey, the bulletin board on the wall behind and to the left of him in the frame has quite a few pieces of paper stuck to it and the window shade to the right is open. During the song, the board is virtually empty and the shade closed during the song (compare the screenshots in Figures 7.1 and 7.2).

Aubrey, of course, would have known that the song was not live. At the beginning of the song, we see Miranda begin to cue up the recording. Aubrey exclaims that this is her "favorite song," but there is a break in the music before the song starts. Still, Krasinki and his team make an effort to convince the viewers that they are seeing Aubrey watch a live performance. When speaking with Aubrey, the cast are all wearing the same clothes and in roughly the same location as in the number. We see shots of Aubrey watching

Figure 7.1 Lin-Manuel Miranda speaks to nine-year-old Aubrey on Zoom.

Figure 7.2 Miranda sings the opening song of *Hamilton*. The background is slightly different than in Figure 7.1.

the video, sometimes filmed from another person's phone in portrait mode, but sometimes from her own web camera. Her video is placed into the Zoom grid of participants to suggest she is not only watching the recording but is present while it is being made. It is not live, but it captured the illusion of liveness at a time when a lengthy absence of live theatre was beginning to be felt by many.

In July of 2020, as described in Chapter Four, Disney streamed the multi-camera recording of *Hamilton* on their relatively new Disney+ streaming service (instead of holding it, as they had originally planned to do, for a theatrical release in 2021). Several other theatre companies also made arrangements with the theatrical unions and guilds to stream recordings from their archives. In November of 2020 the United Kingdom's Southwark Theatre production of Jason Robert Brown's *The Last Five Years* was streamed online for a limited time. In March, Elizabeth Flemming and Ethan Paulini's company, Out of the Box Theatrics, produced Jason Michael Webb's new designed-for-streaming production of the same show. Both were available, per union restrictions, for a limited period and streamed at specified times.

While it would, of course, be possible to film one's screen as the video played, the unions and producers wished to make downloading a high-quality copy of these streamed productions as difficult as possible. In 2020, downloading from existing streaming platforms like YouTube was trivial. Streaming platforms like Netflix, Disney+, Hulu, and even BroadwayHD offered significantly more protection for their content, but were not designed for a very limited or even one-time streaming event like those demanded by union contracts. In May of 2020, Sean Cercone, who had previously founded Broadway Licensing (described in the last chapter), launched Broadway on Demand, a streaming service that offered content producers a wider variety of options for streaming and selling their content.[4] The service was used for streaming the Roundabout Theatre's archival recordings and now hosts several, by subscription, video series that might otherwise be broadcast for free on YouTube (e.g., Laura Heywood's web series *Broadway Fanatic*). In September of 2020, Jim MacCarthy, who had previously founded the "ticket discovery platform" Goldstar, announced his new company, Stellar, which served as the platform for a streaming revival of Michel Legrand's *Amour* with a starry cast that included Adam Pascal and Rachel York performing in front of animated backgrounds.[5]

For amateur and student groups, legal agreements that did not anticipate a global quarantine also complicated performances during the pandemic.

Concord Theatricals negotiated requests to stream their shows on a case-by-case basis.[6] Music Theatre International negotiated with rights holders to make available a set of forty-seven titles for "remote performance" or "streaming" rights (meaning these titles could be licensed by schools to allow a performance on Zoom). The titles available in October of 2020[7] were shows either with small casts (e.g., *The Last Five Years*) or designed for young children (e.g., *Spookley the Square Pumpkin: The Musical*). Musicals that depend on large dancing choruses were understandably mostly missing from the list (though Zoom licenses of *Les Misérables*, *The Drowsy Chaperone*, and *The Pajama Game* were available and presented an interesting challenge for a director).

Most university programs declined to produce a musical for their main-stage season during the pandemic. Although attempts to intentionally limit audiences to those on Zoom (or, in rare instances, in socially distanced physical spaces) may have hidden some productions from search engines and site browsing, in April of 2021 I counted only nine musical productions advertised on the websites of the Princeton Review's top twenty colleges and universities for college theatre.[8] The shows performed were: *Head Over Heels*, *Hair*, *Celebration*, *Urinetown*, *The Last Five Years*, *Beast Mode Cheat*, *This Golden Day*, *Spring Awakening*, and *Edges*. Emerson advertised their production of *Spring Awakening* will take place in a "transmedia platform," and indeed, most of the musicals produced during this period straddled a line between pre-recorded broadcast and live theatre.

In most cases, the musicals produced by schools during this period seem to have been entirely pre-recorded. In rare cases, small cast musicals were recorded with the actors and musicians in the same space in front of a very small live audience (e.g., Wagner College in Staten Island, NY, live streamed their outdoor production of *Celebration* in April of 2021). In other cases, book scenes were performed live but musical numbers featuring more than one person were inserted as pre-recorded moments. The Manhattan School of Music's clever choice to produce the inherently interactive musical *The Mystery of Edwin Drood* helped to create a sense of liveness for the otherwise pre-recorded show by allowing the audience watching the live stream to vote for the variants built into the book and score via text. For the students whose high school or college experience largely occurred during the pandemic, the musicals best suited for digital performance may become part of a personal repertory. Audience exposure to these titles during this period may increase familiarity with previously relatively unknown works with the result that the twenty-first-century musical theatre repertory may include works that could be easily produced on Zoom in 2020.

It seems likely, though, that the event of 2020 that will have the greatest impact on the twenty-first-century repertory will not be the global pandemic, but the societal changes that accelerated that summer after the murder of George Floyd at the hands of the Minneapolis police. The month after the murder, an anonymously authored statement, "Dear White American Theatre," was published online with over three hundred signatures of prominent artists. The open letter called out the ways in which non-white voices are often underpaid, underrecognized, and underproduced and included the statement: "We have watched you program play after play, written, directed, cast, choreographed, designed, acted, dramaturged and produced by your rosters of white theatermakers for white audiences, while relegating a token, if any, slot for a BIPOC play."[9]

Part of the response to this letter included widespread evaluation of the problematic characterizations of race and gender in many of the most-performed musicals in the United States. This evaluation had been underway long before 2020, but many in the industry, especially young students, were no longer willing to participate in works that were not inclusive of the community in which they were performed. Finding the existing repertory unsatisfactory for a number of reasons, many of the colleges and universities with top theatre programs advertised "Devised works" created by faculty and students to respond to both the technical challenges of the pandemic and the demands for equitable inclusion that were at last falling on attentive ears. These works have largely yet to be "fixed in a tangible medium" (or, at least, commercially distributed), but it is likely that the opportunities offered to new writers in educational venues previously dedicated to performing established works has nurtured new creative teams who will shape the repertory in the coming decades.

Despite the traumas of 2020, not all of the work produced during this time was as serious, as one might expect. In late September of 2020, the TikTok app offered a new way of recording "Duets" in which users could easily add their own content to other videos posted on the platform. Almost immediately users began to create musical theatre scenes using the tool. On September 23, Dan Mertzlufft posted a musical scene based on an argument he overheard between a couple in a grocery store.[10] Within ten days, the Mertzlufft's male protagonist had been joined by a female partner, a can of soup, a squeaky shopping cart wheel, and the sprayers that moisten the fresh produce.

Several weeks later, encouraged by the reception to his mini-musical, Mertzlufft arranged and orchestrated a short snippet of a song about the rodent character "Remy" from the 2007 Pixar film *Ratatouille* posted in August 2020 by Emily Jacobsen, an elementary-school teacher from Hartsdale, NY.[11] Mertzlufft's followers rose to the challenge again, and videos inspired by Jacobsen's short melody quickly went viral. Jana Shea and Greg Nobile's production company, Seaview Productions, sought out Mertzlufft, Jacobsen, and the other primary TikTok creators and offered to fully produce the musical as a benefit for the Actors Fund.[12] The production streamed from January 1–4, 2021, on the theatre discount website and app TodayTix and raised around $2 million from over 200,000 ticket buyers.[13]

Several theatre companies experimented with even more innovative technical approaches during the pandemic. Joshua Gelb, a playwright and actor who had previously written musicals based on the making of the 1866 melodrama *The Black Crook* and the 1927 film *The Jazz Singer*, along with choreographer Katie Rose McLaughlin (the associate choreographer for Broadway's *Hadestown*) created a new company aptly named Theatre in Quarantine through which they produced live performances broadcast via YouTube directly from a closet in his apartment. While most of the performances were non-musical dramas, in late 2020 they commissioned composer-lyricist Heather Christian to write a short musical piece. The result was a pre-recorded soundtrack for a one-person show told from the perspective of Mother Theresa. Gelb lip-synched, in drag, to the recorded accompaniment of Heather Christian's voice and music. Gelb performed the work live four times between December 14 and 18, 2020 (all performances were recorded and kept on YouTube for later viewing).[14] The live video was fed through Troikatronix's Isadora, a professional video-manipulation software suite often used by projection designers, to create a digital stage that sometimes included pre-recorded or looped video of Gelb on either side of the live video. At times Gelb's lips, suggesting the mouth of God, were shown, in various rotations, around the main image (see Figure 7.3). Frequently important lyrics were interposed on top of the video, in part to assist the viewer, who might not, on first listen, catch all of Christian's dense lyrics.

Theatre in Quarantine's productions also included less-narrative-based dance works and even an occasional two-person show (e.g., Scott Sheppard's *Blood Meal* featured both Gelb and Lee Minora performing in a digitally assembled dollhouse). Still, the miniscule budget (*Sacred Face* was reportedly made with less than $2,500) and health-and-safety requirements placed

Figure 7.3 Joshua Gelb performs Heather Christian's *I Am Sending You The Sacred Face* live in his closet. Additional scenic and textual elements are added via the video-processing program Isadora before the feed is sent to YouTube.

certain limits on the scope of the productions. Theatre companies with larger budgets, perhaps even eventually Theatre in Quarantine itself, may, post-pandemic, manage to build upon the kind of work that Gelb and McLaughlin created. Although live broadcasts of theatrical performance have long existed, the interplay of digital video processing with live, intentionally theatrical, performance is a new art form and one that might well develop to create its own repertory in coming years.

Theatre in Quarantine's use of YouTube as a streaming platform also provided the option for audience reaction and interaction in the form of a live chat feed. Those watching could react or comment on moments in the performance as the show played. Optionally, the video producer can capture these comments and allow them to play back on future viewings (which Theatre in Quarantine did for performances of *I'm Sending you the Sacred Face* but not all of their works). This opportunity for audience participation provided one of the elements of the theatre experience most clearly missing from the other forms of quarantine theatre, the ability not just to see and listen to actors, but to be seen and heard by one's fellow audience members.

The social experience of watching a show was re-created even more faithfully in a small set of live virtual-reality productions staged over the pandemic. While virtual-reality headsets had been available for decades before the pandemic, relatively inexpensive versions proliferated in the second decade of the twenty-first century. In 2014 Google published plans and released software for a headset that could turn most smartphones into a powerful virtual-reality device with a few cheap lenses and a small cardboard box. Also in 2014, Facebook bought a small startup called Oculus that had previously raised over a quarter of a million dollars through a Kickstarter campaign to make a more powerful and still relatively inexpensive headset. Over the next seven years the technology increased in power and functionality and decreased in price, and in fall of 2020 Facebook released the second edition of their Oculus Quest headset with an entry-level model that cost $300 (about as much as a more traditional gaming console like the Nintendo Switch). The Quest 2 allowed users to freely, physically walk around in a virtual space untethered to any additional sensors or other equipment.

The potential of the technology as a tool for creating theatre was immediately recognized by many artists. In 2014, visual artist and software developer Danny Cannizzaro partnered with director and media-arts scholar Samantha Gorman to create Tender Claws, a digital game studio specializing in virtual reality. In 2019 they released "The Under Presents," a multiplayer virtual world designed for the Oculus that, through 2020, included live actors who would interact with players as they explored a theatrical world. In one section of the game there was a theatre where both "pre-recorded" acts performed by computer-controlled characters and live shows performed by human players (both curated by the New York–based experimental theatre company PieHole) could be seen.

The company also staged live performances in the game including an adaptation of The Tempest, which ran from fall of 2020 to the spring of 2021.[15] In the adaptation, the audience is transported to several locations from Shakespeare's play, led by a character who claims to have been cast to perform Prospero in The Tempest before current events closed the show. The actor/Prospero narrates the plot of the play and performs a few lines and sings several songs taken from Shakespeare's text. Often the actor casts members of the audience in other roles from the play (Ferdinand, Miranda, etc.) and asks them to perform certain actions (e.g., carry wood, appear to be in love). The play ends with a dance party in which the human players' dance moves are approximated by their avatars (see Figure 7.4).

Tender Claw's production of The Tempest felt at times like a university Shakespeare course led by a particularly creative and energetic teacher. The plot and language of Shakespeare's play were, at least in my experience, mostly lost by the severe abridgement of the text and the one-person

Figure 7.4 A screenshot from *The Tempest* on the Tender Claws website (https://tenderclaws.com/tempest).

cast. Still, I found it a startlingly moving experience. In September 2020, when performances of *The Tempest* started, theatres had been closed for six months, and many had been "sheltering in place" in their homes during that time. The experience of joining together with strangers had become rare, and meetings that did take place often happened on video calls in which fellow participants were encountered face-to-face in a grid of boxes rather than side-by-side as one tends to encounter fellow audience members in the theatre. In *The Tempest*, the lead actor's avatar has a human-like body and face, but the audience members are represented as a small sphere floating above an inverted cone. The motion of the shapes tracks the motion of the players in a way that suggests the actual posture and head movements of the players, making each audience member recognizably individualized but also anonymous. In an actual darkened theatre, one's fellow audience members can become humanoid abstractions, not unlike the arrangement of shapes in "The Under Presents." This digital production therefore approximated the anonymous intimacy of a live audience better than most other attempts at digital theatre during the first year of the pandemic.

Audience anonymity is not always assured, however, especially for regular theatre goers within a particular theatre community. In some cases, particularly for small shows in subscription venues or at invited readings, part of the experience of attending theatre is the unscheduled encounters with the friends and colleagues one meets in the lobby at intermission or before or after the show. In 2021, Tim Kashani and his company Apples and Oranges Arts offered several workshops as part of their THEatre Accelerator that familiarized emerging musical theatre writers with augmented- and virtual-reality technologies and encouraged them to consider the platforms as a possible virtual space for future readings.

The technical expertise and time required for designing and building virtual-reality apps (like "The Under Presents") were beyond the reach of most artists. However, by late 2020, several so-called sandbox games (games that provide a virtual space and tools for creating new things using building blocks within the world) had emerged, and several companies attempted to stage new work within them. Several readings of new work took place in Graham Gaylor and Jesse Jourdrey's VRChat and in Microsoft's (now retired) AltspaceVR platform. Kashani produced several virtual readings of musical theatre works in which the audience entered a virtual theatre in AltspaceVR, gathered in a lobby, and chatted until they were led into an auditorium where actors controlling avatars performed both in the theatre space and then, suddenly, in other locations to which the audience was magically transported. During the production the audience could respond to the performances using AltspaceVR's built-in "reaction," which could cause hearts or applauding hands to rise from one's avatar's head. If an audience member moved to the music of a song, their avatar would move in much the same way. All of this helped to give the sense of watching a show together with an audience.

However, the conversations that could be had in the lobby (or in the "reception" after the show) re-created the liminal space between the world of the play and the real world that contributes to the theatrical experience. Unlike a Zoom room where all speakers are heard at the same volume, AltspaceVR allowed many conversations to occur in the same space, and the volume of the conversations corresponded to the proximity of one's avatar to others in the space. In this way, it was possible to overhear a part of a conversation and then join it. The increasingly faithful simulation of this analog experience in virtual space has begun to break down the divisions between live theatre and digitally mediated performance, and also may help us better understand the essence of the theatre-going experience itself.

Theatre in Quarantine's digitally enhanced live video performances and the virtual reality productions staged during the months of the COVID-19 pandemic may seem charmingly rudimentary in the coming years. Perhaps these will soon feel as old fashioned and suggestive of this time of incunabula as the scratchy recordings of *Florodora* or the mostly silent musical film of the *Jazz Singer*. However, they do suggest new forms of live musical theatre that may emerge and become canonical in the coming decades. The abstract avatars of *The Under Presents* or the cartoony self-caricatures that populated AltspaceVR may one day be replaced by photo-realistic re-creations of human beings, and interactions with human-controlled avatars may soon be indistinguishable from computer-controlled ones. At such a time, it may well be that the lobby experience becomes no less part of the text of some musicals than the script, score, or design. As virtual reality expands and artificial intelligence makes the reproduction of human-like interaction possible, we may soon find that audience interactions both during the performance and immediately before and after can also be fixed in a tangible medium and essential to the work of twenty-first-century musical theatre.

Notes

Introduction

1. "17 U.S. Code § 101—Definitions," LII / Legal Information Institute, accessed July 7, 2021, https://www.law.cornell.edu/uscode/text/17/101.
2. Arthur Laurents, Leonard Bernstein, and Stephen Sondheim, *West Side Story*, Licensed Libretto Vocal Book (Music Theatre International, 1958). (The warning is included on nearly every libretto licensed by Music Theatre International, though is here transcribed from a copy of *West Side Story*.)
3. An earlier version of a portion of this text as well as a further examination the Kurt Weill Edition and approaches to editing musical theatre libretti can be found in my unpublished dissertation: Douglas Reside, "The Electronic Edition and the Textual Criticism of American Musical Theatre" (Dissertation, University of Kentucky, 2006).
4. Edward Harsh and Jürgen Selk, "Guide for Volume Editors of the Kurt Weill Edition," 2002, https://www.kwf.org/media/edguide.pdf.
5. Bruce Kirle, *Unfinished Show Business: Broadway Musicals as Works-in-Process*, Theater in the Americas (Southern Illinois University Press, 2005).
6. For instance, the song "I Saw Him once," recorded for the original London cast recording of *Les Misérables*, dropped out of the show and future records by the time the musical reached Broadway.
7. Miles Kreuger, *Show Boat, the Story of a Classic American Musical* (Oxford University Press, 1977), viii.
8. Interview with Harold Prince: Raw Footage, September 9, 2003, NCOX 2167, Theatre on Film and Tape Archive, Billy Rose Theatre Division, New York Public Library for the Performing Arts, New York, NY.
9. Geoffrey Block, *Enchanted Evenings: The Broadway Musical from "Show Boat" to Sondheim and Lloyd Webber* (Oxford University Press, 2009), 41.
10. Kirle, Unfinished Show Business, p. xviii
11. Kirle.
12. Roland Barthes, *Image-Music-Text* (Macmillan, 1977), 163.
13. Kirle, Unfinished Show Business.
14. Laurence Maslon, *Broadway to Main Street: How Show Tunes Enchanted America* (Oxford University Press, 2018).
15. Kelly Kessler, *Broadway in the Box: Television's Lasting Love Affair with the Musical* (Oxford University Press, 2020).
16. Derek Miller, *Copyright and the Value of Performance, 1770–1911* (Cambridge University Press, 2018).

17. Brent S. Salter, *Negotiating Copyright in the American Theatre: 1856–1951* (Cambridge University Press, 2021).

Chapter 1

1. "Musical Play Gets The Pulitzer Award; Mrs. Buck, Pershing Duranty Honored," *New York Times*, May 3, 1932. https://timesmachine.nytimes.com/timesmachine/1932/05/03/100729643.pdf (accessed March 24, 2019).
2. George Jean Nathan, foreword to *Of Thee I Sing*, by George Kaufman, Maurie Ryskind, and Ira Gershwin (A. Knopf, 1932, 4th printing).
3. George Jean Nathan, *The Theatre in the Fifties* (Alfred A. Knopf, 1953), 247.
4. Mary Kay Duggan, "Early Music Printing and Ecclesiastical Patronage," in *Early Music Printing in German-Speaking Lands*, ed. Andrea Lindmayr-Brandl, Elisabeth Giselbrecht and Grantley McDonald (Routledge, 2018).
5. Julie Stone Peters, *Theatre of the Book, 1480–1880: Print, Text, and Performance in Europe* (Oxford University Press, 2003), 16.
6. Peters, 31.
7. Peters, 31.
8. "The Project Gutenberg EBook of The Invention of Lithography, by Alois Senefelder," accessed July 17, 2021, https://www.gutenberg.org/files/40924/40924-h/40924-h.htm.
9. "The Project Gutenberg EBook of The Invention of Lithography, by Alois Senefelder."
10. *Printers' Ink* (Printers' Ink Publishing Company, 1902), 57.
11. Townley Searle, *A Bibliography of Sir William Schwenck Gilbert, with Bibliographical Adventures in the Gilbert & Sullivan Operas* (B. Franklin, 1968), 30, http://archive.org/details/bibliographyofsi0000sear.
12. "Gilbert Interviews—The Tendency of the Modern Stage," accessed October 23, 2021, https://www.gsarchive.net/gilbert/interviews/mod_stage.html.
13. Arthur Sullivan, Thespis, Or, The Gods Grown Old: An Entirely Original Grotesque Opera, in Two Acts (1871).
14. Arthur Sullivan and William Schwenck Gilbert, . . . H.M.S. Pinafore: Or, The Lass That Loved a Sailor. An Entirely Original Comic Opera, in Two Acts (1879).
15. Cecil A. Smith and Glenn Litton, *Musical Comedy in America: From The Black Crook to South Pacific, From The King & I to Sweeney Todd* (Routledge, 2013), 212.
16. Elizabeth L. Wollman, *A Critical Companion to the American Stage Musical* (Bloomsbury Publishing, 2017), 60.
17. John Bush Jones, *Our Musicals, Ourselves: A Social History of the American Musical Theatre* (Brandeis University Press, 2011), 46.
18. Herbert Woodward and Everett Woodward, *Of Making Many Books* (Vail-Ballou Press, Inc., 1950), 45.
19. Woodward and Woodward, 45.
20. Woodward and Woodward, 74.

21. Marc Blitzstein, *The Cradle Will Rock* (Random House, 1938), 6.

22. Blitzstein, 11.

23. "Big Biz in Books from the Boards," *The Publishers Weekly* 164, no. 8 (August 22, 1953): 676.

24. "Big Biz in Books from the Boards," 678.

25. "Big Biz in Books from the Boards," 678.

26. Barbara E. Scott Fisher, "Evening Project of Brineys Becomes 'Fireside Theater': 'We Put Our Hearts Into It,'" *The Christian Science Monitor (1908–)*, December 14, 1951, sec. Women Today.

27. Fisher.

28. Marjorie Dent Candee, ed., *Current Biography: Who's News and Why 1954*, Current Biography (H.W. Wilson, 1954), 117.

29. Fisher, "Evening Project of Brineys Becomes 'Fireside Theater.'"

30. Candee, Current Biography: Who's News and Why 1954, 117.

31. Candee, 117–18.

32. Simi Horwitz, "Stage & Screen Closes the Book . . . And Its Doors," *Backstage*, November 4, 2019, https://www.backstage.com/magazine/article/stage-screen-clo ses-book-doors-19643/ (accessed June 21, 2023).

33. Publishers, "Prologue," *Theatre Arts* 32, no. 3 (1948): 27.

34. Peter Brooker and Andrew Thacker, *The Oxford Critical and Cultural History of Modernist Magazines*, vol. 2: *North America 1894–1960* (Oxford University Press, 2009), 17.

35. "Visualizations | Circulating American Magazines," accessed November 13, 2021, https://sites.lib.jmu.edu/circulating/visualizations/.

36. Jay Thompson, "A Headnote on the Form of 'Double Entry,'" *Theatre Arts* 45, no. 7 (1961): 32.

37. Cecil A. Smith, "The Lyric Theatre," *Theatre Arts Magazine* 31, no. 1 (January 1947): 24–26.

38. Thompson, "A Headnote on the Form of 'Double Entry.'"

39. Richard Rodgers and Oscar Hammerstein II, *6 Plays by Rodgers and Hammerstein* (Modern Library, 1959).

40. Lise Jaillant, "Canonical in the 1930s: Willa Cather's 'Death Comes for the Archbishop' in the Modern Library Series," *Studies in the Novel* 45, no. 3 (2013): 476–99.

41. Stanley Richards, *Ten Great Musicals of the American Theatre*, 1st ed. (Chilton Book Co, 1973).

42. Stanley Richards, *Great Musicals of the American Theatre: Edited, with an Introd. And Notes on the Plays, Authors, and Composers, ByStanley Richards*, 1st ed., vol. 2 (Chilton Book Co, 1976).

43. Stanley Richards, ed., *Great Rock Musicals* (Stein and Day, 1979).

44. Richards, Ten Great Musicals of the American Theatre.

45. George Gershwin et al., *Porgy and Bess: An Opera in Three Acts*, limited edition (Random House, 1935).

46. Betty Comden and Adolph Green, *The New York Musicals of Comden and Green* (Applause, 1999).

47. Stephen Sondheim et al., eds., *Four by Sondheim: Wheeler, Lapine, Shevelove and Gelbart*, The Applause Musical Library (Applause, 2000).

48. Wiley Hausam, ed., *The New American Musical: An Anthology from the End of the Century*, 1st ed. (Theatre Communications Group, 2003).

49. "About | Library of America," accessed June 11, 2022, https://www.loa.org/about.

50. Laurence Maslon, *American Musicals: The Complete Books and Lyrics of Sixteen Broadway Classics: A Library of America Boxed Set*, Box Har/Cr edition (Library of America, 2014).

51. "About | Library of America."

52. Laurence Maslon, *American Musicals: The Complete Books and Lyrics of Sixteen Broadway Classics: A Library of America Boxed Set*, Box Har/Cr edition (Library of America, 2014), xiii.

53. Maslon, xiii.

54. Maslon, xiii.

55. Laurence Maslon, "Curtain Up! Get the Rights!," *Slate*, October 31, 2014, https://slate.com/culture/2014/10/what-are-the-best-musicals-of-broadways-golden-age-behind-the-library-of-america-selections.html (accessed June 21, 2023).

56. Maslon.

57. Laurence Maslon, email to author, July 6, 2022.

58. Maslon, 651.

59. Maslon, American Musicals, 687.

60. Maslon, "Library of America Anthology," July 6, 2022.

61. Most are documented in David Hummel's book *The Collector's Guide to the American Musical Theatre*, and the *My Fair Lady* recording is available in the Biff Liff papers in the Billy Rose Theatre Division at the New York Public Library for the Performing Arts.

62. Bruce Kirle, *Unfinished Show Business: Broadway Musicals as Works-in-Process*, Theater in the Americas (Southern Illinois University Press, 2005), 1.

63. Douglas Larue Reside, "The Electronic Edition and Textual Criticism of American Musical Theatre" (Dissertation, University of Kentucky, 2006).

64. "Rec.Arts.Theatre.* Frequently Asked Questions (FAQ): Part 1/3," accessed June 12, 2022, https://groups.google.com/g/rec.arts.theatre.musicals/c/8yg004zGDaI/m/wBX3NDVXWA4J.

65. "The Pirates of Penzance by W. S. Gilbert and Arthur Sullivan," accessed August 29, 2021, https://www.gsarchive.net/pirates/web_op/operhome.html.

66. "What's New @ Laura's MIDI Heaven!," May 8, 1999, https://web.archive.org/web/19990508050215/http://laurasmidiheaven.com/1new.htm.

67. Dmitry Golovanov, "Transformation of Authors' Rights and Neighbouring Rights in Russia," *IRIS Plus, Legal Observations of the European Audiovisual Observatory*, 2008.

68. "Music Theatre Online," accessed August 29, 2021, https://mith.umd.edu/research/mto/.

69. "Musical of the Month | The New York Public Library," accessed August 29, 2021, https://www.nypl.org/voices/blogs/blog-channels/musical-of-the-month.

Chapter 2

1. "Kyd's Spanish Tragedy, 1615 | The British Library," accessed June 18, 2022, https:// www.bl.uk/collection-items/kyds-spanish-tragedy-1615.

2. "Musical of the Month: The Music of the Black Crook," The New York Public Library, accessed June 18, 2022, https://www.nypl.org/blog/2011/06/16/musi cal-month-music-black-crook.

3. Joseph Whitton, "The Naked Truth!" An Inside History of the Black Crook (H.W. Shaw Co., 1897).

4. David S. Shields, "Photography and the American Stage," Broadway Photographs, accessed June 18, 2022, https://broadway.cas.sc.edu/.

5. David S. Shields, "Charles Deforest Fredricks," Broadway Photographs, accessed June 20, 2023, https://broadway.library.sc.edu/content/charles-deforest-fredricks.html.

6. David S. Shields, "Napoleon Sarony," Broadway Photographs, accessed June 18, 2022, https://broadway.library.sc.edu/content/napoleon-sarony.html.

7. David S. Shields, Still: American Silent Motion Picture Photography (University of Chicago Press, 2013), 40.

8. Erin Pauwels, Acting Out: Cabinet Cards and the Making of Modern Photography (University of California Press, 2020), 34.

9. Lithographic Co. v. Sarony, 111 U.S. 53 (1884).

10. Lithographic Co. v. Sarony, 111 U.S. 53 (1884).

11. David S. Shields, "Joseph Byron," Broadway Photographs, accessed June 20, 2023, https://broadway.library.sc.edu/content/joseph-byron.html.

12. A. I. Bowersox, "Photographers at Home and Abroad," American Journal of Photography 15, no. 176 (August 1894): 343–48.

13. The British Journal of Photography 30, no. 1206 (June 15, 1883): 330.

14. "Photographing by Electric Light," The New York Times, May 2, 1883. https://times machine.nytimes.com/timesmachine/1883/05/02/102817209.html?pageNumber=5 (accessed June 21, 2023).

15. "Photographing by Electric Light."

16. Sidney Allan, "Byron- 'The Stage Is My Studio,'" Wilson's Photographic Magazine, 1907.

17. Allan, 26.

18. Oklahoma!, Advertisement, The New York Times, March 28, 1943. https://timesmach ine.nytimes.com/timesmachine/1943/03/28/issue.html (accessed June 21, 2023).

19. Michael Patrick Hearn, The Art of the Broadway Poster (Ballantine Books, 1980), 22.

20. Hearn, 70.

21. Bosley Crowther, "A Leaf-Not Leap-Through the Playbill," The New York Times, April 11, 1937. https://www.nytimes.com/1937/04/11/archives/a-leafnot-leapthrough-the-playbill-leafing-through-the-playbi.html (accessed June 21, 2023).

22. Vicki Hoskins, "Playbill Takes the Stage: The Rise of America's Foremost Theatrical Program" (Dissertation, University of Pittsburgh, 2020), 75.

23. Hoskins, 81.

24. Hoskins, 131.

25. Hoskins, 132.

26. John Guare,. *Two Gentlemen of Verona: A Re-creation, Complete With Pictures and Sheet Music*, 1st ed. (Holt, Rinehart & Winston, 1973).

27. Martin Charnin, *Annie: A Theatre Memoir*, 1st ed. (Dutton, 1977).

28. Andrew Lloyd Webber and Tim Rice, *Evita: The Legend of Eva Peron, 1919–1952* (Drama Pub, 1979).

29. Andrew Lloyd Webber, *Cats: The Book of the Musical*, 1st ed. (Faber and Faber Ltd, 1981).

30. Andrew Lloyd Webber, John Napier, and T. S. Eliot, *Cats: The Book of the Musical: Based on Old Possum's Book of Practical Cats by T.S. Eliot*, 1st ed, A Harvest/HBJ Book (Harcourt Brace Jovanovich, 1983).

31. George Perry et al., *The Complete Phantom of the Opera* (Pavilion, 1987).

32. Edward Behr, *Les Misérables: History in the Making* (Cape, 1989).

33. Edward Behr, *The Complete Book of Les Misérables* (Arcade Pub, 1989).

34. Kurt Gänzl et al., *The Complete Aspects of Love* (Viking Studio Books, 1990).

35. Edward Behr and Mark Steyn, *The Story of Miss Saigon* (Arcade Pub, 1991).

36. George Perry and Andrew Lloyd Webber, *Sunset Boulevard: From Movie to Musical* (Pavilion Books, 1993).

37. Jonathan Larson et al., *RENT* (Rob Weisbach Books: William Morrow and Co., 1997).

38. Arthur Sullivan, William Schwenck Gilbert, and Isaac Asimov, *Asimov's Annotated Gilbert & Sullivan* (Doubleday, 1988).

39. Stephen Sondheim, *Finishing the Hat: Collected Lyrics (1954–1981) with Attendant Comments, Principles, Heresies, Grudges, Whines and Anecdotes*, illustrated ed. (Knopf, 2010).

40. Stephen Sondheim, *Look, I Made a Hat: Collected Lyrics (1981–2011) with Attendant Comments, Amplifications, Dogmas, Harangues, Digressions, Anecdotes and Miscellany*, illustrated ed. (Knopf, 2011).

41. Lin-Manuel Miranda and Jeremy McCarter, *Hamilton: The Revolution* (Little, Brown Book Group, 2016).

42. "Lin-Manuel Miranda," Genius, accessed June 19, 2022, https://genius.com/artists/Lin-manuel-miranda.

43. Lin-Manuel Miranda, Quiara Alegría Hudes, and Jeremy McCarter, *In the Heights: Finding Home* (Random House, 2021).

44. "Dave Malloy," Genius, accessed June 19, 2022, https://genius.com/artists/Dave-malloy.

45. Steven Suskin and Dave Malloy, eds., *The Great Comet: The Journey of a New Musical to Broadway*, book with CD edition (Union Square & Co., 2016).

46. Laura MacDonald, "Connection in an Isolating Age: Looking Back on Twenty Years of Engaging Audiences and Marketing Musical Theatre Online," in *Broadway: Musical Theatre in the Digital Age*, ed. Jessica Hillman-McCord. (Palgrave Macmillan, 2017).

47. MacDonald, 22.

48. MacDonald, 24.

49. "Logos & Clipart Available Anywhere?," accessed April 21, 2022, https://groups.google.com/g/rec.arts.theatre.musicals/c/UC1PQ1agpRM/m/cfucLj9UhmkJ?pli=1.

50. "Logos & Clipart Available Anywhere?"

51. "Broadway Posters," February 2, 1998, https://web.archive.org/web/19980202074104 fw_/http://www.digitas.harvard.edu/~note/poster.html.

52. "The Les Miserables Home Page," July 11, 1997, https://web.archive.org/web/1997071 1003830/http://www.ot.com/lesmis/.

53. Robert Viagas, "Les Miserables Launches Its Own Website," *Playbill*, March 3, 1997, https://playbill.com/article/les-miserables-launches-its-own-website-com-329103.

54. Steven A. Taylor, "Editorial?!—Or a Place for Me to Say Stuff!," May 24, 1997, https:// web.archive.org/web/19970524171522/http://www.netlink.co.uk/users/nomad/ want.htm.

55. Taylor.

56. Christian Bittler, "Les Misérables Interactive," TDK Collection, 1997.

57. Katharine Stalter, "Spotlight: Interactive Offers Backstage Glimpse," in *Variety (Archive: 1905–2000)* (Penske Business Corporation, March 10, 1997).

58. Stalter.

Chapter 3

1. "Historic Arthur Sullivan Recordings," accessed October 9, 2021, https://web.archive.org/web/20211009135732/https://www.gsarchive.net/sullivan/html/historic.html.

2. "Matrix Numbers in Recordings of Gilbert & Sullivan," accessed April 22, 2022, http://gasdisc.oakapplepress.com/matrix4.htm.

3. Vaclav Smil, *Creating the Twentieth Century: Technical Innovations of 1867–1914 and Their Lasting Impact* (Oxford University Press, 2005), 240; Marc Shepherd, "The G&T 1906 Mikado," accessed April 22, 2022, http://gasdisc.oakapplepress.com/mik1 906.htm.

4. Laurence Maslon, *Broadway to Main Street: How Show Tunes Enchanted America* (Oxford University Press, 2018).

5. Maslon, 28–29.

6. Thom Holmes, *The Routledge Guide to Music Technology*, 1st ed. (Routledge, 2006), 324.

7. Lance W. Brunner, "The Orchestra and Recorded Sound," in *The Orchestra: A Collection of 23 Essays on Its Origins and Transformations*, ed. Joan Peyser (Hal Leonard, 2006), 492–93.

8. "Victor Matrix CS-95387. Porgy and Bess / Helen Jepson; Alexander Smallens; Lawrence Tibbett—Discography of American Historical Recordings," accessed April 22, 2022, https://adp.library.ucsb.edu/index.php/matrix/detail/200021945/CS-95387-Porgy_and_Bess.

9. Maslon, *Broadway to Main Street*, 58.

10. Maslon, 58.

11. Dale Harrison, "Dale Harrison's New York," *The Bristol Herald Courier, Bristol Virginia-Tennessee*, May 18, 1938.

12. bruce d mcclung, *Lady in the Dark: Biography of a Musical*, 1st ed. (Oxford University Press, 2006), 159.

13. Maslon, *Broadway to Main Street*, 59–60.

14. Maslon, 63.

15. Tim Carter, *Oklahoma!: The Making of an American Musical*, illustrated edition (Yale University Press, 2007), 225.

16. Carter, 226.

17. Maslon, *Broadway to Main Street*, 65.

18. Maslon, 67.

19. Laurence Maslon, "How 'Oklahoma!' Revolutionized the Cast Album," *The New York Times*, July 10, 2019, sec. Theater, https://www.nytimes.com/2019/07/10/theater/oklahoma-cast-album.html(accessed June 21, 2023).

20. Carter, *Oklahoma!*, 161.

21. Maslon, *Broadway to Main Street*, 67.

22. Maslon, 25.

23. Louis Untermeyer, liner notes, *Carousel*, Decca 1955 LP release DL 79020.

24. Maslon, *Broadway to Main Street*, 84.

25. Maslon, 54.

26. Geoffrey Block, *Enchanted Evenings: The Broadway Musical from "Show Boat" to Sondheim and Lloyd Webber* (Oxford University Press, 2009), 180.

27. Maslon, *Broadway to Main Street*, 87.

28. Maslon, 116–17.

29. *Les Misérables (1985, Vinyl)*, accessed October 9, 2021, https://www.discogs.com/release/2204934-Alain-Boublil-And-Claude-Michel-Schönberg-Les-Misérables.

30. *Original London Cast—Les Misérables (1985, Double Play, Dolby System, Cassette)*, accessed October 9, 2021, https://www.discogs.com/release/20233711-Original-London-Cast-Les-Misérables.

31. *Les Misérables (1985, CD)*, accessed October 9, 2021, https://www.discogs.com/release/8925565-Alain-Boublil-And-Claude-Michel-Schönberg-Les-Misérables.

32. Edward Behr, *The Complete Book of Les Misérables* (Arcade Pub, 1989), 71.

33. Perhaps coincidentally, yet another version of this song "Who Says It Hurts" is partially preserved in the 1989 making-of documentary *The Heat Is On*. It is sung by Ruthie Henshall just after a scene in which the music copyists are shown erasing part of the score, which one copyist notes "is really out of date."

34. Dan Rebellato, "Playwriting and Globalisation: Towards a Site-Unspecific Theatre," *Contemporary Theatre Review* 16, no. 1 (February 1, 2006): 97–113.

Chapter 4

1. Four years later, the New York Public Library would launch the Theatre on Film and Tape Archive, and Prince's dream was realized.

2. Harold Prince, "Harold Prince Papers" (n.d.), Harold Prince Papers, *T-Mss 1986-006, box 15, folder 1, Billy Rose Theatre Division, New York Public Library for the Performing Arts.

3. Of course, in 1966, the film version of *West Side Story* was five years old, and it preserved much of Robbins' choreography (although adapted for the somewhat more realistic medium of film and with notable excisions including the "Somewhere" ballet).
Prince apparently did not feel enough of the essence of the work had been preserved
in the film version to feel assured that *West Side Story* had been adequately preserved.
Prince seems to argue a filmed version of a stage production would be an adequate
transcription of the essential "text" of a musical, but that the movie adaptation is not.

4. Harold Prince, *Sense of Occasion* (Applause Theatre & Cinema Books, an imprint of
Hal Leonard LLC, 2017), 140.

5. Bruce Kirle, *Unfinished Show Business: Broadway Musicals as Works-in-Process*,
Theater in the Americas (Southern Illinois University Press, 2005), xviii

6. Gerda Taranow, *Sarah Bernhardt: The Art within the Legend* (Princeton University
Press, 1972), 265, http://archive.org/details/sarahbernhardtar0000tara.

7. David B. Lovell, "Tales from the Collection: A Cinematic Wilde Goose Chase," *The
Lovell Collection* (blog), accessed March 25, 2021, https://thelovellcollection.wordpr
ess.com/2021/03/25/tales-from-the-collection-a-cinematic-wilde-goose-chase/.

8. Richard Barrios, *A Song in the Dark: The Birth of the Musical Film*, electronic resource, 2nd ed. (Oxford University Press, 2010), 86, http://TM9QT7LG9G.search.
serialssolutions.com/?V=1.0&L=TM9QT7LG9G&S=JCs&C=TC0000370615&T=
marc&tab=BOOKS.

9. Barry Monush, *The Sound of Music FAQ: All That's Left to Know About Maria, the von
Trapps and Our Favorite Things* (Rowman & Littlefield, 2015).

10. Frederick Wasser, *Veni, Vidi, Video: The Hollywood Empire and the VCR* (University
of Texas Press, 2001), 97.

11. Elissa Nadworny, "The Most Popular High School Plays And Musicals," *NPR*, July 30,
2020, sec. K-12, https://www.npr.org/sections/ed/2019/07/31/427138970/the-most-
popular-high-school-plays-and-musicals.

12. Howard Lindsay and Oscar Hammerstein II, *The Sound of Music: Perusal Libretto*, perusal copy (New York: Concord).

13. Luisa Lyons, "Show Girl," FILMED LIVE MUSICALS, accessed January 28, 2023,
https://www.filmedlivemusicals.com/show-girl.html.

14. Richard Halloran, "TV 'Oh! Calcutta!' Leads to Charges," *The New York Times*, May
20, 1971. https://www.nytimes.com/1971/05/20/archives/tv-oh-calcutta-leads-to-
charges-obscenity-indictments-are-returned.html (accessed June 21, 2023).

15. Kelly Kessler, *Broadway in the Box: Television's Lasting Love Affair with the Musical*, 1st
ed. (New York: Oxford University Press, 2020), 136.

16. John J. O'Connor, "TV: 'Most Happy Fella' and 'Beyond Westworld,'" *The New York
Times*, March 5, 1980. https://www.nytimes.com/1980/03/05/archives/tv-most-
happy-fella-and-beyond-westworld.html (accessed June 21, 2023).

17. "Radio-Television: RCTV Puts Final Touches On Feevee Venture With RCA," *Variety
(Archive: 1905–2000)* (Los Ángeles, CA: Penske Business Corporation, October
7, 1981).

18. "RCA to Offer Video Disc of 'Pippin,'" accessed April 22, 2022, https://www.cedma
gic.com/museum/press/release-1981-06-01-2.html.

19. David Sheehan, interview by Doug Reside with David Sheehan, September 14, 2020.

20. Bob Fosse, "Letter from Bob Fosse to David Sheehan and Hillard Elkins," July 10, 1981.

21. Fosse.

22. "RCA to Offer Video Disc of 'Pippin.'"

23. Jim McCullaugh, "General News: Videocassette Music Growth Slow, Steady," *Billboard (Archive: 1963–2000)* (New York: P-MRC, August 15, 1981).

24. Jim McCullaugh, "General News: Video Music Software Flexes Muscles At CES; More Due," *Billboard (Archive: 1963–2000)* (New York: P-MRC, January 30, 1982).

25. Kathyrn Doby, interview by Doug Reside with Kathyrn Doby, September 21, 2020.

26. Bob Fosse, "Letter to the Cast and Crew of Pippin," November 23, 1981 (digital scan sent to the author by Kathyrn Doby)

27. Fosse.

28. Doby, interview by Doug Reside with Kathyrn Doby.

29. Kevin Winkler, "An Anecdotic Revue," in *Big Deal: Bob Fosse and Dance in the American Musical* (Oxford University Press, 2018), 182.

30. Winkler, 180–181.

31. Michael Zinberg, dir., *Gilmore Girls*, Season 6, Episode 5, "We've Got Magic to Do," aired October 11, 2005, on WB.

32. Mark Cendrowski, dir., *The Big Bang Theory*, Season 12, Episode 10, "The VCR Illumination," aired December 6, 2018, on CBS.

33. Winkler, 180.

34. Doby, interview by Doug Reside with Kathyrn Doby.

35. Luisa Lyons, "Sophisticated Ladies," FILMED LIVE MUSICALS, accessed January 28, 2023, https://www.filmedlivemusicals.com/sophisticated-ladies.html.

36. Kessler, 150.

37. Terry Hughes, interview by Doug Reside with Terry Hughes, September 14, 2020.

38. Hughes.

39. Hughes.

40. Hughes.

41. Sandra Salmans, "How a Cable Channel Flopped," *The New York Times*, February 28, 1983, sec. Business, https://www.nytimes.com/1983/02/28/business/how-a-cable-channel-flopped.html(accessed June 21, 2023).

42. Richard Hummler, "Cable-Television: Legit Cable Hopes Didn't Pan Out, But Showtime Likes 'B'way' Series; HBO Wants More Original Dramas," *Variety (Archive: 1905–2000)* (Penske Business Corporation, May 29, 1985).

43. Hummler, 127.

44. Hummler, "Cable-Television."

45. Harry Haun, "Cable Connection: A New Broadway?," *Daily News* (New York), August 13, 1982.

46. Craig Zadan, *Sondheim & Co.*, 2nd ed. (Harper & Row, Publishers, 1986), vii

47. James Kaplan, "Is Stephen Sondheim God?," *New York Magazine* 27, no. 14 (April 4, 1994).

48. Joseph McLellan, "A 'Miz' Not to Miss," *Washington Post*, March 6, 1996, https://www.washingtonpost.com/archive/lifestyle/1996/03/06/a-miz-not-to-miss/7290ed79-f749-47a0-987f-a9449c9dfed4/ (accessed June 21, 2023).

49. *Les Misérables—The Dream Cast in Concert*, VHS, directed by John Caird and Gavin Taylor (Columbia/Tristar Studios, 1996).

50. Kenneth Jones, "Trim for the New Year: Broadway Les Miz Now Runs 2 Hours 58 Minutes," *Playbill*, December 13, 2000, https://www.playbill.com/article/trim-for-the-new-year-broadway-les-miz-now-runs-2-hours-58-minutes-com-93804 (accessed July 2, 2022).

51. Jones.

52. Stephen Battaglio and Cathy Dunkley, "Lloyd-Webber Ticketed for Vids," *Back Stage,* August 8, 1997, 36.

53. Nigel Hunter, "And Now For Something Really Useful . . .," *Billboard*, October 19, 1996.

54. Battaglio. 3.

55. *A Live Commentary from Andrew: Cats The Musical (1998)*, 2020, https://www.youtube.com/watch?v=sAP7V5KwZCU.

56. Ken Mandelbaum, "Ken Mandelbaum's MUSICALS ON DISC: Video Bundles From Britain," *Playbill*, July 26, 1998, http://www.playbill.com/article/ken-mandelbaums-musicals-on-disc-video-bundles-from-britain-com-76632 (accessed April 22, 2022).

57. Murdoch McBride, "Broadway Digital Entertainment Relaunches 'Archive' Site May 8 | Playbill," *Playbill*, May 25, 2000, https://www.playbill.com/article/broadway-digital-entertainment-relaunches-archive-site-may-8-com-89462 (accessed June 21, 2023).

58. Jeremy Gerard, "Live-Streamed 'Daddy Long Legs' Brought 150K Viewers To Off-Broadway For Free," *Deadline* (blog), December 22, 2015, https://deadline.com/2015/12/live-stream-daddy-long-legs-brought-150k-viewers-off-broadway-1201671199/ (accessed June 21, 2023).

59. Gerard.

60. "Hamilton Will Be Filmed; Mixtape and Documentary Released This Fall," *Playbill*, June 16, 2016, https://playbill.com/article/hamilton-will-be-filmed-mixtape-and-documentary-released-this-fall (accessed June 21, 2023).

61. Ashley Lee, "'We Need to Talk about the Money': Leslie Odom Jr.'s 'Hamilton' Duels, Onstage and Off," *Los Angeles Times*, June 25, 2020, sec. Movies, https://www.latimes.com/entertainment-arts/movies/story/2020-06-25/leslie-odom-jr-hamilton-disney-aaron-burr(accessed June 21, 2023) .

62. Anousha Sakoui, "SAG-AFTRA and Actors Equity Are Fighting: What Is This Union Beef About?," *Los Angeles Times*, October 22, 2020, sec. Company Town, https://www.latimes.com/entertainment-arts/business/story/2020-10-22/sag-aftra-actors-equity-union-fight-hollywood-pandemic(accessed June 21, 2023).

63. The company does still occasionally film in New York. In 2022, for instance, they captured the Broadway production of *Mr. Saturday Night*. Still, as of this writing, a Broadway recording is relatively rare among their recent acquisitions.

Chapter 5

1. "The Bodleian First Folio," accessed October 23, 2021, https://firstfolio.bodleian.ox.ac.uk/book.html.

2. *The Black Crook* is selected as an example here not because it is, as some have suggested, the first musical, but its post–Civil War introduction of European ballet into an immensely popular American melodrama has led many historians to consider it an important early milestone in the development of American musical theatre.

3. Joseph Whitton, *"The Naked Truth!" An Inside History of the Black Crook* (H.W. Shaw Co., 1897), 10.

4. George Dolby, *Charles Dickens As I Knew Him: The Story of the Reading Tours in Great Britain and America* (Lume Books, 2016), 197.

5. Joseph Whitton, *Wags of the Stage* (George H. Rigby, 1902), 246.

6. Whitton, 11.

7. Matthew P. Deady. Reports of Cases Determined in the Circuit and District Courts of the United States of Oregon and California (A.L. Bancroft and Company, 1872), 218.

8. Deady, 218.

9. The Judge further argued that the piece, in its eroticism, is not "suited for public representation" and therefore not copyrightable even if it were considered a dramatic composition (Deady, 222).

10. Charles M. Barras, "The Black Crook: An Original Magical and Spectacular Drama in Four Acts" (Rockwell, Baker & Hill, 1866).

11. Charles M. Barras, *The Black Crook: An Original Magical and Spectacular Drama in Four Acts* (Rounds & James, Printers, 1867).

12. Craig H. Roell, *The Piano in America, 1890–1940* (University of North Carolina Press, 1989).

13. "184.015—Gems From the Black Crook. Original Edition. | Levy Music Collection," accessed July 3, 2022, https://levysheetmusic.mse.jhu.edu/collection/184/015.

14. "053.103—You Naughty, Naughty Men. | Levy Music Collection," accessed July 3, 2022, https://levysheetmusic.mse.jhu.edu/collection/053/103.

15. "185.093—Black Crook. No. 1. March of the Amazons. | Levy Music Collection," accessed July 3, 2022, https://levysheetmusic.mse.jhu.edu/collection/185/093.

16. "186.060—Transformation Polka. | Levy Music Collection," accessed July 3, 2022, https://levysheetmusic.mse.jhu.edu/collection/186/060.

17. Andrew Lamb, *Leslie Stuart: Composer of Florodora* (Routledge, 2020), 78.

18. Lamb, 73.

19. John Philip Sousa, "Publisher and Composer on Musical Piracy," *Musical News*, 1903, 77. (Also cited by Lamb, 136).

20. "Musical News," 1903.

21. Lamb, *Leslie Stuart*, 82.

22. Lamb, 136.

23. Rodgers and Hammerstein Archive of Recorded Sound, "Mapleson Cylinders," December 19, 2018, https://web.archive.org/web/20181219182148/http://digilib.nypl.org/dynaweb/millennium/mapleson.

24. "Paying Dearly for Opera," *New York Times,* February 14, 1884. http://timesmach ine.nytimes.com/timesmachine/1884/02/14/106142485.html(accessed   January 18, 2021).

25. David Hummel, *Collector's Guide to the American Musical Theatre* (Scarecrow Press, Incorporated, 1984).

26. Megan Rosenfeld, "Miles Krueger, The Musicals Man," *Washington Post*, March 19, 1989,   https://www.washingtonpost.com/archive/lifestyle/style/1989/03/19/miles-kreuger-the-musicals-man/96a0c951-b37c-4b45-8129-0c6a4a542904/   (accessed June 21, 2023).

27. Rosenfeld.

28. Olin Downes, "Disks of Yesteryear," *The New York Times*, March 6, 1938, https://times machine.nytimes.com/timesmachine/1938/03/06/578432772.html?pageNumber= 155 (accessed June 21, 2023).

29. "Librarian," *New Yorker*, December 28, 1935, https://archives-newyorker-com.i.ezpr oxy.nypl.org/newyorker/1935-12-28/flipbook/012.

30. "Librarian."

31. Rosenfeld, "Miles Krueger, The Musicals Man."

32. "ABHÖRGERÄTE: Mikrofon Unterm Schlips—DER SPIEGEL 48/1951," accessed February 13, 2021, https://www.spiegel.de/spiegel/print/d-20804174.html.

33. archives.nypl.org—Beatrice Lillie Papers," accessed February 13, 2021, http://archi ves.nypl.org/the/21271.

34. "ABHÖRGERÄTE: Mikrofon Unterm Schlips—DER SPIEGEL 48/1951."

35. "Advertisement: Only WEBCOR Records in Both Directions," *Magnetic Film and Tape Recording*, April 1954, http://thehistoryofrecording.com/Magazines/ Tape%20Recording%20Magazine/Tape-Recording-1954-04.pdf.

36. Robert Schear, interview by Doug Reside with Robert Schear, January 30, 2021.

37. Schear.

38. Schear.

39. Schear.

40. Schear.

41. Howard Klein, "Take the Case of Magda Olivero; Take the Case of Magda Olivero," *New York Times*, November 28, 1971, http://timesmachine.nytimes.com/timesmach ine/1971/11/28/82218406.html.

42. Allan Kozinn, "A Music Lovers' Mecca Is Closing," *The New York Times*, November 7, 1990, https://www.nytimes.com/1990/11/07/arts/a-music-lovers-mecca-is-closing. html (accessed June 21, 2023).

43. Frank Frankly, interview by Doug Reside with "Frank," February 6, 2021.

44. Frankly.

45. Frankly.

46. Frankly.

47. Frankly.

48. Frankly.

49. Frankly.

50. An encyclopedic knowledge of creators and dates seems endemic among the most active bootleggers. Many also seem to have an almost involuntary verbal tic of reciting author and date information when mentioning a title. It is perhaps part of the performance of expertise that demonstrates their bonafides in the community.

51. Frankly, interview by Doug Reside with "Frank."

52. Frankly.

53. Jim Philadelphia, interview by Doug Reside with Jim Philadelphia, January 31, 2022.

54. Philadelphia.

55. Wheeler had contributed additional material to John Weidman's libretto for *Pacific Overtures*.

56. Frankly, interview by Doug Reside with "Frank."

57. Max Boots, interview by Doug Reside with Max Boots, February 1, 2021.

58. Frankly, interview by Doug Reside with "Frank."

59. Frankly.

60. Brad Bennett, interview by Doug Reside with Brad Bennett, January 30, 2022.

61. Bennett.

62. Robert Sher, interview by Doug Reside with Robert Sher, n.d.

63. Doris Ettlinger, "For Many, TV Tape Means Watching More and Loving It," *The New York Times*, August 27, 1977, https://www.nytimes.com/1977/08/27/archives/for-many-tv-tape-means-watching-more-and-loving-it.html (accessed June 21, 2023).

64. David Buckingham, Rebekah Willett, and Maria Pini, "Home Truths?: Video Production and Domestic Life," *Technologies of the Imagination*, 2011, 9.

65. Uncle Louie, interview by Doug Reside with Uncle Louie, February 6, 2021.

66. Louie.

67. Lester Lux, interview by Doug Reside with Lester Lux, February 1, 2021.

68. Lux.

69. Boots, interview by Doug Reside with Max Boots.

70. "VIDEOS—Fair Broadway/ Musical Trades," October 19, 2016, https://web.archive.org/web/20161019055721/https://fairbroadwaymusicaltrades.weebly.com/videos.html.

71. "My Masters/Expected Masters—Phantom Of Broadway," June 25, 2014, https://web.archive.org/web/20140625180848/http://phantomofbroadway.weebly.com/my-mastersexpected-masters.html.

72. "Good/Bad Traders," Broadway Trades, accessed July 3, 2022, http://tradebway.weebly.com/goodbad-traders.html.

73. "How to Start Trading—Theater Trades," August 19, 2018, https://web.archive.org/web/20180819143221/http://theatertrades.weebly.com/how-to-start-trading.html.

74. "FAQ—Theater Trades," August 28, 2018, https://web.archive.org/web/20180828183237/http://theatertrades.weebly.com/faq.html.

75. Nelson Pressley, "After the Curtain Falls, the Web Gets Into the Act," August 31, 2008, http://www.washingtonpost.com/wp-dyn/content/article/2008/08/29/AR2008082900684.html (accessed June 21, 2023).

76. Chris Stokel-Walker, "Illicit Bootlegs on YouTube Are Giving Musicals a Second Life," *Medium*, December 9, 2019, https://ffwd.medium.com/illicit-bootlegs-on-youtube-are-giving-musicals-a-second-life-dd945e23409e (accessed June 21, 2023).

77. *Pacific Overtures* was recorded for Japanese television (as discussed in the previous chapter) but never released commercially in the United States. The full video recording is, however, as of this writing, the first result when one searches for "Pacific Overtures" on YouTube.

78. Mark Eden Horowitz, *Sondheim on Music: Minor Details and Major Decisions*, 2nd ed. (Scarecrow Press, 2010), 236.

79. "Tumblrico," *Tumblrico*, accessed February 15, 2021, https://linmanuel.tumblr.com/post/114774696985/lovesjustachemical-actressingfanatic.

80. Doug Reside, "The Advantages of Floating in the Middle of the Sea: Digital Musical Theatre Research," in *IBroadway: Musical Theatre in the Digital Age*, ed. Jessica Hillman-McCord (Palgrave MacMillan, 2017), 261–82.

81. Ken Mandelbaum, *Not Since Carrie: Forty Years of Broadway Musical Flops* (St. Martin's Publishing Group, 1992), 49.

82. Patrick Healy, "An Outsider Gets a Nicer Date for the Prom," *The New York Times*, February 2, 2012, sec. Theater, https://www.nytimes.com/2012/02/05/theater/carrie-a-huge-stage-flop-is-reinvented-by-mcc-theater.html (accessed June 21, 2023).

83. David Rooney, "'Carrie': Theater Review," *The Hollywood Reporter* (blog), March 1, 2012, https://www.hollywoodreporter.com/news/general-news/carrie-theater-review-296385/(accessed June 21, 2023).

84. Laurence Maslon, *Broadway to Main Street: How Show Tunes Enchanted America* (Oxford University Press, 2018), 185.

Chapter 6

1. Brent S. Salter, *Negotiating Copyright in the American Theatre: 1856–1951* (Cambridge University Press, 2021).

2. Anthea Kraut, *Choreographing Copyright: Race, Gender, and Intellectual Property Rights in American Dance*, illustrated edition (Oxford University Press, 2015).

3. Salter, Negotiating Copyright in the American Theatre, 67.

4. Samuel French Ltd., *Truly Yours: One Hundred and Fifty Years of Play Publishing & Service to the Theatre* (French, 1980), 1.

5. Samuel French Ltd., 1.

6. Samuel French Ltd., 1.

7. Samuel French Ltd., 1.

8. Samuel French Ltd., 1.

9. Derek Miller, *Copyright and the Value of Performance, 1770–1911* (Cambridge University Press, 2018), 195.

10. Miller, 197.

11. Miller, 200.

12. *Truly Yours* mistakenly dates the interview to July 19,1875, before *The Sketch* started publication.

13. "A Chat with Mr. Samuel French," *The Sketch: A Journal of Art and Actuality*, June 19, 1895, 434.

14. "A Chat," 434.

15. "A Chat," 434.

16. Samuel French Ltd., *Truly Yours*, 26.

17. Samuel French Ltd., 26.

18. Samuel French Ltd., 26.

19. Samuel French Ltd., 27.

20. Samuel French Ltd., 28.

21. Samuel French Ltd., 28.

22. Samuel French Ltd., 28.

23. See, for instance, Alan Menken, *Kurt Vonnegut's God Bless You, Mr. Rosewater*, French's Musical Library (S. French, 1980), 2.

24. George Middleton, *The Dramatists' Guild, What It Is and Does, How It Happened and Why*, 5th ed. (Dramatists' Guild, 1966), 27.

25. "Music Libraries End 30-Year War," *The New York Times*, January 11, 1925. https://www.nytimes.com/1925/01/11/archives/music-libraries-end-30year-war-tams-and-witmark-consolidate-opera.html (accessed June 21, 2023).

26. "Music Libraries End 30-Year War."

27. "TAMS—WITMARK MUSIC LIBRARY, INC.," September 17, 2013, https://web.archive.org/web/20130917053917/http://www.tamswitmark.com/latestnews.html.

28. "TAMS—WITMARK MUSIC LIBRARY, INC."

29. "The Rodgers and Hammerstein Organization," February 2, 1999, https://web.archive.org/web/19990202175810fw_/http://rnh.com/theatre/index.html.

30. Ted Chapin, who served as president of Rodgers and Hammerstein Organization from 1981 to 2021, remembers that the decision to reprint the libretti had been made before the purchase of the company by Imagem.

31. Theodore S. Chapin, interview by Doug Reside with Theodore S. Chapin, April 24, 2022.

32. Chapin.

33. Arianne Johnson Quinn, *British and American Musical Theatre Exchanges in the West End (1920–1970): The "Americanization" of Drury Lane* (Palgrave Macmillan, forthcoming).

34. Chapin, interview by Doug Reside with Theodore S. Chapin.

35. An archival video recording was also made of the London production of *South Pacific*, but before the age of YouTube, access was extremely limited, and there is little evidence it was used for later productions.

36. Kara Anne Gardner, *Agnes de Mille: Telling Stories in Broadway Dance*, 1st ed. (Oxford University Press, 2016), 188.

37. Chapin, interview by Doug Reside with Theodore S. Chapin.

38. "About Us," Music Theatre International, August 13, 2014, https://www.mtishows.com/about.

39. Chapin, interview by Doug Reside with Theodore S. Chapin.

40. Karl Gallmeyer, interview by Doug Reside with Karl Gallmeyer, December 13, 2019.

41. Library conservator Melina Avery describes the process, and the instability of the documents created with it, in the 2012 edition of *The Book and Paper Annual* ("Ozalids in the Music Library: Life Before Xerox," 31 [2012]: 7).

42. The process by which a full orchestral score is copied into different books of parts for the individual instruments.

43. "Requiem," Local 802 AFM, October 29, 2019, https://www.local802afm.org/allegro/articles/requeim-november-2019/.

44. Fleagle's stamp was identified by orchestrator Larry Blank via a Facebook message (March 27, 2022).

45. Gallmeyer, interview by Doug Reside with Karl Gallmeyer.

46. Gallmeyer.

47. Erin Schreiner has written a detailed history of the company in an essay written for Medium.com that provides additional background on Jean M. Shepard (Erin Schreiner, "The Small Script-Copying Service That Powered NYC Entertainment for Decades," *Atlas Obscura*, http://www.atlasobscura.com/articles/studio-duplicating-service-script-copying).

48. Grey Shepard, interview by Doug Reside with Grey Shepard, April 1, 2022.

49. Shepard.

50. Joseph Sicari, interview by Doug Reside with Joseph Sicari, April 9, 2022.

51. Shepard, interview by Doug Reside with Grey Shepard.

52. Sicari, interview by Doug Reside with Joseph Sicari.

53. Sicari.

54. Sicari.

55. Sicari.

56. Gallmeyer, interview by Doug Reside with Karl Gallmeyer.

57. Gallmeyer.

58. Gallmeyer.

59. "Theatrical Resources: Music Theatre International—MTI—Musical Theatre," November 26, 2005, https://web.archive.org/web/20051126215415/http://www.mtishows.com/resources.asp.

60. Music Theatre International Catalog, 1994.

61. Music Theatre International Catalog.

62. Apple's early outreach to schools with significant educational discounts in the 1980s and 1990s meant many educational theatre programs were more likely to have Macs than PCs. MTI did not abandon the PC market, though, and in 1999 released a Windows 95 version of the RehearScore that could play the MIDI files through the PC itself (without the need to connect the computer to an external keyboard).

63. "REHEARSCORE," February 15, 1997, https://web.archive.org/web/19970215064240/http://www.mtishows.com/resources/rehrscr.htm.

64. "OrchEXTRA: Music Theatre International—MTI—Musical Theatre," May 8, 2003, https://web.archive.org/web/20030508185348/http://www.mtishows.com/resource_OrchEXTRA.asp.

65. "OrchEXTRA."

66. "OrchEXTRA: Music Theatre International—MTI—Musical Theatre," August 21, 2008, https://web.archive.org/web/20080821110444/http://mtishows.com/resource_OrchEXTRA.asp.

67. jameson, "Fill|Harmonic," *Right on Cue Services* (blog), accessed July 4, 2022, https://rightoncueservices.com/products/fill-harmonic/.

68. Jesse Green, "DO RE MI . . . Q W E R T Y?," *Tampa Bay Times*, August 25, 2007, https://www.tampabay.com/archive/2007/04/15/do-re-mi-q-w-e-r-t-y/ (accessed June 21, 2023).

69. Suzy Evans, "The Man behind the 'Hamilton' Sound: Hidden Beatles References, the 'Hip-Hop Horse' Sample and Why If 'It's All Computerized, There's No Heart to It,'" *Salon*, November 28, 2015, https://www.salon.com/2015/11/27/the_man_behind_the_hamilton_sound_hidden_beatles_references_the_hip_hop_horse_sample_and_why_if_its_all_computerized_theres_no_heart_to_it/ (accessed June 21, 2023).

70. "The MTI Theatrical Resources—Production Slides," August 19, 2000, https://web.archive.org/web/20000819151816/http://www.mtishows.com/resources-slides.htm.

71. "Annie—Digital Scenery and Resources," accessed April 18, 2022, https://www.broadwaymedia.com/category/annie.

72. Those wishing to read more about the history of intellectual property protections for choreographers are directed to Anthea Kraut's *Choreographing Copyright: Race, Gender, and Intellectual Property Rights in American Dance* (Oxford University Press, 2016).

73. Andrew Gans and Zachary Pincus-Roth, "Akron Urinetown Lawsuit Settled," *Playbill*, July 2, 2008, https://playbill.com/article/akron-urinetown-lawsuit-settled-com-151350 (accessed June 21, 2023).

74. Jessica Hillman, "Tradition or Travesty? Radical Reinterpretations of the Musical Theatre Canon," *Theatre Topics* 20, no. 1 (2010): 1–10.

75. Hillman.

Chapter 7

1. Tyler Nagata, "World of Warcraft Video Contest," gamesradar, March 1, 2007, https://www.gamesradar.com/world-of-warcraft-video-contest/(accessed June 21, 2023).

2. Emily Rella, "'Everyone Deserves a Chance to Fly': Family Puts on Sky-High Performances of 'Wicked' for Neighbors," accessed March 20, 2021, https://www.aol.com/news/family-puts-on-performances-wicked-for-neighbors-143430398.html.

3. *Hamilton Cast Zoom Surprise: Some Good News with John Krasinski (Ep. 2)*, 2020, https://www.youtube.com/watch?v=oilZ1hNZPRM&list=PL_7yEns96WJN5JtKJIL7Kw2_HUuiTjPdq&index=8.

4. Trilby Beresford, "Broadway on Demand Streaming Service to Launch in May," *Billboard*, April 16, 2020, https://www.billboard.com/articles/news/broadway/9360213/broadway-on-demand-streaming-service/.

5. "Amour in New York at Art Lab and ShowTown Productions 2021," BroadwayWorld. com, accessed April 25, 2021, https://www.broadwayworld.com/regional/Amour-2811802.

6. "Are We Allowed to Make an Archival Recording of a Past Production Available for Streaming or Online Viewing?—Concord Theatricals Help," accessed July 5, 2022, https://help.concordtheatricals.com/knowledgebase/are-we-allowed-to-make-an-archival-recording-of-a-past-production-available-for-streaming-or-online-viewing/.

7. On October 31, 2020, the musicals available from MTI for "Remote Performance" were: *Annie, Annie Jr., Annie kids, Annie Warbucks, Band Geeks, Band Geeks* (expanded cast), *Disney's Beauty and the Beast Jr., Captain Louie, Captain Louie Jr., Daddy Long Legs, The Drowsy Chaperone, Edges, Elephant & Piggie's: We Are In A Play!, Ernest in Love, Fame, Fame Jr., Disney's Frozen Kids, A Gentleman's Guide to Love and Murder, Hello! My Baby, High School Musical Jr., HONK!, HONK! Jr., Jane Eyre: A Musical Drama, A Killer Party, Knuffle Bunny: A Cautionary Musical, The Last Five Years, Les Misérables School Edition, Disney's The Little Mermaid Jr., A Little Princess, Little Women, Meredith Willson's Miracle on 34th Street: The Musical, Naked Mole Gets Dressed: The Rock Experience, The Pajama Game, School House Rock Live!, School House Rock Live! Jr., School House Rock Live! Too., Singin' in the Rain, Singing in the Rain Jr., Something Rotten, Spookley the Square Pumpkin: The Musical, Spring Awakening, The Story of My Life, The Theory of Relativity, Urinetown, Violet, Winnie the Pooh Kids,* and *Wonderland High.* (https://www.mtishows.com/remote-performance-rights)

8. "Best College Theater | The Princeton Review," accessed April 3, 2021, https://www.princetonreview.com/college-rankings?rankings=best-college-theater.

9. "Statement," We See You W.A.T., accessed April 10, 2021, https://www.weseeyouwat.com/statement.

10. Felicia Fitzpatrick, "How the Viral Grocery Store: A New Musical Was Built Through TikTok Collaborations," *Playbill*, October 7, 2020, http://www.playbill.com/article/how-the-viral-grocery-store-a-new-musical-was-built-through-tiktok-collaborations (accessed June 21, 2023).

11. Isabel Keane, "'Ratatouille' Musical: Westchester Teacher's TikTok Creation Goes Viral," *The Journal News*, January 4, 2021, https://www.lohud.com/story/entertainment/2021/01/04/viral-tiktok-westchester-teacher-emily-jacobsen-ratatouille-musical/4125979001/ (accessed April 10, 2021).

12. Keane.

13. Alexandra Del Rosario and Alexandra Del Rosario, "'Ratatouille: The TikTok Musical' Raises $2M To Become Actors Fund's Most Successful Fundraiser—Update," *Deadline* (blog), January 12, 2021, https://deadline.com/2021/01/ratatouille-the-tiktok-musical-raise-million-the-actors-fund-1234664043/(accessed June 21, 2023).

14. *TiQ / I Am Sending You the Sacred Face*, 2020, https://www.youtube.com/watch?v=T9jGmhHFO6o.

15. "Tempest – Tender Claws," accessed June 21, 2023, https://tenderclaws.com/tempest.

Bibliography

Allan, Sidney. "Byron: 'The Stage Is My Studio.'" *Wilson's Photographic Magazine*, 1907.

"Annie—Digital Scenery and Resources." Accessed April 18, 2022. https://www.broadw aymedia.com/category/annie.

Avery, Melina. "Ozalids in the Music Library: Life Before Xerox." *The Book and Paper Group Annual* 31 (2012): 7.

Baker, Thomas. "Transformation Polka." *Levy Music Collection*. Accessed July 3, 2022. https://levysheetmusic.mse.jhu.edu/collection/186/060.

Barras, Charles M. *The Black Crook: An Original Magical and Spectacular Drama in Four Acts*. Buffalo: Rockwell, Baker & Hill, 1866.

Barras, Charles M. *The Black Crook: An Original Magical and Spectacular Drama in Four Acts*. Chicago: Rounds & James, Printers, 1867.

Barrios, Richard. *A Song in the Dark: The Birth of the Musical Film*. Electronic resource. 2nd edition. Oxford, New York: Oxford University Press, 2010. http://TM9QT7LG9G. search.serialssolutions.com/?V=1.0&L=TM9QT7LG9G&S=JCs&C=TC0000370 615&T=marc&tab=BOOKS.

Barthes, Roland. *Image-Music-Text*. Macmillan, 1977.

Battaglio, Stephen and Cathy Dunkley. "Lloyd-Webber Ticketed for Vids." Back Stage, August 8, 1997, 3, 36.

Behr, Edward. The *Complete Book of Les Misérables*. New York: Arcade Pub, 1989.

Behr, Edward. *Les Misérables: History in the Making*. Cape, 1989.

Behr, Edward, and Mark Steyn. *The Story of Miss Saigon*. New York: Arcade Pub, 1991.

Bennett, Brad. Interview by Doug Reside with Brad Bennett, January 30, 2022.

Beresford, Trilby. "Broadway on Demand Streaming Service to Launch in May." *Billboard*, April 16, 2020. https://www.billboard.com/articles/news/broadway/9360213/broad way-on-demand-streaming-service/ (Accessed April 25, 2021).

Bickwell, G., and T. Kennick. "You Naughty, Naughty Men." *Levy Music Collection*. Accessed July 3, 2022. https://levysheetmusic.mse.jhu.edu/collection/053/103.

"Big Biz in Books from the Boards." *The Publishers Weekly* 164, no. 8 (August 22, 1953).

Bittler, Christian. "Les Misérables Interactive." TDK Collection, 1997.

Blitzstein, Marc. *The Cradle Will Rock*. New York: Random House, 1938.

Block, Geoffrey. *Enchanted Evenings: The Broadway Musical from "Show Boat" to Sondheim and Lloyd Webber*. Oxford University Press, 2009.

Boots, Max. Interview by Doug Reside with Max Boots, February 1, 2021.

Bowersox, A. I. "Photographers at Home and Abroad." *American Journal of Photography* 15, no. 176 (August 1894): 343–48.

The British Journal of Photography 30, no. 1206 (June 15, 1883): 330.

"Broadway Posters." February 2, 1998. https://web.archive.org/web/19980202074104fw_/ http://www.digitas.harvard.edu/~note/poster.html.

Broadway Trades. "Good/Bad Traders." Accessed July 3, 2022. http://tradebway.weebly. com/goodbad-traders.html.

BroadwayWorld.com. "Amour in New York at Art Lab and ShowTown Productions 2021." Accessed April 25, 2021. https://www.broadwayworld.com/regional/Amour-2811802.

Brooker, Peter, and Andrew Thacker. *The Oxford Critical and Cultural History of Modernist Magazines: Volume II: North America 1894–1960*. New York: Oxford University Press, 2009.

Brunner, Lance W. "The Orchestra and Recorded Sound." In *The Orchestra: A Collection of 23 Essays on Its Origins and Transformations*, edited by Joan Peyser. Milwaukee, WI: Hal Leonard, 2006.

Buckingham, David, Rebekah Willett, and and Maria Pini. "Home Truths?: Video Production and Domestic Life." *Technologies of the Imagination*, 2011. https://doi.org/10.3998/toi.9362787.0001.001.

Candee, Marjorie Dent, ed. *Current Biography: Who's News and Why 1954*. Current Biography. New York: H.W. Wilson, 1954. http://archive.org/details/currentbiography1954thom.

Carter, Tim. *Oklahoma!: The Making of an American Musical*. Illustrated edition. New Haven, CT: Yale University Press, 2007.

Chapin, Theodore S. Interview by Doug Reside with Theodore S. Chapin, April 24, 2022.

Charnin, Martin. *Annie: A Theatre Memoir*. 1st edition. New York: Dutton, 1977.

Cendrowski, Mark, dir., *The Big Bang Theory*. Season 12, Episode 10, "The VCR Illumination." December 6, 2018, on CBS.

Comden, Betty, and Adolph Green. *The New York Musicals of Comden and Green*. New York; London: Applause, 1999.

Concord Theatricals. "Are We Allowed to Make an Archival Recording of a Past Production Available for Streaming or Online Viewing?—Concord Theatricals Help." Accessed July 5, 2022. https://help.concordtheatricals.com/knowledgebase/are-we-allowed-to-make-an-archival-recording-of-a-past-production-available-for-streaming-or-online-viewing/.

Crowther, Bosley. "A Leaf-Not Leap-Through the Playbill," *The New York Times*, April 11, 1937. https://www.nytimes.com/1937/04/11/archives/a-leafnot-leapthrough-the-playbill-leafing-through-the-playbi.html (Accessed June 21, 2023).

Deady, Matthew P. *Reports of Cases Determined in the Circuit and District Courts of the United States of Oregon and California*. A.L. Bancroft and Company, 1872.

Doby, Kathyrn. Interview by Doug Reside with Kathyrn Doby, September 21, 2020.

Dolby, George. *Charles Dickens As I Knew Him: The Story of the Reading Tours in Great Britain and America*. Lume Books, 2016.

Downes, Olin. "Disks of Yesteryear." *The New York Times*, March 6, 1938, https://timesmachine.nytimes.com/timesmachine/1938/03/06/578432772.html?pageNumber=155 (Accessed June 21, 2023).

Duggan, Mary K. "Early Music Printing and Ecclesiastical Patronage." In *Early Music Printing in German-Speaking Lands*, ed. Andrea Lindmayr-Brandl, Elisabeth Giselbrecht and Grantley McDonald. New York: Routledge, 2018.

Ettlingler, Doris. "For Many, TV Tape Means Watching More and Loving It." *The New York Times*, August 27, 1977. https://www.nytimes.com/1977/08/27/archives/for-many-tv-tape-means-watching-more-and-loving-it.html (Accessed June 21, 2023).

Evans, Suzy. "The Man behind the 'Hamilton' Sound: Hidden Beatles References, the 'Hip-Hop Horse' Sample and Why If 'It's All Computerized, There's No Heart to It.'" *Salon*, November 28, 2015. https://www.salon.com/2015/11/27/the_man_behind_

the_hamilton_sound_hidden_beatles_references_the_hip_hop_horse_sample_and_ why_if_its_all_computerized_theres_no_heart_to_it/ (Accessed June 21, 2023).

"Everything Broadway, Everything Musical—Encora." Accessed July 3, 2022. https://enc ora-archive.github.io/encora.one/index.html.

"FAQ—Theater Trades." August 28, 2018. https://web.archive.org/web/20180828183237/ http://theatertrades.weebly.com/faq.html.

"Fill|Harmonic." *Right on Cue Services* (blog). Accessed July 4, 2022. https://rightoncues ervices.com/products/fill-harmonic/.

Fisher, Barbara E. Scott "Evening Project of Brineys Becomes 'Fireside Theater': 'We Put Our Hearts Into It.'" *The Christian Science Monitor (1908–)*, December 14, 1951, sec. Women Today.

Fitzpatrick, Felicia. "How the Viral Grocery Store: A New Musical Was Built Through TikTok Collaborations." *Playbill*, October 7, 2020. http://www.playbill.com/article/ how-the-viral-grocery-store-a-new-musical-was-built-through-tiktok-collaborations (Accessed June 21, 2023).

Fosse, Bob. "Letter from Bob Fosse to David Sheehan and Hillard Elkins." July 10, 1981.

Fosse, Bob. "Letter to the Cast and Crew of Pippin." November 23, 1981.

Frankly, Frank. Interview by Doug Reside with "Frank." February 6, 2021.

Gallmeyer, Karl. Interview by Doug Reside with Karl Gallmeyer, December 13, 2019.

Gans, Andrew, and Zachary Pincus-Roth. "Akron Urinetown Lawsuit Settled." *Playbill*. July 2, 2008. https://playbill.com/article/akron-urinetown-lawsuit-settled-com-151 350 (Accessed July 4, 2022).

Gänzl, Kurt, Clive Barda, Jane Rice, and Andrew Lloyd Webber. *The Complete Aspects of Love*. New York: Viking Studio Books, 1990.

Gardner, Kara Anne. *Agnes de Mille: Telling Stories in Broadway Dance*. 1st edition. New York: Oxford University Press, 2016.

Genius. "Dave Malloy." Accessed June 19, 2022. https://genius.com/artists/Dave-malloy.

Genius. "Lin-Manuel Miranda." Accessed June 19, 2022. https://genius.com/artists/Lin-manuel-miranda.

Gerard, Jeremy. "Live-Streamed 'Daddy Long Legs' Brought 150K Viewers to Off-Broadway for Free." *Deadline* (blog), December 22, 2015. https://deadline.com/2015/ 12/live-stream-daddy-long-legs-brought-150k-viewers-off-broadway-1201671199/ (Accessed June 21, 2023).

Gershwin, George, DuBose Heyward, Ira Gershwin, and Dorothy Heyward. *Porgy and Bess: An Opera in Three Acts*. Limited edition. New York: Random House, 1935.

Gioia, Michael, and Blake Ross. "Hamilton Will Be Filmed; Mixtape and Documentary Released This Fall." *Playbill*, June 16, 2016. https://playbill.com/article/hamilton-will-be-filmed-mixtape-and-documentary-released-this-fall (Accessed June 21, 2023).

"Gilbert Interviews—The Tendency of the Modern Stage." Accessed October 23, 2021. https://www.gsarchive.net/gilbert/interviews/mod_stage.html.

Golovanov, Dmitry. "Transformation of Authors' Rights and Neighbouring Rights in Russia." *IRIS Plus, Legal Observations of the European Audiovisual Observatory*, 2008.

Green, Jesse. "DO RE MI . . . Q W E R T Y?" *Tampa Bay Times*, August 25, 2007. https:// www.tampabay.com/archive/2007/04/15/do-re-mi-q-w-e-r-t-y/ (Accessed April 18, 2022).

Guare, John. *Two Gentlemen of Verona: A Re-creation, Complete with Pictures and Sheet Music*. 1st edition. New York: Holt, Rinehart & Winston, 1973.

Halloran, Richard. "TV 'Oh! Calcutta!' Leads to Charges," *The New York Times*, May 20, 1971.   https://www.nytimes.com/1971/05/20/archives/tv-oh-calcutta-leads-to-charges-obscenity-indictments-are-returned.html (Accessed June 21, 2023).

Harrison, Dale. "Dale Harrison's New York." *The Bristol Herald Courier, Bristol Virginia-Tennessee*, May 18, 1938.

Harsh, Edward, and Jürgen Selk. "Guide for Volume Editors of the Kurt Weill Edition." 2002. https://www.kwf.org/media/edguide.pdf.

Haun, Harry. "Cable Connection: A New Broadway?" *Daily News (New York)*, August 13, 1982.

Hausam, Wiley, ed. *The New American Musical: An Anthology from the End of the Century.* 1st edition. New York: Theatre Communications Group, 2003.

Healy, Patrick. "An Outsider Gets a Nicer Date for the Prom." *The New York Times*, February 2, 2012, sec. Theater. https://www.nytimes.com/2012/02/05/theater/carrie-a-huge-stage-flop-is-reinvented-by-mcc-theater.html (Accessed June 21, 2023).

Hearn, Michael Patrick. *The Art of the Broadway Poster.* New York: Ballantine Books, 1980.

"Historic Arthur Sullivan Recordings." Accessed October 9, 2021. https://web.archive.org/web/20211009135732/https://www.gsarchive.net/sullivan/html/historic.html.

Hillman, Jessica. "Tradition or Travesty? Radical Reinterpretations of the Musical Theatre Canon." *Theatre Topics* 20, no. 1 (2010): 1–10.

Holmes, Thom. *The Routledge Guide to Music Technology.* 1st edition. New York: Routledge, 2006.

Horowitz, Mark Eden. *Sondheim on Music: Minor Details and Major Decisions.* 2nd edition. Lanham, MD: Scarecrow Press, 2010.

Horwitz, Simi. "Stage and Screen Closes the Book . . . And Its Doors." *Backstage*, May 14, 2003. https://www.backstage.com/magazine/article/stage-screen-closes-book-doors-19643/ (Accessed June 21, 2023).

Hoskins, Vicki. "Playbill Takes the Stage: The Rise of America's Foremost Theatrical Program." Dissertation, University of Pittsburgh, 2020.

"How to Start Trading—Theater Trades." August 19, 2018. https://web.archive.org/web/20180819143221/http://theatertrades.weebly.com/how-to-start-trading.html.

Hughes, Terry. Interview by Doug Reside with Terry Hughes, September 14, 2020.

Hummel, David. *Collector's Guide to the American Musical Theatre.* Metuchen, NJ: Scarecrow Press, Incorporated, 1984. https://www.biblio.com/book/collectors-guide-american-musical-theatre-david/d/1444995790.

Hummler, Richard. "Cable-Television: Legit Cable Hopes Didn't Pan Out, But Showtime Likes 'B'way' Series; HBO Wants More Original Dramas." In *Variety (Archive: 1905–2000).* Los Angeles, CA: Penske Business Corporation, May 29, 1985.

Hunter, Nigel. "And Now For Something Really Useful . . ." *Billboard*, October 19, 1996.

Interview with Harold Prince: Raw Footage. September 9, 2003. NCOX 2167. Theatre on Film and Tape Archive. Billy Rose Theatre Division. New York Public Library for the Performing Arts, New York, NY.

Jaillant, Lise. "Canonical in the 1930s: Willa Cather's 'Death Comes for the Archbishop' in the Modern Library Series." *Studies in the Novel* 45, no. 3 (2013): 476–99.

Jones, John Bush. *Our Musicals, Ourselves: A Social History of the American Musical Theatre.* Waltham: Brandeis University Press, 2011.

Jones, Kenneth. "Trim for the New Year: Broadway Les Miz Now Runs 2 Hours 58 Minutes." *Playbill.* December 13, 2000. https://www.playbill.com/article/

trim-for-the-new-year-broadway-les-miz-now-runs-2-hours-58-minutes-com-93804 (Accessed July 2, 2022).

Kaplan, James. "Is Stephen Sondheim God?" *New York Magazine* 27, no. 14 (April 4, 1994).

Keane, Isabel. "'Ratatouille' Musical: Westchester Teacher's TikTok Creation Goes Viral." *The Journal News*. January 4, 2021. https://www.lohud.com/story/entertainment/2021/01/04/viral-tiktok-westchester-teacher-emily-jacobsen-ratatouille-musical/4125979001/ (Accessed April 10, 2021).

Kessler, Kelly. *Broadway in the Box: Television's Lasting Love Affair with the Musical.* Oxford University Press, 2020.

Kirle, Bruce. *Unfinished Show Business: Broadway Musicals as Works-in-Process.* Theater in the Americas. Carbondale: Southern Illinois University Press, 2005.

Klein, Howard. "Take the Case of Magda Olivero; Take the Case of Magda Olivero." *New York Times*, November 28, 1971. http://timesmachine.nytimes.com/timesmachine/1971/11/28/82218406.html (Accessed February 14, 2021).

Kozinn, Allan. "A Music Lovers' Mecca Is Closing." *The New York Times*, November 7, 1990. https://www.nytimes.com/1990/11/07/arts/a-music-lovers-mecca-is-closing.html (Accessed June 21, 2023).

Krasinski, John, et al. *Hamilton Cast Zoom Surprise: Some Good News with John Krasinski*, episode 2, 2020. https://www.youtube.com/watch?v=oilZ1hNZPRM&list=PL_7yEns96WJN5JtKJIL7Kw2_HUuiTjPdq&index=8.

Kraut, Anthea. *Choreographing Copyright: Race, Gender, and Intellectual Property Rights in American Dance.* Illustrated edition. Oxford, New York: Oxford University Press, 2015.

Kreuger, Miles. *Show Boat, the Story of a Classic American Musical.* Oxford University Press, 1977.

"Kyd's Spanish Tragedy, 1615 | The British Library." Accessed June 18, 2022. https://www.bl.uk/collection-items/kyds-spanish-tragedy-1615.

Lamb, Andrew. *Leslie Stuart: Composer of Florodora.* Routledge, 2020.

Larson, Jonathan, Evelyn McDonnell, Kathy Silberger, Larry Fink, Stewart Ferebee, and Kate Giel. *Rent.* New York: Rob Weisbach Books: William Morrow and Co., 1997.

Laurents, Arthur, Leonard Bernstein, and Stephen Sondheim. *West Side Story.* Licensed Libretto Vocal Book. Music Theatre International, 1958.

Lee, Ashley. "'We Need to Talk about the Money': Leslie Odom Jr.'s 'Hamilton' Duels, Onstage and Off." *Los Angeles Times*, June 25, 2020. https://www.latimes.com/entertainment-arts/movies/story/2020-06-25/leslie-odom-jr-hamilton-disney-aaron-burr (Accessed June 21, 2023).

Les Misérables—The Dream Cast in Concert. VHS. Directed by John Caird and Gavin Taylor. Columbia/Tristar Studios, 1996.

"The Les Miserables Home Page." July 11, 1997. https://web.archive.org/web/19970711003830/http://www.ot.com/lesmis/.

"Librarian." *New Yorker*, December 28, 1935.

Library of America. "About | Library of America." Accessed June 11, 2022. https://www.loa.org/about.

LII / Legal Information Institute. "17 U.S. Code § 101—Definitions." Accessed July 7, 2021. https://www.law.cornell.edu/uscode/text/17/101.

Lindsay, Howard, and Oscar Hammerstein II. *The Sound of Music: Perusal Libretto.* Perusal copy. New York: Concord, 2010.

Lloyd Webber, Andrew, John Napier, and T. S. Eliot. *Cats: The Book of the Musical: Based on Old Possum's Book of Practical Cats by T.S. Eliot.* 1st edition. A Harvest/HBJ Book. San Diego: Harcourt Brace Jovanovich, 1983.

Local 802 AFM. "Requiem." Accessed June 21, 2023. https://www.local802afm.org/alle gro/articles/requeim-november-2019/.

"Logos and Clipart Available Anywhere?" Accessed April 21, 2022. https://groups.google. com/g/rec.arts.theatre.musicals/c/UC1PQ1agpRM/m/cfucLj9UhmkJ?pli=1.

Louie, Uncle. Interview by Doug Reside with Uncle Louie, February 6, 2021.

Lovell. David B. "Tales from the Collection: A Cinematic Wilde Goose Chase." *The Lovell Collection* (blog), March 25, 2021. https://thelovellcollection.wordpress.com/2021/ 03/25/tales-from-the-collection-a-cinematic-wilde-goose-chase/ (Accessed June 21, 2023).

Lux, Lester. Interview by Doug Reside with Lester Lux, February 1, 2021.

Lyons, Luisa. "Show Girl." *FILMED LIVE MUSICALS.* Accessed January 28, 2023. https:// www.filmedlivemusicals.com/show-girl.html.

Lyons, Luisa. "Sophisticated Ladies." *FILMED LIVE MUSICALS.* Accessed January 28, 2023. https://www.filmedlivemusicals.com/sophisticated-ladies.html.

MacDonald, Laura. "Connection in an Isolating Age: Looking Back on Twenty Years of Engaging Audiences and Marketing Musical Theatre Online." in *iBroadway: Musical Theatre in the Digital Age,* edited by Jessica Hillman-McCord. Palgrave Macmillan, 2017.

Mandelbaum, Ken. "Ken Mandelbaum's MUSICALS ON DISC: Video Bundles From Britain." *Playbill,* July 26, 1998. https://playbill.com/article/ken-mandelbaums-music als-on-disc-video-bundles-from-britain-com-76632 (Accessed April 22, 2022).

Mandelbaum, Ken. *Not Since Carrie: Forty Years of Broadway Musical Flops.* St. Martin's Publishing Group, 1992.

Maslon, Laurence. *American Musicals: The Complete Books and Lyrics of Sixteen Broadway Classics: A Library of America Boxed Set.* Box Har/Cr edition. New York: Library of America, 2014.

Maslon, Laurence. *Broadway to Main Street: How Show Tunes Enchanted America.* New York: Oxford University Press, 2018.

Maslon, Laurence. "Curtain Up! Get the Rights!" *Slate,* October 31, 2014. https://slate. com/culture/2014/10/what-are-the-best-musicals-of-broadways-golden-age-behind- the-library-of-america-selections.html (Accessed June 23, 2023).

Maslon, Laurence. "How 'Oklahoma!' Revolutionized the Cast Album." *The New York Times,* July 10, 2019, sec. Theater. https://www.nytimes.com/2019/07/10/theater/oklah oma-cast-album.html (Accessed June 21, 2023).

"Matrix Numbers in Recordings of Gilbert and Sullivan." Accessed April 22, 2022. http:// gasdisc.oakapplepress.com/matrix4.htm.

McBride, Murdoch. "Broadway Digital Entertainment Relaunches 'Archive' Site May 8 | Playbill." *Playbill,* May 25, 2000. https://www.playbill.com/article/broadway-digital- entertainment-relaunches-archive-site-may-8-com-89462 (Accessed June 21, 2023).

mcclung, bruce d. *Lady in the Dark: Biography of a Musical.* 1st edition. New York: Oxford University Press, 2006.

McCullaugh, Jim. "General News: Videocassette Music Growth Slow, Steady." In *Billboard (Archive: 1963–2000).* New York: P-MRC, August 15, 1981.

McCullaugh, Jim. "General News: Video Music Software Flexes Muscles At CES; More Due." In *Billboard (Archive: 1963–2000).* New York: P-MRC, January 30, 1982.

McLellan, Joseph. "A 'Miz' Not to Miss." *Washington Post*, March 6, 1996. https://www.was hingtonpost.com/archive/lifestyle/1996/03/06/a-miz-not-to-miss/7290ed79-f749-47a0-987f-a9449c9dfed4/ (Accessed June 21, 2023).

Menken, Alan. *Kurt Vonnegut's God Bless You, Mr. Rosewater.* French's Musical Library. New York: S. French, 1980.

Middleton, George. *The Dramatists' Guild, What It Is and Does, How It Happened and Why.* 5th edition. New York: Dramatists' Guild, 1966.

"Mikrofon Unterm Schlips." *Der Spiegel* 48 (1951). Accessed February 13, 2021. https://www.spiegel.de/spiegel/print/d-20804174.html.

Miller, Derek. *Copyright and the Value of Performance, 1770–1911.* Cambridge University Press, 2018.

Miranda, Lin-Manuel, Quiara Alegría Hudes, and Jeremy McCarter. *In the Heights: Finding Home.* New York: Random House, 2021.

Miranda, Lin-Manuel, and Jeremy McCarter. *Hamilton: The Revolution.* Boston: Little, Brown Book Group, 2016.

Monush, Barry. *The Sound of Music FAQ: All That's Left to Know About Maria, the von Trapps and Our Favorite Things.* Rowman & Littlefield, 2015.

"Music Libraries End 30-Year War." *New York Times*, January 11, 1925.

Music Theatre International. "About Us." August 13, 2014. https://www.mtishows.com/about.

Music Theatre International. "The MTI Theatrical Resources—Production Slides." August 19, 2000. https://web.archive.org/web/20000819151816/http://www.mtishows.com/resources-slides.htm.

Music Theatre International. *Music Theatre International Catalog.* 1994.

Music Theatre International. "OrchEXTRA: Music Theatre International—MTI—Musical Theatre." May 8, 2003. https://web.archive.org/web/20030508185348/http://www.mtishows.com/resource_OrchEXTRA.asp.

Music Theatre International. "REHEARSCORE." February 15, 1997. https://web.archive.org/web/19970215064240/http://www.mtishows.com/resources/rehrscr.htm.

Music Theatre International. "Theatrical Resources: Music Theatre International—MTI—Musical Theatre." November 26, 2005. https://web.archive.org/web/2005112 6215415/http://www.mtishows.com/resources.asp.

"My Masters/Expected Masters—Phantom Of Broadway." June 25, 2014. https://web.arch ive.org/web/20140625180848/http://phantomofbroadway.weebly.com/my-masterse xpected-masters.html.

Nadworny, Elissa. "The Most Popular High School Plays And Musicals." *NPR*, July 30, 2020, sec. K–12. https://www.npr.org/sections/ed/2019/07/31/427138970/the-most-popular-high-school-plays-and-musicals.

Nagata, Tyler. "World of Warcraft Video Contest." gamesradar. Accessed January 1, 2021. https://www.gamesradar.com/world-of-warcraft-video-contest/.

Nathan, George Jean. *The Theatre in the Fifties.* New York: Alfred A. Knopf, 1953.

Nathan, George Jean. Foreword to Of Thee I Sing, by George Kaufman, Maurie Ryskind, and Ira Gershwin. A. Knopf, 1932, 4th printing.

The New York Times. "Musical Play Gets The Pulitzer Award; Mrs. Buck, Pershing, Duranty Honored." May 3, 1932. https://timesmachine.nytimes.com/timesmachine/1932/05/03/100729643.pdf (accessed March 24, 2019).

Oklahoma!. Advertisement, *The New York Times*, March 28, 1943. https://timesmachine.nytimes.com/timesmachine/1943/03/28/issue.html (accessed June 21, 2023).

O'Connor, John J. "TV: 'Most Happy Fella' and 'Beyond Westworld.'" *The New York Times*, March 5, 1980. https://www.nytimes.com/1980/03/05/archives/tv-most-happy-fella-and-beyond-westworld.html (Accessed June 21, 2023).

"Only WEBCOR Records in Both Directions." Advertisement in *Magnetic Film and Tape Recording*, April 1954. http://thehistoryofrecording.com/Magazines/Tape%20Record ing%20Magazine/Tape-Recording-1954-04.pdf.

Pauwels, Erin. *Acting Out: Cabinet Cards and the Making of Modern Photography*. Oakland: University of California Press, 2020.

"Paying Dearly for Opera." *New York Times*, February 14, 1884. Accessed January 18, 2021. http://timesmachine.nytimes.com/timesmachine/1884/02/14/106142485.html.

Perry, George, Jane Rice, Clive Barda, and Andrew Lloyd Webber. *The Complete Phantom of the Opera*. London: Pavilion, 1987.

Perry, George, and Andrew Lloyd Webber. *Sunset Boulevard: From Movie to Musical*. London: Pavilion Books, 1993.

Peters, Julie Stone. *Theatre of the Book, 1480–1880: Print, Text, and Performance in Europe*. New York: Oxford University Press, 2003.

Philadelphia, Jim. Interview by Doug Reside with Jim Philadelphia, January 31, 2022.

"Photographing by Electric Light." *The New York Times*, May 2, 1883.

"PHOTOGRAPHY AND THE AMERICAN STAGE | Broadway Photographs." Accessed June 18, 2022. https://broadway.cas.sc.edu/.

Pressley, Nelson. "After the Curtain Falls, the Web Gets Into the Act." August 31, 2008. http://www.washingtonpost.com/wp-dyn/content/article/2008/08/29/AR2008082900 684.html (Accessed June 21, 2023).

Prince, Harold. *Sense of Occasion*. Milwaukee, WI: Applause Theatre & Cinema Books, an imprint of Hal Leonard LLC, 2017.

Princeton Review, The. "Best College Theater." Accessed April 3, 2021. https://www.prin cetonreview.com/college-rankings?rankings=best-college-theater.

Printers' Ink. Printers' Ink Publishing Company, 1902.

Publishers. "Prologue." *Theatre Arts* 32, no. 3 (1948): 27.

Quinn, Arianne Johnson. *British and American Musical Theatre Exchanges in the West End (1920–1970): The "Americanization" of Drury Lane*. Palgrave Macmillan, Forthcoming.

"Radio-Television: RCTV Puts Final Touches On Feevee Venture With RCA." In *Variety (Archive: 1905–2000)*. Los Angeles, CA: Penske Business Corporation, October 7, 1981.

"RCA to Offer Video Disc of 'Pippin.'" Accessed April 22, 2022. https://www.cedmagic. com/museum/press/release-1981-06-01-2.html.

Rebellato, Dan. "Playwriting and Globalisation: Towards a Site-Unspecific Theatre." *Contemporary Theatre Review* 16, no. 1 (February 1, 2006): 97–113.

"Rec.Arts.Theatre.* Frequently Asked Questions (FAQ): Part 1/3." Accessed June 12, 2022. https://groups.google.com/g/rec.arts.theatre.musicals/c/8yg004zGDaI/m/ wBX3NDVXWA4J.

Rella, Emily. "'Everyone Deserves a Chance to Fly': Family Puts on Sky-High Performances of 'Wicked' for Neighbors." Accessed July 4, 2022. https://www.yahoo.com/lifestyle/ family-puts-on-performances-wicked-for-neighbors-143430398.html.

Reside, Douglas Larue. "The Advantages of Floating in the Middle of the Sea: Digital Musical Theatre Research." in *iBroadway: Musical Theatre in the Digital Age*, edited by Jessica Hillman-McCord, 261–82. Palgrave MacMillan, 2017.

Reside, Douglas Larue. "The Electronic Edition and Textual Criticism of American Musical Theatre." Dissertation, University of Kentucky, 2006.

Reside, Douglas Larue. "Music Theatre Online." Accessed August 29, 2021. https://mith.
    umd.edu/research/mto/.
Reside, Douglas Larue. "Musical of the Month: The Music of the Black Crook."
    Accessed June 18, 2022. https://www.nypl.org/blog/2011/06/16/musical-month-
    music-black-crook.
Reside, Douglas Larue. "Musical of the Month | The New York Public Library."
    Accessed August 29, 2021. https://www.nypl.org/voices/blogs/blog-channels/musi
    cal-of-the-month.
Richards, Stanley. Great Musicals of the American Theatre: Edited, with an Introd. and
    Notes on the Plays, Authors, and Composers, By Stanley Richards. 1st edition. Vol.
    2. Radnor, PA: Chilton Book Co., 1976.
Richards, Stanley, ed. Great Rock Musicals. New York: Stein and Day, 1979.
Richards, Stanley. Ten Great Musicals of the American Theatre. 1st edition. Radnor,
    PA: Chilton Book Co., 1973.
Rodgers, Richard, and Oscar Hammerstein II. 6 Plays by Rodgers and Hammerstein.
    New York: Modern Library, 1959.
Rodgers and Hammerstein Archives of Recorded Sound, The New York Public Library at
    Lincoln Center. "The Mapleson Cylinders." https://web.archive.org/web/20181219182
    148/http://digilib.nypl.org/dynaweb/millennium/mapleson.
"The Rodgers and Hammerstein Organization." Accessed July 4, 2022. https://web.arch
    ive.org/web/19990202175810fw_/http://rnh.com/theatre/index.html.
Roell, Craig H. The Piano in America, 1890–1940. Chapel Hill: University of North
    Carolina Press, 1989. http://archive.org/details/pianoinamerica1800roel.
Rooney, David. "'Carrie': Theater Review." The Hollywood Reporter (blog), March 1, 2012.
    https://www.hollywoodreporter.com/news/general-news/carrie-theater-review-296
    385/ (Accessed June 21, 2023).
Rosario, Alexandra Del, and Alexandra Del Rosario. "'Ratatouille: The TikTok Musical'
    Raises $2M To Become Actors Fund's Most Successful Fundraiser—Update." Deadline
    (blog), January 12, 2021. https://deadline.com/2021/01/ratatouille-the-tiktok-musi
    cal-raise-million-the-actors-fund-1234664043/ (Accessed June 21, 2023).
Rosenfeld, Megan. "Miles Krueger, The Musicals Man." Washington Post, March 19, 1989.
    https://www.washingtonpost.com/archive/lifestyle/style/1989/03/19/miles-kreu
    ger-the-musicals-man/96a0c951-b37c-4b45-8129-0c6a4a542904/ (Accessed   June
    21, 2023).
Sakoui, Anousha. "SAG-AFTRA and Actors Equity Are Fighting: What Is This Union
    Beef About?" Los Angeles Times, October 22, 2020. https://www.latimes.com/entert
    ainment-arts/business/story/2020-10-22/sag-aftra-actors-equity-union-fight-hollyw
    ood-pandemic (Accessed June 21, 2023).
Salmans, Sandra. "HOW A CABLE CHANNEL FLOPPED." The New York Times,
    February 28, 1983, sec. Business. https://www.nytimes.com/1983/02/28/business/
    how-a-cable-channel-flopped.html (Accessed June 21, 2023).
Salter, Brent S. Negotiating Copyright in the American Theatre: 1856–1951. Cambridge
    University Press, 2021.
Samuel French Ltd. Truly Yours: One Hundred and Fifty Years of Play Publishing and
    Service to the Theatre. London: French, 1980.
Schear, Robert. Interview by Doug Reside with Robert Schear, January 30, 2021.
Schönberg, Claude-Michel, and Alain Boublil. Les Misérables. CD, 1985.

Schönberg, Claude-Michel, and Alain Boublil. *Les Misérables*. Double Play, Dolby System, Cassette, 1985.

Schönberg, Claude-Michel, and Alain Boublil. *Les Misérables*. Vinyl, 1985.

Schreiner, Erin. "The Small Script-Copying Service That Powered NYC Entertainment for Decades." *Atlas Obscura*. http://www.atlasobscura.com/articles/studio-duplicating-service-script-copying (Accessed June 21, 2023).

Searle, Townley. *A Bibliography of Sir William Schwenck Gilbert, with Bibliographical Adventures in the Gilbert and Sullivan Operas*. New York: B. Franklin, 1968. http://arch ive.org/details/bibliographyofsi0000sear.

Senefelder, Alois. "The Project Gutenberg EBook of The Invention of Lithography." Accessed July 17, 2021. https://www.gutenberg.org/files/40924/40924-h/40924-h.htm.

Shakespeare, William. "The Bodleian First Folio." Accessed October 23, 2021. https://fir stfolio.bodleian.ox.ac.uk/book.html.

Sheehan, David. Interview by Doug Reside with David Sheehan, September 14, 2020.

Shepard, Grey. Interview by Doug Reside with Grey Shepard, April 1, 2022.

Shepherd, Marc. "The G&T 1906 Mikado." Accessed April 22, 2022. http://gasdisc.oakapp lepress.com/mik1906.htm.

Sher, Robert. Interview by Doug Reside with Robert Sher, n.d.

Shields, David S. "Charles Deforest Fredricks | Broadway Photographs." Accessed June 20, 2023. https://broadway.library.sc.edu/content/charles-deforest-fredricks.

Shields, David S. "Joseph Byron | Broadway Photographs." Accessed June 20, 2023. https:// broadway.library.sc.edu/content/joseph-byron.

Shields, David S. "Napoleon Sarony | Broadway Photographs." Accessed June 20, 2023. https://broadway.library.sc.edu/content/napoleon-sarony.

Shields, David S. *Still: American Silent Motion Picture Photography*. Chicago: University of Chicago Press, 2013.

Sicari, Joseph. Interview by Doug Reside with Joseph Sicari, April 9, 2022.

The Sketch: A Journal of Art and Actuality. "A Chat with Mr. Samuel French." June 19, 1895. https://catalog.hathitrust.org/Record/000531640.

Smil, Vaclav. *Creating the Twentieth Century: Technical Innovations of 1867–1914 and Their Lasting Impact*. Oxford University Press, 2005.

Smith, Cecil A. "The Lyric Theatre." *Theatre Arts Magazine* 31, no. 1 (January 1947): 24–26.

Smith, Cecil A., and Glenn Litton. *Musical Comedy in America: From The Black Crook to South Pacific, From The King and I to Sweeney Todd*. New York: Routledge, 2013.

Sondheim, Stephen. *Finishing the Hat: Collected Lyrics (1954–1981) with Attendant Comments, Principles, Heresies, Grudges, Whines and Anecdotes*. Illustrated edition. New York: Knopf, 2010.

Sondheim, Stephen. *Look, I Made a Hat: Collected Lyrics (1981–2011) with Attendant Comments, Amplifications, Dogmas, Harangues, Digressions, Anecdotes and Miscellany*. Illustrated edition. New York: Knopf, 2011.

Sondheim, Stephen, Burt Shevelove, Larry Gelbart, Hugh Wheeler, and James Lapine, eds. *Four by Sondheim: Wheeler, Lapine, Shevelove and Gelbart*. The Applause Musical Library. New York: Applause, 2000.

Sousa, John Philip. "Publisher and Composer on Musical Piracy." *Musical News*, 1903.

Stalter, Katharine. "Spotlight: Interactive Offers Backstage Glimpse." In *Variety (Archive: 1905–2000)*. Los Angeles, CA: Penske Business Corporation, March 10, 1997.

Stigler, Emil. "Black Crook. No. March of the Amazons." *Levy Music Collection*. Accessed July 3, 2022. https://levysheetmusic.mse.jhu.edu/collection/185/093.

Stokel-Walker, Chris. "Illicit Bootlegs on YouTube Are Giving Musicals a Second Life." Medium, December 9, 2019. https://ffwd.medium.com/illicit-bootlegs-on-youtube-are-giving-musicals-a-second-life-dd945e23409e (Accessed June 21, 2023).

Sullivan, Arthur. *Thespis, Or, The Gods Grown Old: An Entirely Original Grotesque Opera, in Two Acts*, 1871.

Sullivan, Arthur, and William Schwenck Gilbert. . . . *H.M.S. Pinafore: Or, The Lass That Loved a Sailor. An Entirely Original Comic Opera, in Two Acts*. 1879.

Sullivan, Arthur, and William Schwenck Gilbert. "The Pirates of Penzance by W. S. Gilbert and Arthur Sullivan." Accessed August 29, 2021. https://www.gsarchive.net/pirates/web_op/operhome.html.

Sullivan, Arthur, William Schwenck Gilbert, and Isaac Asimov. *Asimov's Annotated Gilbert and Sullivan*. Doubleday, 1988.

Suskin, Steven, and Dave Malloy, eds. *The Great Comet: The Journey of a New Musical to Broadway*. Book with CD edition. New York: Union Square & Co., 2016.

"TAMS—WITMARK MUSIC LIBRARY, INC." September 17, 2013. https://web.archive.org/web/20130917053917/http://www.tamswitmark.com/latestnews.html.

Taranow, Gerda. *Sarah Bernhardt: The Art within the Legend*. Princeton, NJ: Princeton University Press, 1972. http://archive.org/details/sarahbernhardtar0000tara.

Taylor, Steven A. "Editorial?!—Or a Place for Me to Say Stuff!" May 24, 1997. https://web.archive.org/web/19970524171522/http://www.netlink.co.uk/users/nomad/want.htm.

"Tempest—Tender Claws." Accessed June 21, 2023. https://tenderclaws.com/tempest.

Thompson, Jay. "A Headnote on the Form of 'Double Entry.'" *Theatre Arts* 45, no. 7 (1961): 32.

TiQ / I Am Sending You the Sacred Face. 2020. https://www.youtube.com/watch?v=T9jGmhHFO6o.

Tumblrico. "Tumblrico." Accessed February 15, 2021. https://linmanuel.tumblr.com/post/114774696985/lovesjustachemical-actressingfanatic.

Lithographic Co. v. Sarony, 111 U.S. 53 (1884).

Viagas, Robert. "Les Miserables Launches Its Own Website." *Playbill*. March 3, 1997. https://playbill.com/article/les-miserables-launches-its-own-website-com-329103 (Accessed April 21, 2022.).

"Victor Matrix CS-95387. Porgy and Bess / Helen Jepson; Alexander Smallens; Lawrence Tibbett - Discography of American Historical Recordings." Accessed April 22, 2022. https://adp.library.ucsb.edu/index.php/matrix/detail/200021945/CS-95387-Porgy_and_Bess.

"VIDEOS—Fair Broadway/ Musical Trades." October 19, 2016. https://web.archive.org/web/20161019055721/https://fairbroadwaymusicaltrades.weebly.com/videos.html.

"Visualizations | Circulating American Magazines." Accessed November 13, 2021. https://sites.lib.jmu.edu/circulating/visualizations/.

Wasser, Frederick. *Veni, Vidi, Video: The Hollywood Empire and the VCR*. Austin: University of Texas Press, 2001.

We See You W.A.T. "Statement." Accessed April 10, 2021. https://www.weseeyouwat.com/statement.

Webber, Andrew Lloyd. *Cats: The Book of the Musical*. 1st edition. London: Faber and Faber Ltd., 1981.

Webber, Andrew Lloyd. "A Live Commentary from Andrew: Cats The Musical (1998)." 2020. https://www.youtube.com/watch?v=sAP7V5KwZCU.

Webber, Andrew Lloyd, and Tim Rice. *Evita: The Legend of Eva Peron, 1919–1952.* New York: Drama Pub, 1979.

"What's New @ Laura's MIDI Heaven!" May 8, 1999. https://web.archive.org/web/199 90508050215/http://laurasmidiheaven.com/1new.htm.

Whitton, Joseph. *"The Naked Truth!" An inside History of the Black Crook.* H.W. Shaw Co., 1897.

Whitton, Joseph. *Wags of the Stage.* George H. Rigby, 1902.

Wollman, Elizabeth L. *A Critical Companion to the American Stage Musical.* London: Bloomsbury Publishing, 2017.

Woodward, Herbert, and Everett Woodward. *Of Making Many Books.* Binghamton, NY: Vail-Ballou Press, Inc., 1950.

Wright, David, director. *The Heat Is On.* Thames Television, 1989.

Zinberg, Michael, dir. *Gilmore Girls.* Season 6, Episode 5, "We've Got Magic to Do." Aired October 11, 2005, on WB.

Archival collections

Beatrice Lillie Papers. *T-Mss 1990-025. Billy Rose Theatre Division, New York Public Library for the Performing Arts.

Harold Prince Papers. *T-Mss 1986-006. Billy Rose Theatre Division, New York Public Library for the Performing Arts.

The Theatre on Film and Tape Archive. Billy Rose Theatre Division, New York Public Library for the Performing Arts.

Index

For the benefit of digital users, indexed terms that span two pages (e.g., 52–53) may, on occasion, appear on only one of those pages.

Figures are indicated by *f* following the page number

Goldstar (ticket platform), 157
Goodspeed Opera House, 111
Google, 161–62
Google Video, 118
GOPHER (online search tool), 28, 45
Gordon, Joanne, 85
Gordon, Ricky Ian, 67
Gordon, Witold, 39, 40
Gorman, Samantha, 162
Grease (Jacobs, Casey), 129
Great Depression, 39
Great Musicals of the American Theatre, Volume 2 (anthology, ed. Richards), 23–24
Great Performances (PBS series), 75, 86
Great Rock Musicals (anthology, ed. Richards), 23–24
Green, Adolph, 85, 113
Green, Paul, 17
Greenberg, Joshua M., 74
Griffith, Robert, 70
Grooveshark, 68–69
Grun, Bernard, 129
Guettel, Adam, 67
Gypsy (Styne, Sondheim, Laurents), 23–24, 27
  bootleg recording of final performance, 102–5

H.M.S. Pinafore (Sullivan, Gilbert), 15
Hadestown (Mitchell), 160
Hair (MacDermot, Rado, Ragni), 158
  show logo, 45–46
Hairspray (Shaiman, Wittman, Meehan, O'Donnell), 44
  companion book, 44
  video bootlegs, 118
Hamilton (Miranda), 43–44, 68–69, 91, 96, 121, 149, 155–57, 156*f*
  bootleg videos, 121–22
  companion book, 43–44
  livestream, 157
  published libretto, 44
Hamilton's America (PBS documentary), 91
  Hammerstein, Oscar II, 17, 18–19, 23–24, 30, 57–61, 62, 67, 71–73, 96, 134, 136, 138. See also *Allegro*; *Carousel*; *Desert Song, The*; *King and I, The*; *Me and Juliet*; *Oklahoma!*; Rodgers, Richard; *Show Boat*; *Six Plays by Rodgers and Hammerstein*; *Sound of Music, The*; *South Pacific*; *State Fair*
Hansberry, Lorraine, 109
Harbach, Otto, 72
Harcourt Brace Jovanovich (publishers), 42
Harms, T.B. (publisher), 17
Harris, Jeremy O., 120, 121
Harrison, Dale, 56–57
Harry Fox Agency, 30
Haun, Harry, 84
Hausam, Wiley, 24
HBO, 75
Head Over Heels (Whitty, Magruder), 158
Healy, Patrick, 122–23
Hearn, Michael Patrick, 39
Heathers (O'Keefe, Murphy), 125
Hello, Dolly! (Herman, Stewart), 34–35, 40–41
Hellzapoppin (Johnson, Olsen), 40
Her First Roman (Drake)
  live audio recording, 112
Herbert, Victor, 52, 99. *See also* ASCAP; *Babes in Toyland*
Heywood, Laura, 157
Hillman-McCord, Jessica, 10–11, 44–45, 121, 151
  "Tradition or Travesty? Radical Reinterpretations of the Musical Theatre Canon," 151
Hirson, Roger O., 77, 80. See also *Pippin*
Hollywood Reporter, 122–23
Holt, Rinehart, and Wilson (publishers), 41
Home Sweet Homer (Leigh, Burr, Marre, Kibbee), 122
Hoskins, Vicki, 39
"How Can Love Survive" (*The Sound of Music*), 73–74
Howe, Tina, 85
Hoyt, Charles, 36–37
HTML, 29–30, 31
HTTP (Hypertext Transfer Protocol), 28
Hughes, Terry, 82–83, 84
Hugo, Victor, 47, 49*f*
Hulu (streaming platform), 157
Hummel, David, 99–100, 118, 124–25